Microsoft® Windows®98
At a Glance

Microsoft Press

PUBLISHED BY
Microsoft Press
A Division of Microsoft Corporation
One Microsoft Way
Redmond, Washington 98052-6399

Library of Congress Cataloging-in-Publication Data
Joyce, Jerry, 1950–

    Microsoft Windows 98 At a Glance / Jerry Joyce and Marianne Moon.
      p.   cm.
    Includes index.
    ISBN 1-57231-631-4
    1. Microsoft Windows (Computer file).   2. Operating systems (Computers).
    I. Moon, Marianne. II. Title.
    QA76.76.063J6933   1998
    005.4'469—dc21
                             98-9352
                                CIP

Printed and bound in the United States of America.

    8 9 QEQE 3 2 1 0

Distributed to the book trade in Canada by ITP Nelson, a division of Thomson Canada Limited.

A CIP catalogue record for this book is available from the British Library.

Microsoft Press books are available through booksellers and distributors worldwide. For further information about international editions, contact your local Microsoft Corporation office, or contact Microsoft Press International directly at fax (425) 936-7329. Visit our Web site at mspress.microsoft.com.

Acquisitions Editor: Kim Fryer   **Technical Editor:** Jerry Joyce
Project Editor: Maureen Williams Zimmerman   **Manuscript Editor:** Marianne Moon

Dedicated with love to the memory of Uncle David.
We are among the many who will always miss you.

Contents

Windows 98 is your working headquarters.

See page 5

Windows remembers where things belong.

See page 21

Find a folder or a file.
See pages 28–29

Meet Windows Explorer.
See page 36

"Look, Ma, I'm multitasking!"

See page 44

Create a picture.
See page 58

4 Working with Programs   **43**

5 Networking   **65**

"I want my print job to jump the queue!"

See page 86

Put a Web page on your Desktop.
See page 110

Associate a sound
with an event.
See page 122

Work in MS-DOS.
See pages 123–138

Reply to e-mail.
See pages 148–149

Classic view,
Web view, or a
Custom blend?

See pages 209–212

Choose a
Desktop Theme.
See pages 224–225

Change or redesign
the Start menu.
See pages 232–234

Scheduled Task Wizard

See page 251

Add fonts.
See page 260

Acknowledgments

This book is the result of the combined efforts of people whose work we trust and admire and whose friendship we value highly. Ken Sánchez, our talented typographer, meticulously laid out the complex design. Herb Payton refined and produced the interior graphics and then cheerfully reworked them as the inevitable interface changes occurred. Sue Bishop provided the hand-drawn art, and we're happy to have her distinctive sketches in our book. We've worked with Alice Copp Smith on many other books. Alice does so much more than proofread: her gentle and humorous chiding always teaches us to write better. And our indexer, Kari Bero, seems to inhale the soul of a book and magically exhale a comprehensive index. Thanks also to Kristin Ziesemer for her help with the graphics, and to Kari Becker for her good deeds.

At Microsoft Press, we thank Lucinda Rowley for making it possible for us to write this book and our previous books in the *At a Glance* series. Thanks also to Maureen Williams Zimmerman, Kim Fryer, Jenny Benson, Kim Eggleston, Mary DeJong, and Bill Teel, all of whom gave us help and advice along the way.

Thanks to the Windows 98 Beta Team for invaluable technical information about every aspect of Windows 98, and to Don Schuman and Ron Jones of Parallel Technologies, Inc., for detailed information about cables for the Direct Cable Connection.

On the home front, Roberta Moon-Krause and Rick Krause allowed their puppies, Baiser and Pierre, to grace some of our pages with their furry little images. Roberta brought wondrous edible treats to sustain us as we toiled, and Rick provided luxurious transportation for many a chapter. Thanks, kids—you're the greatest!

About This Book

If you want to get the most from your computer and your software with the least amount of time and effort—and who doesn't?—this is the book for you. You will find *Microsoft Windows 98 At a Glance* to be a straightforward, easy-to-read reference tool. With the premise that your computer should work for you, not you for it, this book's purpose is to help you get your work done quickly and efficiently so that you can get away from the computer and live your life.

No Computerese!

Let's face it—when there's a task you don't know how to do but you need to get it done in a hurry, or when you're stuck in the middle of a task and can't figure out what to do next, there's nothing more frustrating than having to read page after page of technical background material. You want the information that you need—nothing more, nothing less—and you want it now! *And* it should be easy to find and understand.

That's what this book is all about. It's written in plain English—no technical jargon and no computerese. There's no single task in the book that takes more than two pages. Just look the task up in the index or the table of contents, turn to the page, and there's the information, laid out step by step and accompanied by graphics that add visual clarity. You don't get bogged down by the whys and wherefores: just follow the steps, look at the illustrations, and get your work done with a minimum of hassle.

Occasionally you might have to turn to another page if the procedure you're working on has a "See Also" in the left column. That's because there's a lot of overlap among tasks, and we didn't want to keep repeating ourselves. We've also scattered some useful tips here and there, and thrown in a "Try This" once in a while, but by and large we've tried to remain true to the heart and soul of the book, which is that the information you need should be available to you at a glance.

Useful Tasks...

Whether you use Windows 98 for work, play, or some of each, we've tried to pack this book with procedures for everything we could think of that you might want to do, from the simplest tasks to some of the more esoteric ones.

...And the Easiest Way to Do Them

Another thing we've tried to do in *Windows 98 At a Glance* is to find and document the easiest way to accomplish a task. Windows often provides a multitude of methods to accomplish a single end result, which can be daunting or delightful, depending on the way you like to work. If you tend to stick with one favorite and familiar approach, we think the methods described in this book are the way to go. If you like trying out alternative techniques, go ahead! The intuitiveness of Windows invites exploration, and you're likely to discover ways of doing things that you think are easier or that you like better than ours. If you do, that's great!

It's exactly what the creators of Windows 98 had in mind when they provided so many alternatives.

A Quick Overview

First and foremost, this book isn't meant to be read in any particular order. It's designed so that you can jump in, get the information you need, and then close the book and keep it near your computer until the next time you need to know how to get something done. But that doesn't mean we scattered the information about with wild abandon. If you were to read the book from front to back, you'd find a logical progression from the simple tasks to the more complex ones. Here's a quick overview.

First, because so many of today's computers come with Windows 98 preinstalled, we assume that Windows is already installed on your machine. If it's not, the Setup Wizard makes installation so simple that you won't need our help anyway. So, unlike most computer books, this one doesn't start out with installation instructions and a list of system requirements. You've already got that under control.

Sections 2 through 5 of the book cover the basics: starting Windows; starting programs and managing program windows; using shortcut menus; creating, finding, and organizing files and folders; working with programs, including some of the programs that come with Windows 98; and an introduction to networking— the different types of networks you're likely to encounter, how to find what you need on your network, and how to use the power of a network to your best advantage.

Sections 6 through 9 describe tasks that are a little more technical but really useful: everything you need to know about printing; setting up your Windows Desktop so that it looks and works exactly as you want it to, including turning it into an *Active* Desktop; and working with multimedia, including sound, video, and TV. If you think these tasks sound complex, rest assured that they're not—Windows makes them so easy that you'll sail right through them. There's also a small section here for all you faithful MS-DOS fans.

Sections 10 through 12 are about communicating with your coworkers and using Windows 98 as your window on the world at large: surfing the Internet and using all the tools that go along with working and playing in cyberspace, including easy ways to telecommute and videoconference directly from your computer.

The final sections, 13 through 15, deal with more advanced topics: changing the look of your computer and the way it works—drastically, if you want, or just a little; adding and removing software components; tuning up the system so that it works more efficiently; and taking care of a variety of problems. And you'll find out how to get all sorts of information, help, and tools directly from Microsoft.

One Click or Two?

Windows 98 lets you choose the way you use your little friend the mouse to access programs and folders. You can stick with the traditional way—that is, point and click to select an item, and then double-click to open it—or you can work in Windows as if you were working on a Web page: point to an item to select it and then open it with a single click. If neither of these methods is exactly right for you, you can incorporate elements from both working styles to create your own custom-blended Windows style.

However, because our working style is somewhat traditional, and because Windows 98 is initially set up to run in the traditional style, that's what we've described in the procedures and graphics throughout the book.

A Final Word (or Two)

We had three goals in writing this book, and here they are:

◆ Whatever you *want* to do, we want the book to help you get it done.

◆ We want the book to help you discover how to do things you *didn't* know you wanted to do.

◆ And, finally, if we've achieved the first two goals, we'll be well on the way to the third: we want the book to help you *enjoy* doing your work with Windows 98. We think that would be the best gift we could give you as a "thank you" for buying our book.

We hope you'll have as much fun using this book as we've had writing it. The best way to learn is by doing, and that's how we hope you'll use *Windows 98 At a Glance*.

Jump right in!

2

Jump Right In

Microsoft Windows 98 is designed to work for you, not you for it. Don't be afraid to jump right in, look around, and try out some features. You'll find that there are often several ways to accomplish one task. Why? Because people work differently. Because different tasks have different requirements. And so that you can find the way that works best for you, get your work done quickly, and get away from the computer!

You'll find that most of the procedures are simple and straightforward and that Windows often uses automated methods to help you get the more complex chores done easily. This doesn't mean that you can't get stuck or get into trouble, but there are so many safeguards built into Windows 98 and so many places to get help that you'll have to work pretty hard to get into *real* trouble.

This section of the book covers the really basic stuff, from starting up Windows 98 through shutting it down. There's also a handy visual glossary on the following two pages that will help you become familiar with the names of the various parts of the Windows 98 environment.

Don't change or delete anything just yet, though—you want to feel comfortable with the basics before you do any customizing. The best way to learn about running programs, managing windows, and getting help if you *do* get into trouble is to jump right in and try things out.

Windows 98 at a Glance

Windows 98 is your working headquarters—the *operating system* that makes it possible for you to run different programs simultaneously and share information between programs if you need to. Most of the programs you'll use have common characteristics that were designed to work together in the Windows environment—meaning that once you learn how to do something in one program, you know how to do it in other programs. Take a look at

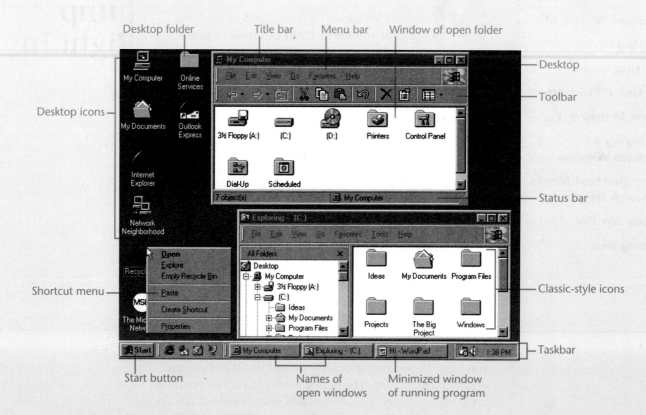

Desktop folder
Title bar
Menu bar
Window of open folder
Desktop
Toolbar
Desktop icons
Status bar
Shortcut menu
Classic-style icons
Taskbar
Start button
Names of open windows
Minimized window of running program

the different parts of the Windows environment that are displayed on these two pages—what they do and what they're called—and you'll be on the road to complete mastery! As you use Windows 98, you might change the way some of these items look and the way some of them work, but the basic concepts are the same. And if you need to, you can always come back to this visual glossary for a quick refresher on Windows terminology.

2

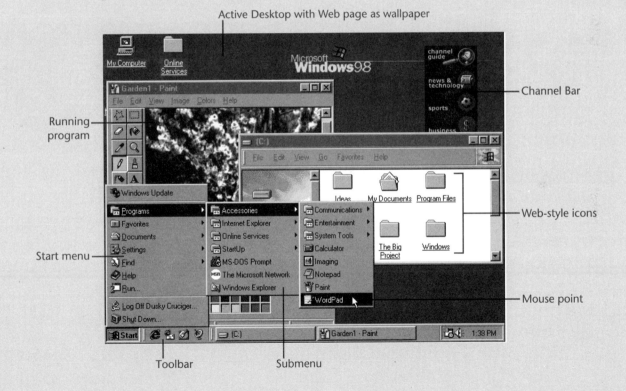

Active Desktop with Web page as wallpaper

Channel Bar

Running program

Start menu

Web-style icons

Mouse point

Toolbar

Submenu

Starting Up

When you turn on your computer, you're also starting Windows 98. The time your computer takes to start up depends on its speed and configuration (including network connections) and on the programs that are set up to start when Windows starts.

TIP

Your computer can have several states of resting other than simply being turned off. Before you touch an On/Off switch, try pressing a key to see if the computer comes back to life.

SEE ALSO

"Changing Your Passwords" on page 78 for information about changing or disabling your passwords.

"Customizing a Computer for Different Users" on page 231 for information about adding users to the Windows Family logon list.

"Starting a Program When Windows Starts" on page 237 for information about specifying which programs start when Windows starts.

Start Windows

1 Turn on your computer, your monitor, and any peripheral devices—your printer, for example.

2 Wait for Windows 98 to load and for the Password dialog box to appear.

3 Do either of the following:

◆ In the User Name text box of the Windows logon or the Network logon dialog box, type the name you've been assigned if it's not already there, and press the Tab key.

◆ In the Windows Family logon dialog box, select the name you've been assigned, and press the Tab key.

4 Type your password in the Password text box. For a network logon, be sure to use the correct capitalization!

5 If you're logging on to a LAN, the domain name will probably be filled in for you already. If not, press Tab again and type the network domain name.

6 Click OK.

Windows logon. If you're the only person who uses your computer, and you're not a member of a workgroup, the logon dialog box might not appear.

Network logon. If you're connected to a client-server network, you'll usually be asked for your user name, password, and domain name.

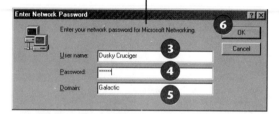

Windows Family logon

Shutting Down

Shutting down your computer used to be a simple matter—you just turned it *off!* But in Windows 98, just as starting the computer takes longer, shutting it down takes a bit more time while Windows closes any open programs and saves all your current settings.

TIP

You don't need to shut down Windows if you want to log on to the computer as a different user. Instead, use the Logoff command on the Start menu.

SEE ALSO

"Quitting When You're Stuck" on page 63 if you have problems when you try to quit Windows.

"Customizing a Computer for Different Users" on page 231 for information about logging off so that someone else can log on to your computer.

Shut Down and Turn Off Your Computer

1 Click the Start button, and choose Shut Down.

2 Click to turn on the appropriate option. The options available depend on the configuration of your computer.

3 Click OK. If you choose to shut down, your computer will probably shut itself off. If it doesn't, wait for the message that tells you it's safe to turn off your computer, and then turn it off.

Exits Windows.

Switches computer to low-power state. Windows remains loaded.

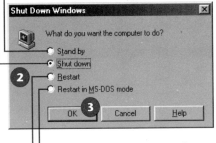

Shut Down Windows

What do you want the computer to do?

- ○ Stand by
- ● Shut down
- ○ Restart
- ○ Restart in MS-DOS mode

[OK] [Cancel] [Help]

Exits Windows and restarts the computer in MS-DOS mode.

Exits and then reloads Windows. (You'll probably want to restart Windows if you have software problems or when you've made changes to the computer's configuration.)

Starting a Program

Despite all the hype, the real work of an operating system is to run your software programs. Windows usually gives you several different ways to start up your programs, so you can choose the way that's easiest for you or that you like the best.

SEE ALSO

"Mouse Maneuvers" on pages 12–13 for detailed information about using a mouse.

"Creating a Shortcut" on page 33 for more information about accessing programs from the Windows Desktop.

Start a Program from the Start Menu

1 Click the Start button.

2 Point to the Programs menu item.

3 Continue pointing to groups as the submenus cascade out. If you don't see the program you want, point to a group where it might be located.

4 When you see the program you want, point to it and click to choose it.

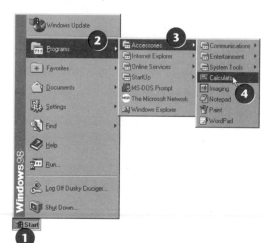

Start a Program from the Desktop

Point to the program icon and double-click. (Remember that if you're in Web view, you need to click the icon only once.)

Double-click to start

TIP

Start a Program from a CD. *Many CDs have a feature called AutoPlay—you simply insert your disc into the CD-ROM drive, and Windows starts the program automatically. If you want to grab some files from the CD without starting the program, hold down the Shift key when you insert the CD, and continue holding it down until the CD is up to full speed.*

SEE ALSO

"Exploring Windows with Windows Explorer" on page 37 if you want to try another way of navigating through your drives and folders to start programs.

"Switching Views" on page 212 for information about switching between Classic-style icons and Web-style icons, and for information about displaying the contents of your folders in separate windows as shown in the graphic.

Start a Program from My Computer

1. Double-click the My Computer icon. (Remember that if you're in Web view, you need to click the icon only once.)

2. Double-click the drive that contains the program you want to start.

3. Double-click the folder that contains the program.

4. If the program is in a subfolder, continue double-clicking the subfolders until you reach the program you want.

5. Double-click the program icon.

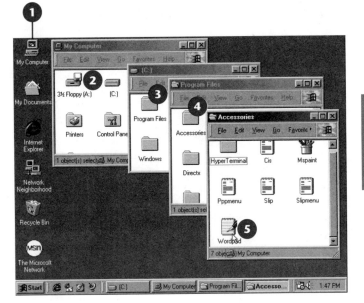

Mouse Maneuvers

Navigating with a mouse is like traveling in a helicopter: you can lift off from any spot, fly a straight line over hills and canyons, and set down wherever you want. Using the keyboard to navigate is like taking the scenic route: you'll run into detours in a program's topography, and you might need a good map to navigate through menus and shortcut keys to reach your destination. You might prefer the longer keyboard route—you get to explore the road less traveled, and you might even come across features and techniques that are new to you. But to finish your tasks as quickly as possible—and to take advantage of some of Windows' best features—give your mouse the job!

Before you fly off on your mouse wings, though, you might need some Mouse Basics. At Mouse School, we believe there are no bad mice (okay, mouse devices)—only bad mouse operators. Here you'll learn to point, click, double-click, right-click, select, drag and drop, and spin the wheel on a wheel mouse. Don't be too surprised if the mouse acts a bit differently from the way you expect it to. Windows gives you numerous options for customizing the way your mouse works, so be patient, experiment a bit, and read pages 224–227 and 248–250 for information about getting your mouse to work the way you want it to.

Point: Move the mouse until the mouse pointer (either a small arrow-shaped pointer or a tiny hand) is pointing to the item you want.

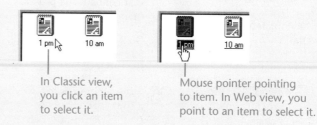

In Classic view, you click an item to select it.

Mouse pointer pointing to item. In Web view, you point to an item to select it.

Click: Point to the item you want, and then quickly press down and release the left mouse button.

Double-click: Point to the item you want, and then quickly press down and release the left mouse button twice, making sure that you don't move the mouse between clicks.

Right-click: Point to the item you want, and then quickly press down and release the right mouse button.

Select: Click the item you want in Classic view; point to the item you want in Web view. A selected item is usually a different color from other similar items or is surrounded by a frame.

Multiple-select: Point above and to the left of the first item, hold down the left mouse button, move the mouse pointer below and to the right of the last item to be selected, and release the mouse button. To select non-sequential items, hold down the Ctrl key and click each item you want. Only certain windows and dialog boxes permit multiple selection.

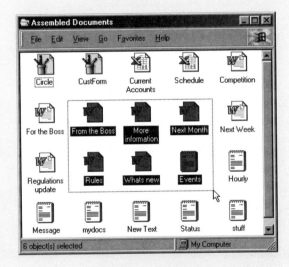

Drag and drop: Select the item you want. Then, keeping the mouse pointer on the selected item, hold down the left mouse button, move the mouse until the item is at the desired location, and then release the left mouse button to "drop" the item.

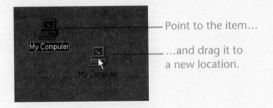

Point to the item…

…and drag it to a new location.

Rotate the wheel: If you're using a mouse equipped with a wheel, rotate the wheel forward or backward. The functionality depends on the program you're using but is usually associated with scrolling. However, the functionality can change when you hold down the Ctrl, Shift, or Alt key.

Click the wheel: Press down and release the wheel. A wheel-click might have special functions, or it might function like the third button on a three-button mouse, depending on the active program.

Managing a Program Window

"Managing" a window means bossing it around: you can move it, change its size, and open and close it. Most programs are contained in windows. Although these windows might have some different features, most program windows have more similarities than differences.

Use the Buttons to Switch Between Sizes

1 Click the Maximize button, and the window enlarges and fills the screen. (If the window is already maximized, you won't see the Maximize button.)

2 Click the Restore button, and the window gets smaller. (If the window is already restored, you won't see the Restore button.)

3 Click the Minimize button, and the window disappears but you see its name on a button on the taskbar.

4 Click the window's name on the taskbar, and the window zooms back to the size it was before you minimized it.

Program title bar

Buttons for switching between window sizes

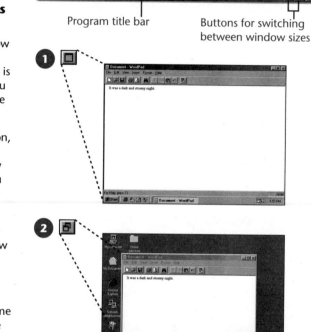

SEE ALSO

"Mouse Maneuvers" on pages 12–13 for information about dragging and dropping.

"Managing Multiple Programs" on page 44 for information about automatically arranging all your program windows.

TIP

Move Your Mouse...*over a side border to change the window's width; over a top or bottom border to change the window's height; over a corner to change both the height and the width.*

TRY THIS

Double-click the title bar of a window, and then double-click it again—another way to resize a window!

Use the Mouse to Resize a Window

1 Click the Restore button if the window is currently maximized. (You can't manually size a maximized window.)

2 Move the mouse over one of the borders of the window until the mouse pointer changes into a two-headed arrow. The directions of the arrowheads show you the directions in which you can move the window border.

3 Drag the window border and drop it when the window is the size you want.

Move a Window

1 Point to the title bar.

2 Drag the window and drop it at a new location.

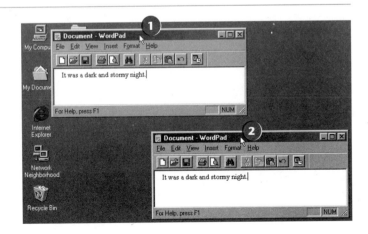

Using Shortcut Menus for Quick Results

Windows 98 and the programs that work with it were designed to be intuitive—that is, they anticipate what you're likely to want to do when you're working on a particular task, and they place the appropriate commands on a shortcut menu that you open by clicking the *right* mouse button. These shortcut menus are *dynamic*, which means that they change depending on the task in progress.

Use a Shortcut Menu Command

1. Right-click an item.

2. Choose a command from the shortcut menu to accomplish the task at hand. (A few items and the shortcut menus they produce when right-clicked are shown here.)

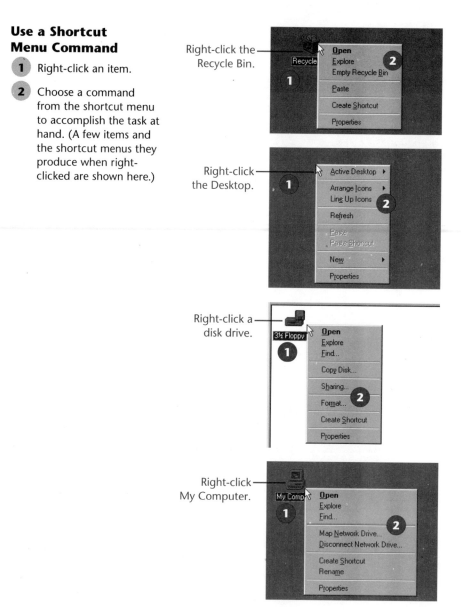

Right-click the Recycle Bin.

Right-click the Desktop.

Right-click a disk drive.

Right-click My Computer.

Dialog Box Decisions

You're going to be seeing a lot of *dialog boxes* as you use Windows 98, and if you're not familiar with them now, you soon will be. Dialog boxes appear when Windows or a program (WordPad, let's say) needs you to make one or more decisions about what you want to do. Sometimes all you have to do is click a Yes, No, or OK button; at other times, there'll be quite a few decisions to make in one dialog box. The Print dialog box, shown below, is one you'll probably be seeing frequently, so take a look at its components and how they work.

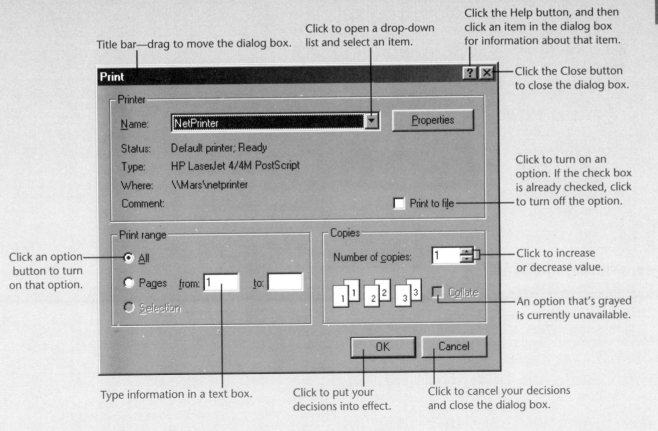

Title bar—drag to move the dialog box.

Click to open a drop-down list and select an item.

Click the Help button, and then click an item in the dialog box for information about that item.

Click the Close button to close the dialog box.

Click to turn on an option. If the check box is already checked, click to turn off the option.

Click an option button to turn on that option.

Click to increase or decrease value.

An option that's grayed is currently unavailable.

Type information in a text box.

Click to put your decisions into effect.

Click to cancel your decisions and close the dialog box.

Getting Help

What's big and colorful; packed with information, procedures, and tools; and sadly underutilized? The Help program! Of course, it couldn't possibly replace this book, but you can use it to find concise step-by-step procedures to help you diagnose and overcome problems, and to learn how to accomplish your tasks faster and more easily than you ever imagined.

TIP

The Contents tab provides a link to the "Getting Started Book: Online Version"—the electronic version of the Windows manual—for additional reference material.

Get Basic Information

1. Click the Start button, and choose Help.

2. On the Contents tab, click the main topic of interest.

3. Click a subtopic, if necessary.

4. Click the item of interest.

5. Read the topic.

6. Repeat steps 2 through 5 to review other topics.

7. Use the Back or Forward button to return to topics you've already reviewed.

8. Click Options, and choose Print to print a topic for handy reference.

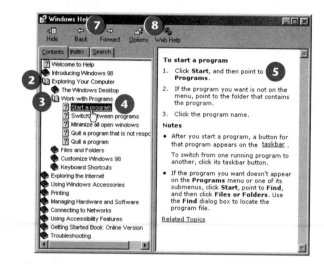

TIP

To read the Help information while working with a window, click the Hide button to see only the topic information; click the Show button to return to the list of topics.

SEE ALSO

"Using Help to Solve Problems" on page 275 and "Searching the Knowledge Base" on page 280 for information about obtaining additional help.

TIP

If you can't find what you're looking for on the Contents or Index tab, try the Search tab. The search looks for your keyword in the text of each Help topic.

Get Specific Help

1 Click the Index tab.

2 Type a word (or part of a word) that describes what you want to do.

3 Double-click the related word or phrase in the list box.

4 If a dialog box appears, listing several topics, select a topic and click Display.

5 Read the topic.

6 Click the Close button when you've finished.

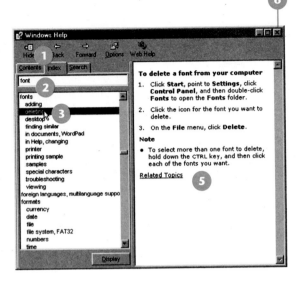

Use Dialog Box Help

1 In any Windows dialog box, click the Help button.

2 Click the item you want more information about.

3 Read the Help information, and then click anywhere to close Help.

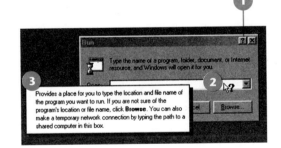

3

Navigating Windows

Using Microsoft Windows 98 is like having a super-efficient office assistant. When you open a folder, Windows shows you an inventory of every document, or file, in the folder. When you tell Windows what you want to do, it hurries off to do your bidding—fetch a file, copy a document and put the copy away in another folder, toss old files into the Recycle Bin, and so on.

The filing system in Windows is structured like a paper-filing system, with its equivalents of filing cabinets, drawers, folders, and documents. The My Computer icon on the Windows Desktop is a gateway to this system. You can open any drawer, dig through any folder, and pull out any document. Also sitting on your Desktop is a folder appropriately named My Documents, which is likely to be your most frequently used folder.

If you'd rather work with files and folders using the basic "tree-structure" filing system that you're familiar with from MS-DOS or from earlier versions of Windows, you can do that too. Using Windows Explorer, you can gain direct access to any file, folder, or drive without having to step through a series of other folders.

Whether you use My Computer, Windows Explorer, or both depends on the way you work and your personal preferences. We'll explore both systems so that you can decide which one works best for you.

Exploring Windows

Sitting on the Windows Desktop is the My Documents folder, where you can store your documents and other files. When you need to navigate elsewhere on your computer, you can use the My Computer icon on your Windows Desktop to open windows to the world of *your* computer. You can then move to any folder and find any file anywhere on your computer.

TIP

To move back from a subfolder to its parent folder, press the Backspace key.

TIP

When you're viewing your folders in a single window, use the Back and Forward buttons to return to folders you opened previously.

Open My Documents

1 Double-click the My Documents folder on the Windows Desktop.

2 Use the scroll bars, if necessary, to view all the files.

3 Click the Close button when you've finished.

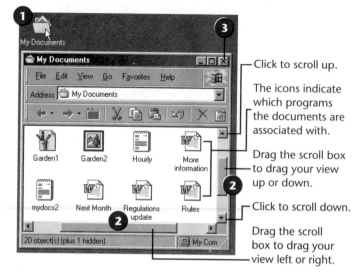

Click to scroll up.

The icons indicate which programs the documents are associated with.

Drag the scroll box to drag your view up or down.

Click to scroll down.

Drag the scroll box to drag your view left or right.

Open a Folder

1 Double-click the My Computer icon on the Windows Desktop.

2 Click a drive icon (for example, [C:]) to open a window for that drive.

3 Click a folder icon to open a window for that folder.

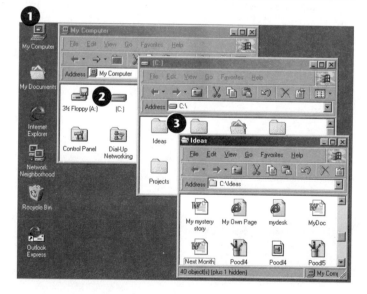

SEE ALSO

"Managing Files with Windows Explorer" on page 38 for information about managing files and folders with Windows Explorer.

"The Views Go On" on page 42 for information about additional views.

"Navigating with Toolbars" on page 98 for information about navigating around Windows.

"Switching Views" on page 212 for information about using a single window or multiple windows to display the contents of your folders.

"Customizing a Folder Window on page 214 for information about changing the look of your folder windows.

"Changing Your Click" on page 230 for information about changing the way an item responds to a click.

TIP

If your computer is set up to show multiple folder windows and you want to close a series of windows in one fell swoop, hold down the Shift key while you click the Close button on the last window you opened—all the windows on the direct route back from that last window to My Computer will close.

Change the Display

1 Click the View menu.

2 Choose a view, as follows:

- ◆ Large Icons to see files or folders with large representative icons arranged in rows

- ◆ Small Icons to see small representative icons arranged in rows from left to right

- ◆ List to see small representative icons arranged from top to bottom in columns

- ◆ Details to see small representative icons and detailed file information arranged in a single column

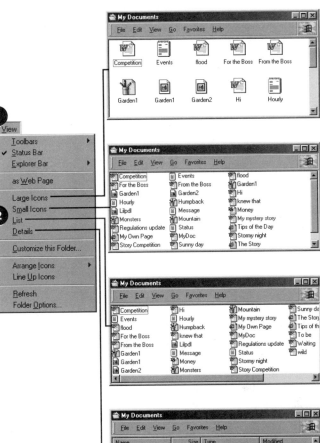

Sorting the File Listings

Depending on the contents of your files and your own idiosyncrasies, you might want Windows to list files alphabetically, by date of most recent edit, by size, or by some other criterion. Windows can also reverse the sorting order—listing names from Z to A, for example—in an opened window.

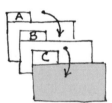

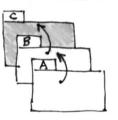

Sort the Files

1 Open the folder you want to examine.

2 Click the View menu and point to Arrange Icons.

3 From the submenu, choose the type of sorting you want:

- ◆ By Name to order the files by their filenames

- ◆ By Type to order the files by their type— Bitmap Image, Microsoft Excel Worksheet, Microsoft Word Document, and so on

- ◆ By Size to order the files by their size

- ◆ By Date to order the files by the date they were created or most recently modified

Smallest file

Most recent file

SEE ALSO

"Locating a File" on page 28 for information about locating a file when you don't know which folder it's in.

"Switching Views" on page 212 for information about using a single window or multiple windows to display the contents of your folders.

"Changing Your Click" on page 230 for information about changing the way an item responds to a click.

TRY THIS

Window Treatments.
In Large Icons or Small Icons view, you can drag the icons to new locations in the window and rearrange the icons however you want them. If you want to straighten up the arrangement but still leave existing gaps between icons, choose Line Up Icons from the View menu. If you want the icons to automatically fill in any gaps and rearrange themselves to fit the width of the window, point to Arrange Icons on the View menu and choose Auto Arrange from the submenu.

Reverse the Order

1 Choose Details from the View menu.

2 Click a label button (Name, Size, Type, or Modified) to choose the type of sorting you want.

3 Click the same label button to reverse the sort order.

Smallest file   Click the Size button to sort by file size.

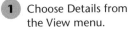
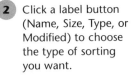

Largest file

Folders and the File Structure

As we mentioned at the beginning of this section, the filing system in Windows is structured very much like a paper-filing system: My Computer is the filing cabinet; the drives are the drawers of the filing cabinet; the folders in the drives are the folders in the drawers; and sometimes, in each system, there are folders inside folders. And, just as with the paper-filing system, you store your documents, or files, inside the folders.

Windows maintains the basic structure for you—My Computer, the drives, the folders for your programs—but if you want to organize your files with a little more detail, you can create your own series of folders to define your own structure, as shown below.

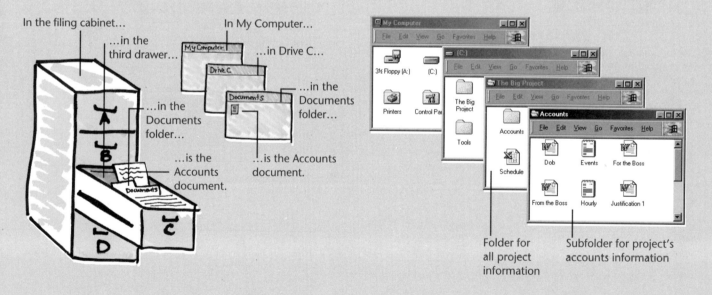

In the filing cabinet...

...in the third drawer...

...in the Documents folder...

...is the Accounts document.

In My Computer...

...in Drive C...

...in the Documents folder...

...is the Accounts document.

Folder for all project information

Subfolder for project's accounts information

Getting More Information About a File or Folder

Windows records information and statistics on every file and folder that you can access from Windows. The information depends on the type of file or what's contained in the folder. This information is called the file's or the folder's *properties*.

TIP

Unless you have a good reason to do so, don't change the Attributes settings. Programs use this information in their own file-management processes, and changes can cause unexpected results.

SEE ALSO

"Find a Folder or a File Somewhere on Your Computer" on page 28 for information about locating files or folders.

Review the Properties of a File or Folder

1. Find the file or folder you want to examine.

2. Right-click the file or folder.

3. Choose Properties from the shortcut menu.

4. Review the information in the Properties dialog box.

5. Click OK.

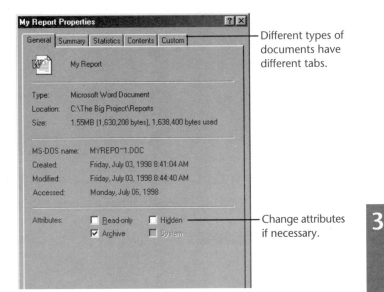

Different types of documents have different tabs.

Change attributes if necessary.

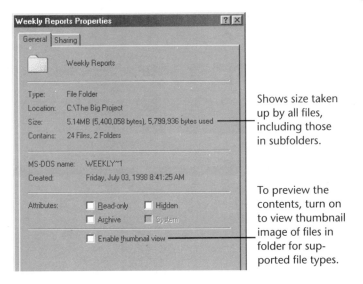

Shows size taken up by all files, including those in subfolders.

To preview the contents, turn on to view thumbnail image of files in folder for supported file types.

Locating a File

If you don't know where a file is located, you can waste a lot of time trying to find it no matter which method you use to explore your windows. Fortunately, Windows can find it for you.

TIP

Depending on the programs and connections you have installed, you can use the Find command on the Start menu to search other locations. For example, you can use it to search for computers on your network or for friends and colleagues in your Address Book or on the Internet.

TIP

When you've located a document, double-click it to open it, drag it and drop it to move it, or select it and open the File menu for additional options.

Find a Folder or a File Somewhere on Your Computer

1 Click the Start button, point to Find, and choose Files Or Folders from the submenu.

2 Type the name, or as much of it as you can remember, in the Named box.

3 Select the location to be searched.

4 Turn on the Include Subfolders check box to search all subfolders.

5 Click Find Now.

6 Examine the results.

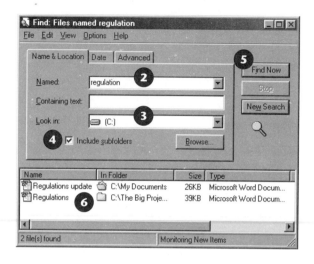

Find a File on a Network

1 Click the Browse button.

2 Select a server, a workgroup computer, or a folder on the server or workgroup computer, and click OK.

3 Click Find Now.

Find a File by Its Content, Date, Type, or Size

1 On the Name & Location tab, type as much information as you can about the document's name.

2 Type any text contained in the document that you want to use as a search parameter.

3 Specify a location for the search.

4 On the Date tab, specify

◆ All Files to skip any date restrictions.

◆ Find All Files to specify whether the files you want were created, modified, or last accessed within a specific time period, and the time period you want the search restricted to. Use the drop-down calendar to specify dates.

5 On the Advanced tab, specify

◆ The type of document to search for.

◆ Any size restrictions for the document.

6 Click Find Now.

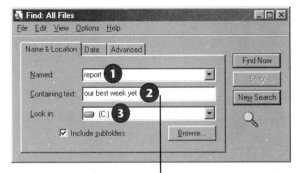

Leave blank if you don't want to search for content.

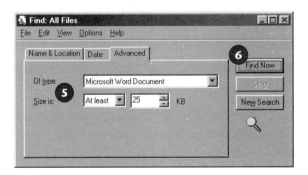

Organizing Your Folders

Windows provides the basic filing structure for you—drives and ready-made folders such as Program Files and Windows. You can customize the filing system by adding your own folders, or even adding folders inside folders (subfolders).

TIP

Off Limits! *There are some locations in which you can't create your own folders—for example, the Printers and Control Panel folders, or any network folder to which you don't have full access. In these cases, the New command won't be on the submenu.*

SEE ALSO

"Switching Views" on page 212 for information about using a single window or multiple windows to display the contents of your folders.

Create a Folder

1. Open the window of the destination folder, drive, or other location.

2. Point to a blank spot on the window and right-click.

3. Point to New.

4. Choose Folder.

5. Type a name, and press Enter.

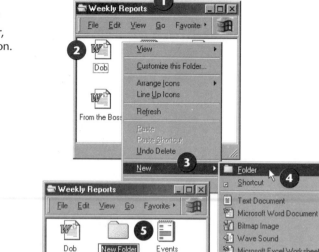

Move or Copy a Folder into Another Folder

1. Open the window containing the folder to be moved or copied, and open the destination folder.

2. Click to the folder to be moved or copied.

3. Hold down the right mouse button, drag the folder, and drop it in the destination-folder window.

4. Choose a menu command to move or copy the folder.

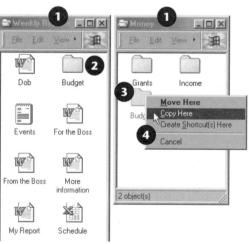

Organizing Your Files

If you have a limited number of files, you can easily keep them all in a single folder. However, if you have many files, or files dealing with different projects, you'll probably want to organize them by placing them in individual folders.

TIP

To select a series of contiguous files, select the first file, hold down the Shift key, and then select the last file. To deselect one of the files, hold down the Ctrl key and click the selected file.

SEE ALSO

"Exploring Windows with Windows Explorer" on page 37 for information about moving files among several different folders.

"Switching Views" on page 212 for information about using a single window or multiple windows to display the contents of your folders.

Move a File into a Subfolder

1. Open the window containing the file.

2. Select the file to be moved. (Hold down the Ctrl key to select multiple files.)

3. Drag the file and drop it on top of the subfolder.

Move or Copy a File into Another Folder

1. Open the window containing the file(s) to be moved or copied.

2. Open the destination folder.

3. Select the file to be moved or copied, hold down the right mouse button, drag the file, and drop it in a blank spot in the destination-folder window.

4. Choose the menu command to move or copy the file.

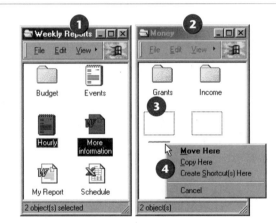

3

Renaming or Deleting a File or Folder

It's quick and easy to rename your files or folders, or to edit a name you've misspelled. Deleting a file or folder is even easier—in fact, it's *so* easy that Windows asks you for confirmation. However, if you delete a file or folder accidentally, don't panic—you can usually retrieve it from the Recycle Bin.

SEE ALSO

"Recovering a Deleted Item" on page 34 for information about retrieving a deleted file or folder from the Recycle Bin.

TIP

It's Gone! *Take the Windows confirmation check seriously. When you delete a folder or a file from a floppy disk or network location, you won't be able to recover it. Lose an important file this way just once, and you'll quickly become a believer in routine backups!*

Rename a File or Folder

1. Right-click the file or folder.

2. Choose Rename from the shortcut menu.

3. With the name selected, type a new name, or click to position the insertion point and then edit the name.

4. Press Enter.

Delete a File or Folder

1. Open the drive or folder containing the file(s) or folder(s) to be deleted.

2. Select the file or folder, or hold down the Ctrl key to select multiple files or folders.

3. Press the Delete key.

4. Click Yes to delete the folder or file and send it to the Recycle Bin.

5. If you're deleting a folder that contains files, click the appropriate button if Windows asks you to confirm the deletion of some types of files.

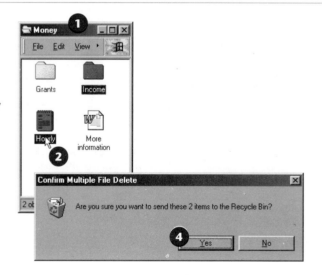

Creating a Shortcut

If you use a particular folder or file frequently, you can access it quickly by putting a shortcut to it on the Windows Desktop or on the Start menu. A shortcut to a document opens the file; a shortcut to a program file starts that program; a shortcut to a folder opens the folder in a window.

TIP

You can also create shortcuts to network, intranet, and Internet locations.

SEE ALSO

"Creating Quick Access to a Network Resource" on page 71 for information about creating a shortcut to a network location.

"Changing the Start Menu" on page 232 for information about adding items to and arranging them on the Start menu.

Create a Shortcut to a Folder or a File

1. Open the window containing the folder or file.

2. Right-click the folder or file.

3. Choose Create Shortcut from the shortcut menu.

4. Drag the shortcut and drop it in any of the following places:
   - On the Windows Desktop
   - In a folder
   - On top of the Start button to add the shortcut to the Start menu

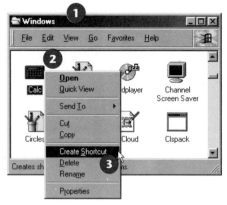

Opens the file in Word.

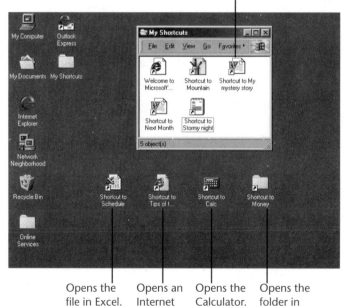

Opens the file in Excel.

Opens an Internet document.

Opens the Calculator.

Opens the folder in a window.

Recovering a Deleted Item

If you delete a file, folder, or shortcut by mistake, you can quickly recover it by either undoing your action or restoring the deleted item from the Recycle Bin. The Recycle Bin holds all the files you've deleted from your hard disk(s) until you empty the bin or until it gets so full that the oldest files are automatically deleted.

Undo a Deletion

1. Point to a blank spot on the Windows Desktop or to a blank spot in any folder window, and right-click.

2. Choose Undo Delete from the shortcut menu.

Available only if the deletion was your last action

Restore an Item from the Recycle Bin

1. Double-click the Recycle Bin icon on the Windows Desktop.

2. Select the item or items to be recovered.

3. Right-click one of the selected items.

4. Choose Restore from the shortcut menu.

5. Click the Close button to close the Recycle Bin.

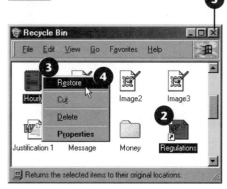

Accessing Everything

You're not limited to exploring your own computer from the My Computer icon. You can use toolbars in any window to go to any location you have permission to access, whether it's part of your workgroup, a network, a company intranet, or the Internet.

TIP

The Links toolbar contains preset connections to Internet locations that you can customize. These are the same links shown in Internet Explorer and in the Links folder on the Favorites menu.

TIP

The Menu bar can be expanded, contracted, and scrolled just like a toolbar. You can place the Menu bar and toolbars on the same line, or drag and stack them one above the other. You can also resize the Menu bar or a toolbar by dragging its left edge.

Display the Toolbars

1. Point to Toolbars on the View menu and choose the toolbar you want to display. Repeat to display several toolbars.

2. If only part of a toolbar is displayed, double-click the "raised" bar or the toolbar's name to expand it.

3. If the entire toolbar is still not fully displayed, click the left or right arrow at the left or right end of the toolbar to scroll the toolbar and see the hidden section.

Go to a Different Location

1. Display the Address Bar.

2. Do either of the following:

   ◆ Open the Address list and click the new location to display it in the current window.

   ◆ Type the address of a location: the drive and path to a folder or document, the name of a computer on your network, or an Internet or intranet Web page.

Copy item to Clipboard.

"Raised" bar

Move up one level.

Undo last action.

Display properties of selected item.

Address Bar

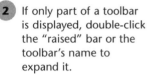

Cut item to Clipboard.

Delete item.

Change view.

Links toolbar

Standard Buttons toolbar

Paste item from Clipboard.

Move backward or forward through sites you've already visited.

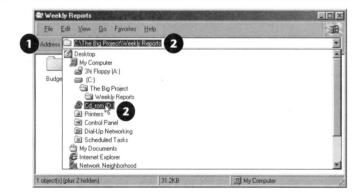

3

Meet Windows Explorer

Windows Explorer has functions similar to those of the folder windows that you reach from My Computer. The list of computers, disks, and folders (often called a *directory tree*) in the left pane gives you direct access to any drive or folder on your computer or on a network. You click the plus sign next to a drive or folder name to expand that branch of the tree structure and see the subfolders it contains, and then you click the minus sign to collapse the branch and hide the subfolders again. The right pane shows you the contents of whatever item you've selected in the left pane.

Left pane shows the tree structure in outline form.

Right pane shows contents of item selected in left pane.

Exploring Windows with Windows Explorer

If you're new to Windows, take a few minutes to go exploring with Windows Explorer. If you're a long-time Windows user, and you liked using File Manager in Windows version 3, you'll feel right at home with Windows Explorer.

TIP

If you don't see a list of drives and folders in Windows Explorer's left pane, open the View menu, point to Explorer Bar, and choose All Folders from the submenu.

TIP

You can also use the toolbars on your Windows Desktop to navigate around Windows.

Explore

1 Click the Start button, point to Programs, and choose Windows Explorer from the submenu.

2 Click through the drives and folders in the left pane to reach the folder that you want to explore. Use the plus or minus signs to display or hide subfolders.

3 Click any folder to see a listing of its contents displayed in the right pane.

Click a plus sign to expand the listing and display the folders it contains.

Click a minus sign to collapse the listing and hide the folders it contains.

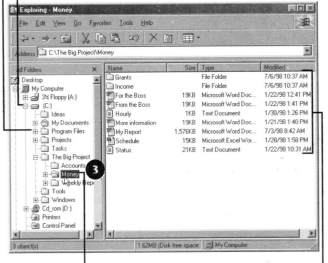

Click a folder...   ...to see what it contains.

Managing Files with Windows Explorer

With Windows Explorer you can quickly and easily copy or move any files or folders on any drive that is accessible to your computer.

TIP

To select several contiguous files to be copied, moved, or deleted, click the first file, hold down the Shift key, and click the last file. All the contiguous files will be selected. To select noncontiguous files, hold down the Ctrl key and click each file you want. All the noncontiguous files will be selected. If Windows is set to the Web style, point to the files while holding down the Shift or Ctrl key to select the files.

TIP

If you start dragging an icon but the window moves too fast and you lose your place, press the Esc key to cancel the drag-and-drop action before you release the mouse button.

Move or Copy Files or Folders

1 Expand the drive and any folders to display the folder containing the files or folders to be moved or copied.

2 Click the folder to display its contents in the right pane.

3 Select the files or folders.

4 Hold down the right mouse button and drag and drop the files or folders into the destination folder.

5 Choose Move Here or Copy Here from the shortcut menu.

Drop when destination folder becomes selected.

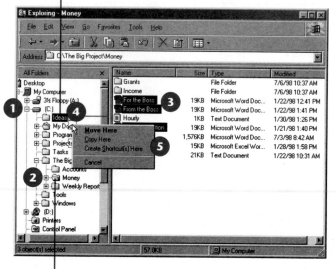

Folder that contains the files or folders to be moved or copied

TIP

If you don't want to see the Confirm File Delete dialog box each time you delete files, right-click the Recycle Bin icon on the Desktop, choose Properties from the shortcut menu, and turn off the Display Delete Confirmation Dialog Box option.

TIP

Files or folders deleted from your hard disk are sent to the Recycle Bin, from which you can recover them if they were deleted accidentally. Files or folders deleted from a network drive or a floppy disk are permanently deleted. If you try to delete a program, Windows informs you that you won't be able to run this program or edit some documents. If you want to remove a program from your computer, use the Windows Uninstall feature.

SEE ALSO

"Removing a Software Program" on page 259 for information about using the Windows Uninstall feature to delete programs and their associated files.

Create a Folder

1. Select the drive or folder that is to contain the new folder.

2. Right-click a blank spot in the right pane.

3. Choose New from the shortcut menu.

4. Choose Folder.

5. Type a name for the new folder, and press Enter.

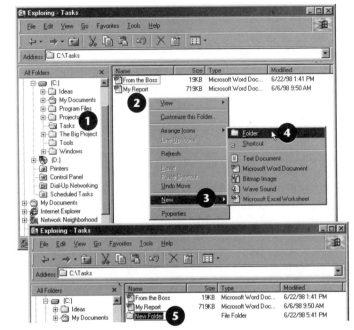
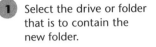

Delete a File or Folder

1. In the right pane, select the file or folder on your computer to be deleted.

2. Press the Delete key.

3. Click Yes to delete the item and send it to the Recycle Bin.

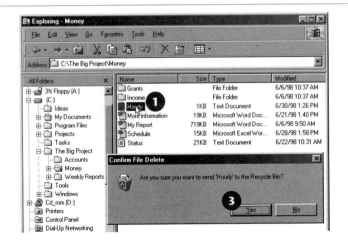

Storing Information on a Floppy Disk

If you use floppy disks to transport or archive information, Windows provides easy access to your disks. If you have a disk that's not preformatted, or if you want to quickly erase and reuse a disk, you'll need to format the disk before you can use it.

TIP

When you format a disk, you remove all the information it contains, including all hidden and system files. This is usually fine with a floppy disk, but—and we can't stress this enough—do not use the Format command on any of your fixed disks unless you know what you're doing and you intend to reinstall everything on that disk.

Format a Floppy Disk

1 Place the disk in your floppy drive.

2 Double-click My Computer on the Windows Desktop.

3 Right-click the floppy drive.

4 Choose Format from the shortcut menu.

5 Choose the formatting option(s) you want:

- ◆ Quick (Erase) to erase the directory and overwrite all files on the disk

- ◆ Full for disks that have not been formatted before, or are not properly formatted

- ◆ Copy System Files Only to add the operating-system files to the disk

6 Type a name for the disk if you want one (up to 11 characters long), and make any changes you want under Other Options.

7 Click Start.

8 Click Close when formatting has been completed.

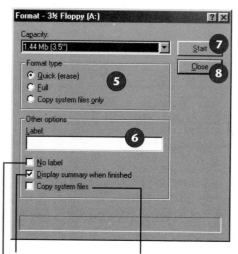

Shows a summary to verify the formatting.

Adds system files to the disk you're formatting.

Removes label from disk.

Copy a File or Folder to a Floppy Disk

1 Place a disk in your floppy drive.

2 Open the window containing the file or folder to be copied.

3 Select and then right-click the file or folder to be copied.

4 Point to Send To on the shortcut menu.

5 Click the floppy drive that contains the disk.

Duplicate a Floppy Disk

1 Place the disk to be duplicated in your floppy drive.

2 Open the My Computer window, right-click the drive containing the disk, and choose Copy Disk from the shortcut menu.

3 Select the drives to be used.

4 Click Start.

5 Click Close when copying has been completed.

You can copy only between drives of the same type. If you're using a single drive, switch disks when requested.

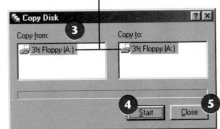

The Views Go On

The versatility that's built into Windows 98 is tremendously helpful in its ability to adapt to your working style, but it can be a bit overwhelming. The Explorer Bar, for example, which you can turn on from the View menu of most folder windows, is a specialized type of toolbar that can pop up all over the place—in a folder window, in Windows Explorer, in Internet Explorer, and even in the Channel Viewer. When you're navigating through folders, the Explorer Bar is a handy tool if you like the view it provides, but you can get along just fine without it if you'd rather stick with your familiar navigation methods. The Explorer Bar is at its most helpful when you're cruising on the Internet or on your company's intranet.

Another specialized view that Windows provides is Thumbnail view. You have to enable this view for a folder before you can see thumbnail views of any documents, and you can enable the view only for file types that support thumbnail views. If you want to try it out, you'll find information about enabling Thumbnail view in "Getting More Information About a File or Folder" on page 27. Thumbnail views are useful mostly for folders with graphics or HTML documents, or for documents from layout programs that supply thumbnail views.

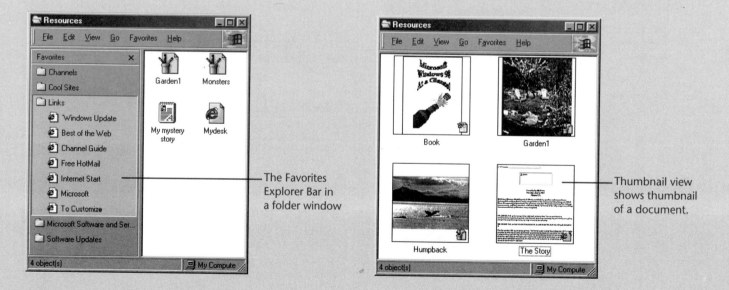

The Favorites Explorer Bar in a folder window

Thumbnail view shows thumbnail of a document.

Working with Programs

Getting to know the programs that come with Microsoft Windows 98 is a bit like moving into a new house or apartment. Just as your new abode has the basics—stove, refrigerator, bathtub, and (dare we say it?) windows—the Windows operating system comes with several useful accessories and tools. Just as you'll add dishes, furniture, rugs, and all the other accoutrements that transform empty rooms into a comfortable home, you'll add other programs to Windows to utilize its full potential as you work (and play).

But take a look at the basics first. There's WordPad, a handy little word processor for quick notes, and Paint, an easy-to-use graphics program. Windows comes with other useful goodies, too: mail and news-reader capabilities, multimedia, and lots of accessory programs— but we'll save those for later. Right now we'll cover some quick ways to accomplish everyday tasks: inserting characters that don't exist on your keyboard, such as © and é; creating and editing plain or formatted text; switching between programs with a single mouse-click; and copying items between documents that were created in different programs. And if you work with information that changes frequently, you'll appreciate being able to create links between related documents so that updates can occur automatically.

Managing Multiple Programs

Windows 98 lets you run several programs at the same time. You can have more than one open program window on your screen and can easily switch between programs. If you prefer, you can park your running programs neatly on the taskbar, where they'll sit snoozing quietly until you need them.

TRY THIS

Look, Ma, I'm Multitasking!
Arrange your program windows by tiling them: right-click a blank spot on the taskbar and choose to tile horizontally or vertically. To make the full screen available as you work in one program, click the Maximize button. When you want to switch to another program, click the Restore button to return the first program to its tiled position.

TIP

To switch between programs using the keyboard, press Alt+Tab.

Switch Between Program Windows

1 If you have several overlapping program windows on your Desktop, click in any visible part of an open window to bring it to the front of your screen and make it the active program—that is, the program you're working on now.

2 Click the Minimize button to remove a window from the Desktop but keep it running as a program button on the taskbar.

3 If the program window is minimized or obscured by other windows, click the program button on the taskbar. To see the full name of the program and the document, position the mouse pointer over the program button until a tooltip appears.

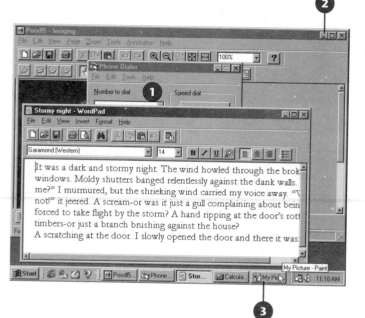

Windows, and Windows in Windows

Windows is called "Windows" because everything in Windows is contained in a window. Well, *almost* everything. In Windows 98, the icons on the Desktop have escaped from their windows, and the taskbar, the toolbars, and the Start menu are free of window restraints. There are a few other items that work outside of windows, too—the wizards and some of the dialog boxes, for example. But, by and large, every program lives in a window. Some programs even have windows inside their main window.

WordPad and Microsoft Word are good examples of the difference between a program that uses a single window and one that uses *document windows.*

Document windows work just like program windows, except that when you close a document window, you are closing only the document or the file that lives in that window; the main program window stays open. Likewise, when you move, size, maximize, or minimize a document window, it is still contained within the program window.

Most programs that have document windows also have a Window menu that you can use to arrange the windows and to switch between them.

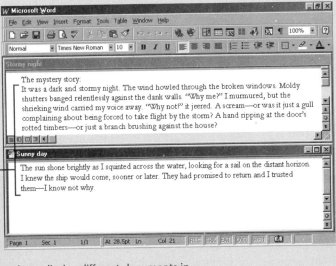

WordPad can display only one document at a time.

Word can display different documents in separate windows within the Word window.

4

Copying Material Between Documents

It's usually very easy to copy material from a document that was created in one program into a document that was created in another program. How you insert the material depends on what it is. If the material is similar to and compatible with the receiving document—text that's being copied into a Word document, for example—it's usually inserted as is and can be edited in the receiving document's program. If the item is dissimilar—a sound clip, say, inserted into a Word document—either it's *encapsulated*, or isolated, as an object and can be edited in the originating program only, or you simply are not able to paste that item into your document.

Copy and Insert Material

1. In the source document, select the material to be copied.

2. Choose Copy from the Edit menu. Windows places copied items on the Clipboard. You can copy only one item at a time, so always paste the Clipboard contents into your document before you copy anything else, or you'll lose whatever was on the Clipboard.

3. Switch to the destination document.

4. Click where you want to insert the material.

5. Choose Paste from the Edit menu.

Many, but not all, programs support drag and drop. If you can't drop a document into the program window, copy the document to the Clipboard, switch to the destination program, and paste the document. If the source document doesn't have a Copy command or the destination document doesn't have a Paste command, try pressing Ctrl+C to copy and Ctrl+V to paste.

Objects are either embedded or linked. An embedded object places all its information, or data, into the document in which the object is placed. A linked object keeps most of its information in a separate file, and inserts only enough information so that the linked file can be located when necessary.

"Mouse Maneuvers" on pages 12–13 for information about using drag and drop.

"Linking to Information That Changes" on page 48 for information about copying a document and linking to files.

Use a Different Format

1 Copy the material from the source document and click in the destination document.

2 Choose Paste Special from the Edit menu.

3 Select the format in which you want to insert the copied material.

4 Click OK.

The source document

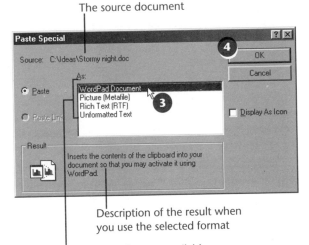

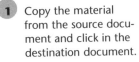

Description of the result when you use the selected format

The different formats available

Copy and Insert an Entire Document

1 Use My Computer to locate and select the document to be copied.

2 Drag the document to the destination document, and drop it where you want it to appear.

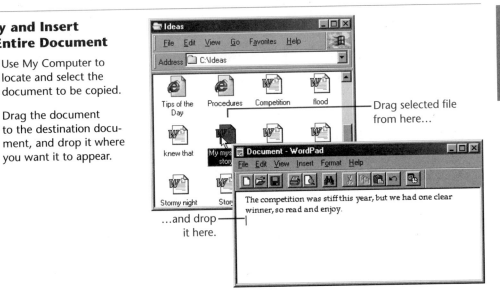

Drag selected file from here...

...and drop it here.

4

Linking to Information That Changes

When the content of an item you've inserted into your document is likely to change in the source document, you can make sure that those changes will be automatically updated in your document. You do this by *linking* to the source document. When the content of the source document changes, the changes appear in your document. But because the content resides in the source document and not in your document, the source document must be available whenever you work in your document. If you change the location of the source document, you must change the link, because the link contains the full path to the document.

Link to a Source Document

1 Locate the source document and right-click it.

2 Choose Copy from the shortcut menu.

3 Switch to the destination document.

4 Click at the location where you want to insert the item.

5 Choose Paste Special from the Edit menu.

6 Select the Paste Link option.

7 Click OK.

Source document

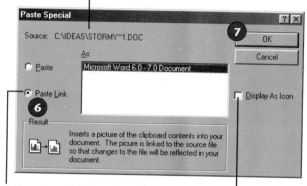

Links the inserted content to an external document.

Check to display icon instead of content. Double-click the icon to display the contents of the linked document.

Change the Link

1. In your document, select the linked information.

2. Choose Links from the Edit menu.

3. Select the current link.

4. Make the changes.

Current link

Click to browse and locate moved document, or to use different document.

Click to edit document in its source program.

Click to update content from source document.

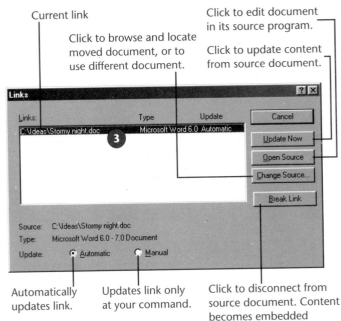

Automatically updates link.

Updates link only at your command.

Click to disconnect from source document. Content becomes embedded in your document.

4

Editing Inserted Material

When material from a document that was created in a different program has been inserted in your document as an *embedded object,* you can edit the inserted item *in place*—that is, in your document—using the tools of the program it which it was created.

Edit Inserted Material in Place

1 Double-click the inserted item.

2 Use the toolbar buttons, menu commands, and whatever other tools are provided by the source program to make your editing changes.

3 Click outside the selected area to return the material into the embedded object and to restore the toolbars, menus, and other tools of your original program.

Paint tools   Paint menus   WordPad window

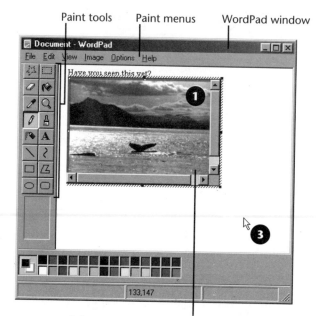

Paint program activated in WordPad window

Inserting Special Characters

Windows provides a special accessory program called Character Map that lets you insert into your programs characters and symbols that aren't available on your keyboard. Character Map displays all the characters that are available for each of the fonts on your computer.

TIP

The Windows Clipboard is a temporary "holding area" for items you want to copy and paste. The Clipboard can hold only one item at a time, so do your pasting right after you've done your copying.

SEE ALSO

"Adding or Removing Windows Components" on page 256 for information about installing Character Map if it's not already installed on your system.

Insert Special Characters

1. Click the Start button, point your way through Programs, Accessories, and System Tools, and choose Character Map from the submenu.

2. Select a font.

3. Click the special character you want to insert.

4. Click Select. Repeat steps 2 and 3, and click Select to insert additional characters.

5. Click Copy to place the character or characters on the Clipboard.

6. Switch to your program, click where you want the character or characters inserted, and paste from the Clipboard.

7. Close Character Map when you've copied all the characters you want.

Displays the character or characters you've selected to be copied to the Clipboard.

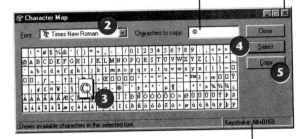

Shows the keyboard shortcut for the selected character. Hold down the Alt key, and use the numeric keypad to enter the numbers.

Working with Plain Text

Sometimes you need to work with pure, unadulterated text that doesn't contain fancy fonts or paragraph formatting. Text documents are the most compatible file formats for transferring text between programs, and they are useful in editing such files as the autoexec.bat and config.sys configuration files.

TIP

By default, text documents are associated with Notepad, so when you double-click a text file, it will open in Notepad unless you've changed the association setting.

SEE ALSO

"File Associations, File Extensions, and Registered Programs" on page 246 for information about the associations between file types and programs.

Create a Text Document

1 Click the Start button, point to Programs and then to Accessories, and choose Notepad from the submenu.

2 From the Edit menu, choose options to change the appearance of the text in this window (word wrap and font information are not saved with the text):

♦ Choose Word Wrap (if it's not already checked) to fit all the text into the width of the current window.

♦ Choose Set Font to select a single font in which to format the entire document.

3 Type, delete, or copy and paste text to create or modify the document. Press Enter when you want to start a new line.

A text document is saved with no formatting and no word wrap.

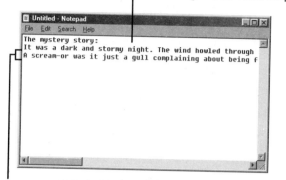

A new line begins only when you press Enter.

Text formatting applies to all the text in the window. Word wrap moves words to the next line so that the text fits into the width of the window.

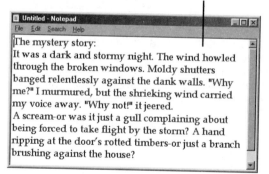

Save the File

1 Choose Save from the File menu to save the document.

2 Navigate to the location where you want to save the file.

3 Type a name for the file.

4 Click Save.

Open to navigate to a location. View Desktop.

Create a new folder.

List view

Details view

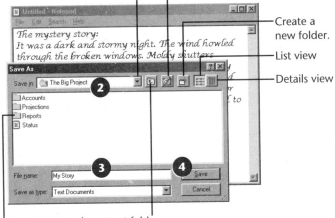

Move up to the parent folder.

Double-click a folder to open it.

Print the Document

1 Choose Page Setup from the File menu. Specify paper size, orientation, and margins. Use the preview to observe your settings.

2 In the Header and Footer text boxes, type text or any of the codes shown in the table that will produce the result you want at the top or bottom of each page.

3 Click OK, and then choose Print from the File menu.

NOTEPAD HEADER AND FOOTER CODES	
Code	**Result**
&f	Filename
&d	Current date
&t	Current time
&p	Page number
&l	Left-aligns header or footer.
&c	Center-aligns header or footer.
&r	Right-aligns header or footer.

4

Working with Formatted Text

WordPad—a program that comes with Windows—can create and open Microsoft Word 6/95 documents, Rich Text Format (RTF) documents, and text documents. It can open, but cannot create, Windows Write documents. WordPad isn't a full-featured word processor, but it's ideal for quick notes. For anything more ambitious, you'll want to use a program such as Microsoft Word.

Start WordPad, and Format the Page

1. Click the Start button, point to Programs and then Accessories, and choose WordPad.

2. Choose Page Setup from the File menu.

3. Specify paper size, paper source, orientation, and margins.

4. Click OK.

5. Save the document.

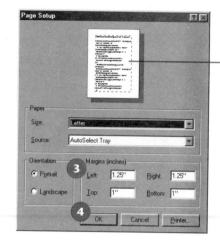

Portrait orientation, shown here, is a page that's longer than it is wide. Landscape orientation is a page that's wider than it is long.

Enter and Format Text

1. Use the View menu to display the Standard and the Formatting toolbars if they're not already visible.

2. Use the drop-down lists and buttons to format the text you're going to type.

3. Type your text.

4. Select any text you want to reformat, and use the formatting tools.

5. Save the document.

Click a "pushed-in" button to turn off formatting.

Click a button to turn on formatting.

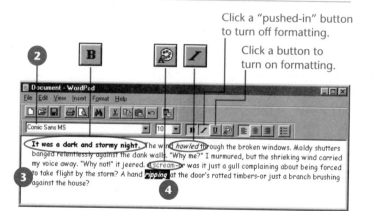

SEE ALSO

"Copying Material Between Documents" on page 46, *"Linking to Information That Changes"* on page 48, and *"Editing Inserted Material"* on page 50 for information about adding pictures and other objects to a WordPad document.

"Adding or Removing Windows Components" on page 256 for information about installing Windows components.

Format the Paragraphs

1 Choose Ruler from the View menu if the ruler isn't displayed.

2 Click in the paragraph to be formatted, or select all the paragraphs that you want to have the same formatting.

3 Use any of the formatting tools:

- ◆ Alignment buttons
- ◆ Bullets button
- ◆ Indent markers
- ◆ Tab markers

4 Save the document.

Drag for left indent.

Drag for first-line indent.

Click to set tab.

Click to set alignment.

Bullets button

Drag for right indent.

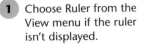

We received many new ideas in the competition. Initially we had a very difficult time determining the winners, but once we re-examined our priorities, we came to unanimous conclusions. Our criteria were quite simple:

- Originality
- Quality
- Contributions to the Foundation

Here is just a sampling of the best entries:

It was a dark and stormy night. The wind howled through the broken windows. Moldy shutters *banged* relentlessly against the dank walls. "Why me?" I murmured, but the shrieking wind carried my voice away. "Why not!" it jeered. A scream-or was it just a gull complaining about being forced to take flight by the storm? A hand *ripping* at the door's rotted timbers-or just a branch brushing against the house?

The sun shone brightly as I squinted across the water, looking for a sail on the distant horizon. I knew the ship would come, sooner or later. They had promised to return and I trusted them-I know not why.

Bulleted list

Center-aligned paragraph

Left-aligned paragraph with left indent and first-line indent

4

Editing a Document in WordPad

You can use WordPad to edit Microsoft Word 6.x, Microsoft Write, Rich Text Format (RTF), or text-only (ANSI and ASCII) documents. When you use WordPad to edit a document that was created in Word, however, you'll lose any special formatting that WordPad doesn't support.

TIP

WordPad can open and save documents in Word 6.0/95 format, which is the format for both Word 6 and Word 95. To open a document created in Word 97 or later, open the document in Word and save it in Word 6.0/95 format.

TIP

If you want to keep a copy of the original unedited document in addition to your edited version, use the Save As command on the File menu to save the edited document under a different filename.

Open a Document

1 Start WordPad if it's not already running.

2 Click the Open button on the toolbar.

3 Select the type of document to be opened.

4 Find and select the document.

5 Click Open.

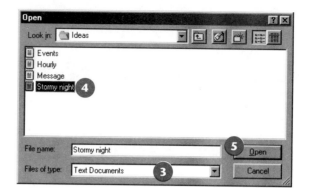

Insert and Delete Text

1 Click where you want to insert the text.

2 Type the text.

3 Select text to be deleted by dragging the mouse pointer over the text.

4 Press the Delete key to delete the text.

1

It was a dark night. The wind nearly howled through the broken windows. Moldy shutters banged relentlessly against the dank walls. "Why me?" I murmured, but the

2

It was a dark and stormy night. The wind nearly howled through the broken windows. Moldy shutters banged relentlessly against the dank walls. "Why me?" I murmured,

3

It was a dark and stormy night. The wind nearly howled through the broken windows. Moldy shutters banged relentlessly against the dank walls. "Why me?" I murmured,

4

It was a dark and stormy night. The wind howled through the broken windows. Moldy shutters banged relentlessly against the dank walls. "Why me?" I murmured, but the

TIP

When Microsoft Word is installed on your computer, Word documents and RTF documents will be associated with Word. You'll notice, too, when you open a window from My Computer or Windows Explorer, that the file displays a Word icon, not a WordPad icon.

TIP

Presto Change-o. *To replace repetitive words or phrases throughout a document, use the Replace command on the Edit menu.*

SEE ALSO

"Save the File" on page 53 for information about navigating to a folder in a dialog box.

"Working with Formatted Text" on page 54 for information about changing the format of text.

"Print a Document Using a Specific Printer" on page 83 to print your document using a printer other than the default printer.

Replace Text

1 Select the text to be replaced by dragging the mouse pointer over the text.

2 Type the new text. The selected text is deleted.

Move Text

1 Select the text to be moved by dragging the mouse pointer over the text.

2 Point to the selected text.

3 Drag the text and drop it in a new location.

Save and Print a Document

1 Click the Save button to save the document in the same format and with the same name.

2 Click the Print button to print the document using the default printer.

Selected text is replaced...

It was a dark and stormy night. The wind howled through the broken windows. Moldy shutters banged relentlessly against the wet walls. "Why me?" I murmured, but the

...when you type new text.

It was a dark and stormy night. The wind howled through the broken windows. Moldy shutters banged relentlessly against the dank walls. "Why me?" I murmured, but the

Drag the selected text to a new location.

It was a dark and stormy night. The wind howled through the broken windows. Moldy shutters banged relentlessly against the dank walls. "Why me?" I murmured, but the wind shrieking hurried my voice away. "Why not!" it jeered. A scream—or was it just a gull complaining about

It was a dark and stormy night. The wind howled through the broken windows. Moldy shutters banged relentlessly against the dank walls. "Why me?" I murmured, but the shrieking wind carried my voice away. "Why not!" it jeered. A scream—or was it just a gull complaining about

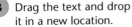

4

Creating a Picture

If you're feeling artistic, you can create a picture in Paint. The Paint program comes with Windows 98 and was designed to create and edit bitmap pictures. (A bitmap is just that: a map created from small dots, or bits. It's a lot like a piece of graph paper with some squares filled in and others left blank to create a picture.) Although you can print your picture if you want to, Paint pictures are usually inserted into other documents as *embedded* or *linked objects*. You can also create a Paint picture and use it as the wallpaper for your Windows Desktop.

SEE ALSO

"Copying Material Between Documents" on page 46 for information *about embedding an object in a document.*

"Linking to Information That Changes" on page 48 for information about linking an object.

Create a Picture

1 Click the Start button, point to Programs and then Accessories, and choose Paint from the submenu.

2 Click a drawing tool.

3 Click the color you want to use.

4 Click an option for the selected tool.

5 Click to start the drawing.

6 Drag the end or corner of the shape and drop it to create the shape you want.

7 Keep choosing appropriate tools, colors, and options to complete your picture.

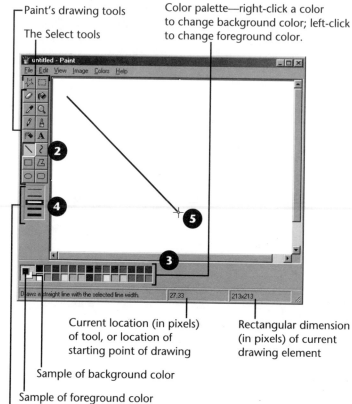

Paint's drawing tools

The Select tools

Color palette—right-click a color to change background color; left-click to change foreground color.

Current location (in pixels) of tool, or location of starting point of drawing

Rectangular dimension (in pixels) of current drawing element

Sample of background color

Sample of foreground color

Options for selected tool

TRY THIS

Here's how to create your own Desktop wallpaper. Start a new Paint picture. Choose Attributes from the Image menu, and set the Width and Height to the dimensions of your screen in pixels (800 x 600, for example). Create your picture, save it, and then choose Set As Wallpaper (Centered) from the File menu.

SEE ALSO

"Changing the Look of the Desktop" on page 108 for information about removing your Desktop wallpaper.

TIP

To add text to a picture, draw a text box, and just start typing. As long as the text box is active, you can edit the text, change the font, and even resize the text box. When you click outside the text box, the text is turned into a bitmap image that can be edited just like any other picture element.

TIP

Use the Undo command on the Edit menu to remove your last drawing. Use the Undo command again to remove the previous drawing.

Use the Tools

1. Hold down a mouse button and drag the shapes you want:

   ◆ Hold down the left mouse button to draw with the foreground color.

   ◆ Hold down the right mouse button to draw with the background color.

2. Hold down the Shift key for special effects when drawing shapes:

   ◆ The Ellipse tool creates a circle.

   ◆ The Rectangle tool creates a square.

   ◆ The Rounded Rectangle tool creates a square with rounded corners.

   ◆ The Line tool draws a horizontal, vertical, or diagonal line.

3. Keep choosing appropriate tools, colors, and options to complete your picture.

4. Save the picture periodically.

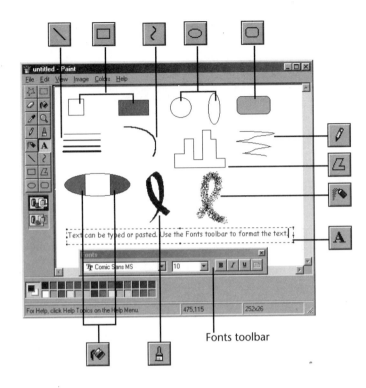

Fonts toolbar

4

Editing a Picture

It's easy and fun to modify an existing bitmap picture to customize it, or to create a new picture using only part of the original picture. However, the picture must be a bitmap; if it isn't, you'll need a program other than Paint in which to edit it.

TIP

To replace one color with another, set the foreground color to the color to be replaced and the background color to the replacement color. Select the Eraser tool, and then hold down the right mouse button and drag the Eraser over the area where you want to replace the color.

TIP

If you don't see a thumbnail version of your picture, choose Zoom from the View menu, and then choose Show Thumbnail.

Edit a Picture

1 Start Paint if it isn't already running.

2 Choose Open from the File menu, locate the bitmap picture you want to edit, and click Open.

3 Use the drawing tools to edit the picture.

4 Use the Magnifier tool to magnify the details, and use the drawing tools to fine-tune your edits; click the Magnifier tool again, and choose 1x magnification to restore the view to Normal Size.

5 Press Ctrl+G to turn on the grid (shown in the picture at the right) if it's not already turned on. Use the Pencil tool to edit individual pixels, clicking the left mouse button for the foreground color and the right mouse button for the background color.

6 Save the picture. If you want to rename the file, choose Save As from the File menu, and type a new name for the picture.

Use the Magnifier tool.

Thumbnail shows context for the magnified area.

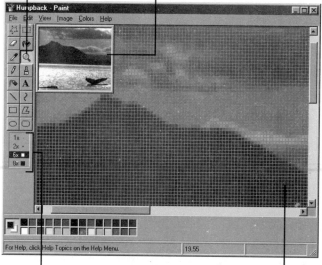

Select the level of magnification.

Use the grid when you need to edit individual pixels.

SEE ALSO

"Editing Inserted Material" on page 50 for information about editing a picture that's contained in another document.

"Changing the Look of the Desktop" on page 108 for information about using the patterns and pictures that come with Windows.

TRY THIS

Click the Select tool, select the Opaque Paste option, and paste in a picture. With the inserted picture still selected, in the Color Box right-click the color that is the main background color for the inserted picture. With the inserted picture still selected, click the Transparent Paste button.

TIP

To save only part of a picture, use one of the Select tools to select the part you want, and then choose Copy To from the Edit menu. To insert an existing picture into your picture, choose Paste From from the Edit menu. To create a picture of something on your computer screen, press the Print Screen button, paste the captured image into Paint, and save it.

Modify Shapes

1 Use one of the Select tools to select the part of the picture you want to work on. The illustration at the right shows a few examples of what you can do.

2 Use the Eraser tool to replace all colors with the background color. To replace a large area with the background color, use the Select tool to select the area, and then press the Delete key.

Hold down the Shift key and drag the selection to create a series of copies.

Drag a handle... ...to resize the selection.

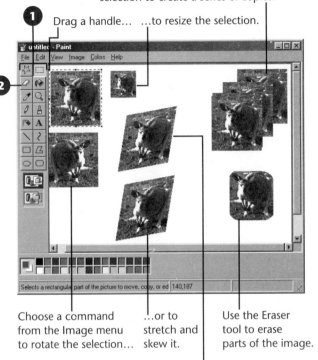

Choose a command from the Image menu to rotate the selection... ...or to stretch and skew it.

Use the Eraser tool to erase parts of the image.

Hold down the Ctrl key, drag the selection, and drop a copy.

4

Viewing a Document Quickly

You can view the contents of many different types of documents to verify that you've found the document you're looking for, and you can do so without spending the time it takes to start the document's program. Quick View lives up to its name!

SEE ALSO

"Adding or Removing Windows Components" on page 256 for information about installing Quick View.

TIP

If you've installed a viewer for a specific program—Microsoft Word Viewer, for example—that viewer will be listed instead of Quick View on a shortcut menu. This type of program-specific viewer has more capabilities than Quick View, including the ability to print a document.

View a Document

1. Right-click the document you want to view.

2. Choose Quick View from the shortcut menu.

3. Use the Increase Font Size or Decrease Font Size button to change your view of the document. Font size changes affect only your *view* of a document—they don't change any information in the file.

4. Use the Page View or Landscape command on the View menu to change your view of the document.

5. Click the Close button when you've finished.

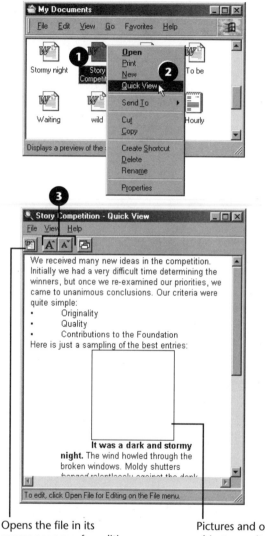

Opens the file in its source program for editing.

Pictures and other objects aren't shown.

Quitting When You're Stuck

If a program isn't working properly and doesn't respond when you try to close it, Windows gives you an alternative course of action, which is known as "ending the task." If you can't end a specific program, you might need to shut down Windows or even turn off your computer. Whatever you do, you'll probably lose any unsaved work in the problem program.

SEE ALSO

"If Disaster Strikes..." on page 274 for information about using tools to diagnose problems in programs.

End the Task or the Windows Session

1 Press Ctrl+Alt+Delete to display the Close Program dialog box.

2 Select the program that's misbehaving.

3 Click the End Task button.

4 Wait for Windows to respond. If Windows asks you whether you want to wait or end the task, click the End Task button. You'll lose any unsaved work.

5 If the program won't close, close all other running programs and shut down Windows.

6 If Windows won't shut down, press Ctrl+Alt+Delete twice. You'll lose any unsaved work and Windows settings.

7 If Windows still refuses to shut down, turn off your computer. When you restart, Windows will recognize an abnormal shutdown and will run a repair utility before you can log on.

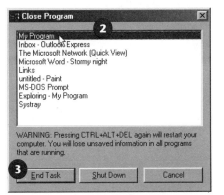

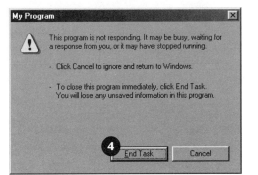

5

Networking

No, this section isn't about schmoozing with people at power breakfasts or "working the tables" at luncheons, handing out business cards and trying to get the inside track on everything. This kind of networking is a lot better!

From your computer network, you can reach out and communicate with people in your immediate workgroup or, if you work for a company that has national or international branches, with people in distant parts of the country or on the other side of the world. You're all part of the Windows 98 Network Neighborhood—and that makes it possible for you to exchange information quickly and productively with your coworkers in Athens, Georgia or Athens, Greece.

This section of the book will guide you through most of what you'll want or need to do if you're new to networking. You'll learn about the different networking systems that you're likely to encounter, as well as some techniques that will help you successfully navigate your particular network.

If you need help setting up your computer to work on a network, or if you're already set up but are experiencing problems, read your company's networking guidelines or talk to your network administrator.

Different Ways of Networking

Working with networks means that you could be dealing with a *client-server network* system, a *peer-to-peer network* system, or both. What's the difference?

A client-server network is the conventional corporate-type network in which one computer (the server) hosts, or provides network services to, other computers (the clients). Almost everything on the network has to pass through the server, which is at the center of this networking universe. The server is managed by a tyrannical overlord known as the *network administrator,* who dictates what each client is allowed to do on the network and can sometimes even prescribe how each client computer is set up.

Servers in a client-server network are often linked so that users have access to other servers. A collection of servers is usually grouped into a management unit called a *domain.* When you log on, you are usually logging on to a domain, which gives you access to all the servers and computers that are part of that domain. Because so many different programs are used to run networks, and because the network administrator can customize the system, you need to refer to your company's networking guidelines for the technical details about your network.

A peer-to-peer network, as its name implies, is a more democratic structure than a client-server network. In this kind of network, all computers are created equal and the users of the computers decide whether and what they will share with other people. Any computer in the workgroup can be a server (sharing its files, for example), a client (using someone else's printer), or both. When you connect to another computer in a workgroup, either as part of a larger network or as a small stand-alone network, you are using peer-to-peer networking.

Why the different systems? It's mostly a matter of scale. Peer-to-peer systems are the easiest to use but can quickly become overloaded as computers are added to the workgroup. A client-server system with one or more powerful server computers and sophisticated management software is designed to handle very large volumes of network traffic.

A generally accepted standard is that for a small office with 10 or fewer computers, you'll probably want a stand-alone peer-to-peer network. For a company with more than 10 computers, you'll probably need a client-server network set up with workgroups.

Client-Server Network

Peer-to-Peer Network

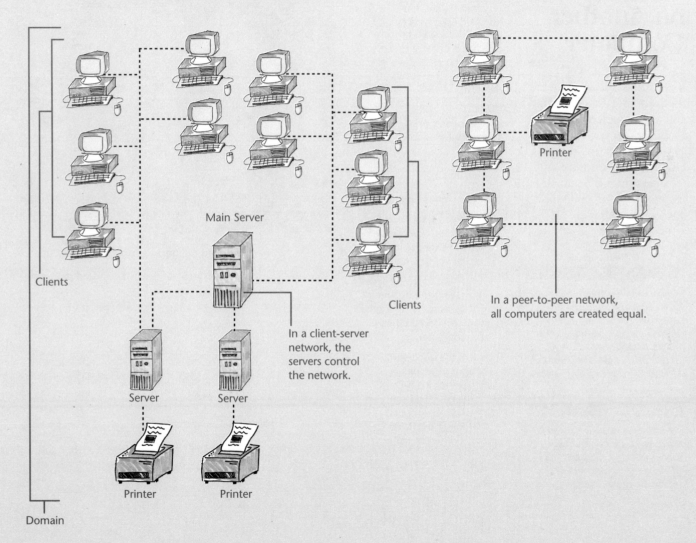

Clients

Main Server

In a client-server network, the servers control the network.

Server

Server

Printer

Printer

Clients

Domain

Printer

In a peer-to-peer network, all computers are created equal.

5

Opening a Document on Another Computer

If you know the name of the computer, the folder, and the document that you want to open, you can simply type the address. Like a document on your own computer, a document on another computer will open in the program it's associated with.

TIP

Only computers that have been set up for sharing are accessible. Depending on how such computers are shared, you might be denied access or you might need to use a password.

SEE ALSO

"Finding a File on a Network" on page 70 for information about finding a file when you don't know the exact name or location of a computer or folder.

Open a Document

1. In any Address toolbar (on the Desktop, My Computer, or Windows Explorer, for example), type the full path and name of the document in the form *computer**folder**document*.

2. Press Enter.

3. If you're asked for a password, provide the password, and click OK.

4. Work with the document.

5. Save your changes.

   ◆ If you have Read-Only access, you can save the changes in a folder on your computer.

   ◆ If you have Full access, saving the document saves it in the original folder on the network computer.

   ◆ If the document (not the folder) is set for Read-Only access, you can save it in the original folder by giving it a different name.

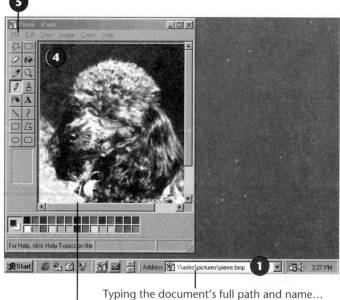

Typing the document's full path and name...

...opens the document in its associated program.

TIP

The Address toolbar on the Windows Desktop remembers the addresses you enter, so, to return to a previously visited site, open the Address list and click the appropriate address.

SEE ALSO

"Creating Quick Access to a Network Resource" on page 71 for information about creating a shortcut to a folder on a computer.

"Navigating with Toolbars" on page 98 for information about using the Address toolbar on the Desktop.

TIP

Many documents contain hyperlinks that take you to a particular location. When you click a hyperlink, it provides the computer with an address—just as you do when you enter an address in the Address toolbar. If an address in a document isn't a hyperlink, you can select and copy it, click in the Address toolbar, and press Ctrl+V to paste the address into the Address toolbar.

Open a Folder

1. In the Address toolbar, type the name of the computer and the shared folder in the form \\computer\folder or \\computer\folder\subfolder.

2. Press Enter.

3. If you're asked for a password, provide the password, and click OK.

4. Locate the document you want in the folder window that appears.

As you type, Windows completes the address with the best match.

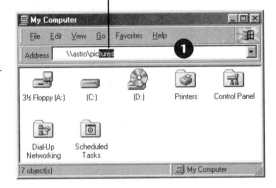

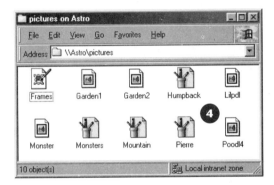

Finding a File on a Network

If you don't know the exact name or location of a computer or folder, you can browse your workgroup or the network to find the computer and then the folder.

TIP

If you know the name of the computer but you can't find it by browsing, use the Find command on the Start menu to search for the computer.

TIP

You can also explore your Network Neighborhood from Windows Explorer.

TRY THIS

Find Yourself. *Open Network Neighborhood, find your own computer, and click it. You'll see what everyone else sees— that is, only the folders that are shared, and any customization you applied to any of those folders.*

Browse

1 Double-click the Network Neighborhood icon on the Desktop.

2 Double-click the name of a computer in your workgroup.

3 If the computer isn't part of your workgroup, double-click Entire Network.

4 Double-click the name of the workgroup or network that contains the computer.

5 Explore.

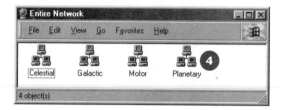

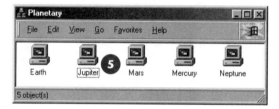

Creating Quick Access to a Network Resource

If you frequently need access to another computer, or to a folder that's on another computer, you can either create a shortcut to the folder or assign a drive letter to the folder. Although the shortcut is the easier connection, you might want to assign a drive letter when you're using certain programs. How do you know which way to go? When you want direct access to a folder, create a shortcut. When you're working with a program that requires a drive letter to access network resources, assign a drive letter.

SEE ALSO

"Creating Your Own Toolbars" on page 99 for information about using a toolbar to gain access to a folder on a network.

Create a Shortcut

1. Double-click the Network Neighborhood icon on the Desktop.

2. Locate the computer and the folder you want.

3. Click the folder to select it.

4. Hold down the right mouse button, drag the folder, and drop it on the Desktop.

5. Choose Create Shortcut(s) Here from the shortcut menu.

Dropping the folder on your Desktop and creating a shortcut…

…gives you easy access to a folder on another computer.

Assign a Drive Letter

1. Use the Network Neighborhood window to locate the computer and the folder you want.

2. Right-click the folder.

3. Choose Map Network Drive from the shortcut menu.

4. Click OK.

Accept the proposed drive letter or select a different unused drive letter.

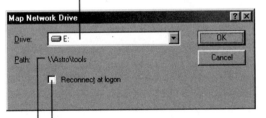

Turn on if you want to create this connection each time you log on to the network.

Check the path to verify that you've connected to the correct computer and folder.

5

Sharing Your Computer

When you need to share files that are on your computer, you must set up your network connection to allow others access to your computer. There are two ways to do this: you can create password-only access to certain folders, or you can specify the names of those individuals on your network who are allowed to access the folders.

TIP

Any subfolder that's contained within a shared folder is also shared.

SEE ALSO

"Sharing a Printer" on page 92 for information about sharing your printer with others.

Turn On Sharing

1. Click the Start button, point to Settings, and choose Control Panel from the submenu.

2. Double-click the Network icon to display the Network dialog box.

3. On the Configuration tab, click the File And Print Sharing button.

4. Specify the items you want to be able to share.

5. Click OK.

6. Click OK.

Shares your files with other people on your network.

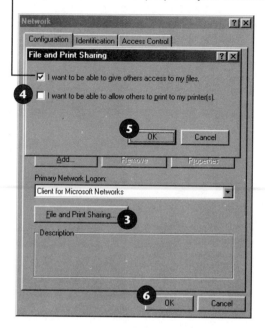

Many companies have rigid policies about what information may be shared and with whom. Before you adjust any sharing settings, check with the network administrator and verify that you're not violating company security standards. If the network administrator has set up your computer for remote administration, don't change the access control or remove sharing from a drive or folder. If you do, you could disable the remote administration.

You can have only one type of access control for your computer, so make your choice before you start sharing folders. If you change your mind and switch the access control, all the folders that were shared will no longer be shared.

Use the Identification tab to change the name of your computer, the workgroup you belong to, or the description of your computer.

Select the Type of Sharing

1 In the Network dialog box, click the Access Control tab.

2 Turn on the type of sharing you want:

◆ Share-Level Access Control to specify the level of access for each folder.

◆ User-Level Access Control to specify which users can access each folder. This requires connection to a server that verifies user names and permissions.

3 Click OK.

4 Restart your computer to implement the changes.

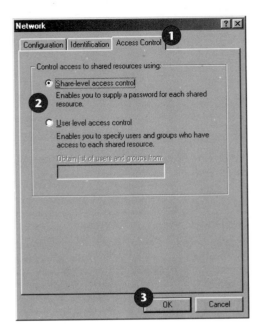

5

Sharing Folders Using Passwords

When you set up your computer for *share-level access control,* you specify which folders are to be shared and what type of access you will allow. You create a password to limit access to the specified folders, and you give the password to the people who may access those folders. You can customize the level of access even further by creating one password for full access and another password for read-only access.

TRY THIS

You can prevent unauthorized changes to your shared files but still make them available for viewing without a password. For the access type, select Depends On Password. Then specify a Full Access Password, but leave Read-Only Password blank. Users who enter the correct password will be granted full access; those who cancel the password prompt can open, but cannot change the content of, shared files.

Share a Folder

1 Locate the folder you want to share.

2 Right-click the folder and choose Sharing from the shortcut menu.

3 On the Sharing tab, turn on the Shared As option.

4 Type a new name for the folder if you want to change the proposed name.

5 Type a comment if you want one.

6 Specify the type of access.

7 Enter the password or passwords required for access:

   ◆ A Read-Only Password if you selected the Read-Only or Depends On Password option

   ◆ A Full Access Password if you selected the Full or Depends On Password option

8 Click OK.

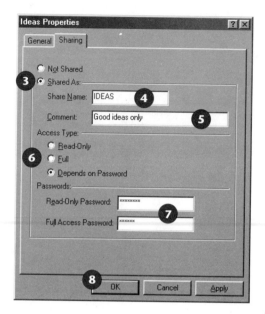

SEE ALSO

"Sharing Your Computer" on page 72 for information about setting up your computer to share folders.

"Sharing Folders with Individuals" on page 76 for information about specifying individual access to shared folders.

Protect Individual Files

1 Open the shared folder.

2 Select the file or files you want to protect.

3 Right-click the selected file or one of the selected files, and choose Properties from the shortcut menu.

4 Turn on the Read-Only check box.

5 Click OK.

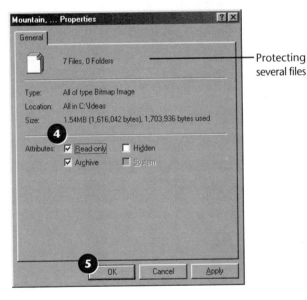

Protecting a single file

Protecting several files

Sharing Folders with Individuals

When you set up your computer for *user-level access control*, you can share folders with individuals or with the entire network if you so desire. You use the names stored on your main network server to specify which individuals have what type of access.

SEE ALSO

"Select the Type of Sharing" on page 73 for information about setting up your computer for user-level access control.

TIP

Different networks use different naming services, so your access list might look different from the one shown in the Add Users dialog box at the right. The examples shown here are based on using a Microsoft Windows NT Server 4.0.

Share a Folder

1. Locate the folder you want to share.

2. Right-click the folder and choose Sharing from the shortcut menu.

3. On the Sharing tab, turn on the Shared As option.

4. Type a name for the folder if you want to change the proposed name.

5. Type a comment if you want one.

6. Click the Add button.

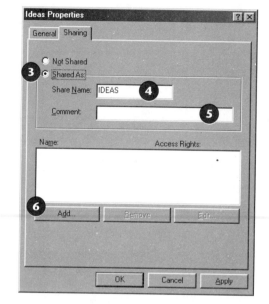

Specify the Access

1. Select the individuals or groups whom you want to have read-only access.

2. Click the Read Only button to add them to the list.

3. Select the individuals or groups whom you want to have full access.

4. Click the Full Access button to add them to the list.

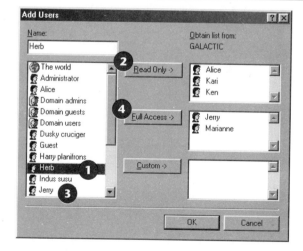

Customize the Access

1 In the Add Users dialog box, select the individuals or groups whom you want to have customized access.

2 Click the Custom button to add them to the list.

3 Click OK.

4 Specify the types of access.

5 Click OK.

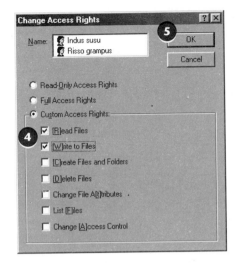

Individualize the Access

1 On the Sharing tab, select an individual whose access you want to modify.

2 Click the Edit button.

3 Change the access specifications in the Change Access Rights dialog box, and click OK.

4 Click OK.

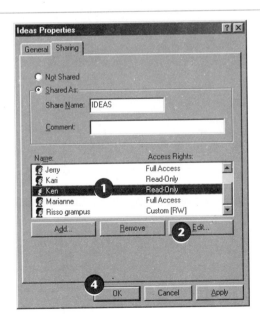

Changing Your Passwords

As if it's not difficult enough to remember your passwords, security procedures—not to mention ruthless network administrators—often require you to change your passwords periodically. Windows simplifies the process by letting you change several passwords at the same time.

TIP

If you set your network password to be the same as your Windows password when you're changing the Windows password, you'll need to enter your password only once when logging on, skipping the password for logging on to your network.

TIP

Some networks require you to use different tools for changing your network password. If the procedures described here don't work, consult your network administrator.

Change Your Windows Password

1. Click the Start button, point to Settings, and choose Control Panel from the submenu.

2. Double-click the Passwords icon.

3. Click the Change Windows Password button.

4. To change only your Windows password, turn off the check box for any network password options shown. To make the Windows and network passwords the same, turn on the check box for the network option.

5. Click OK.

6. Type your old password, and then type a new one. Type the new password again to confirm it, and click OK.

7. Click OK.

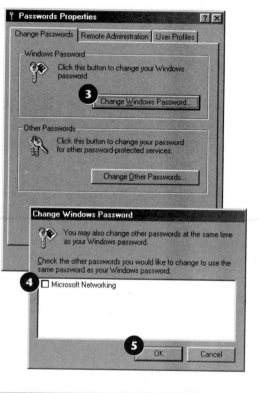

Forgotten passwords are a constant source of problems with computers and networking. You can guard against this particular problem by using the same word for all your passwords, writing the word down, and storing it in a safe place (not on the wall next to the computer!). Be careful to use the correct capitalization when you write the word down.

Your Windows password isn't case-sensitive, but many network passwords are. If you're sure you typed the correct password but it was rejected, check to make sure the Caps Lock key isn't turned on, and type the password again. If the password is rejected yet again, try typing a couple of different capitalizations. If none of them works, you'll be so glad that your password is written down and stored in that safe place!

Change Your Network Password

1 Click the Change Other Passwords button.

2 Select the network access for which you want to change your password.

3 Click the Change button.

4 Type your old password, and then type a new one. Type the new password again to confirm it, and click OK.

5 Click OK when Windows confirms the change.

6 Click Close.

6

Printing

Whether you're printing your documents on a printer that's attached directly to your computer or on a shared printer on a company network, you're using the print services provided by Microsoft Windows 98. These services include sending the correct types of codes to the printer, organizing print jobs so that they print in an orderly succession, and managing output to different printers.

We'll cover some useful techniques in this section. For example, you'll find out how to print to a file when you can't access a printer; then, when a printer is available, you'll be able to print your document without having to open the program it's associated with. You'll learn how simple it is to set up your computer so that you can share your printer with other people in your workgroup. If you and your computer are part of a company network, you'll also learn how to connect to a network printer. And, should you run into trouble when you try to print from an MS-DOS–based program on a network printer, you'll learn how to trick the program into thinking it's printing from a standard printer port.

If, as many people do, you feel a bit daunted by the printing process because of previous unpleasant experiences, this section of the book will guide you painlessly through the printing maze.

Printing from a Program

In most situations, the easiest way to print a document is to use the Print command, which you'll usually find on the program's File menu. Depending on the program, you can specify which printer to use, how many copies you want, and so on. You might encounter some differences among programs, but most programs give you the same basic options.

Print

1 Create and save your document.

2 Choose Print from the File menu.

3 Use the Print dialog box to specify your print options.

4 Click OK to print the document.

General information about the printer

Click to fine-tune the printer settings.

Current printer. Select a different printer from the drop-down list.

Turn on to have pages of a multipage document printed in consecutive order, one set at a time, when printing more than one copy.

Specify the number of copies of this document to be printed.

Turn on to create a print file to use on another computer.

Specify which part of a document is to be printed. When printing only a section of a document, specify the beginning and ending page numbers.

Printing a Document

When you want to print only one copy of a document that doesn't need any modification, you can print that document—or several different documents—directly from Windows without first starting the program in which the document resides. This doesn't mean that you don't need the program; it is still required for printing, but Windows will take care of the details for you.

TIP

Some programs require the use of the system default printer. For documents associated with such programs, you'll either have to print using the default printer, or switch the default-printer designation to the printer you want to use.

SEE ALSO

"Switching the Default Printer" on page 84 for information about designating another printer as the default printer.

Print a Document Using the Default Printer

1 Select the document(s) to be printed.

2 Right-click a selected document and choose Print from the shortcut menu. Windows will use the program, or a special viewer for a program—Word Viewer, for example—if it's installed, to print the document.

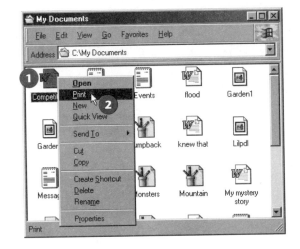

Print a Document Using a Specific Printer

1 Click the Start button, point to Settings, and choose Printers from the submenu to open the Printers folder.

2 Select the document to be printed.

3 Drag the selected document to the Printers folder and drop it on the printer you want to use.

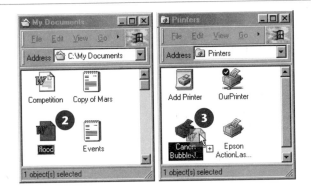

6

Switching the Default Printer

Some programs are set up to print only to the system default printer; other programs are set up to print to the default printer but will allow you to "target," or change to, a different printer. If several printers are available, you can designate any one of them as the default printer.

SEE ALSO

"Printing from a Program" on page 82 for information about printing to a nondefault printer.

TIP

If you can't output or export text or data from a program the way you want, double-click the Add Printer icon, and install the Generic/Text Only printer. Set it to File to send output from a program to a text file. You'll be able to edit the text file or import it into a second program that isn't fully compatible with the original program.

Change the Default

1 Click the Start button, point to Settings, and choose Printers from the submenu.

2 Right-click the printer you want to use as the default printer.

3 Choose Set As Default from the shortcut menu.

4 Verify that the printer has a check mark next to it.

5 Close the Printers folder when you've finished.

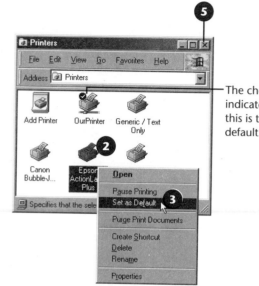

The check mark indicates that this is the current default printer.

Printing Without a Printer

When you're not connected to your usual printer, or if your printer is misbehaving, you can still print your documents. Well, not *exactly*. What you can do is create *print jobs*—that is, the documents stay in the printer *queue* until you and the printer are ready, and then the print jobs are sent to the printer as if you had been connected all the time.

TIP

If a document won't print after the printer is back on line, select the document and turn off the Pause Printing option on the Document menu.

SEE ALSO

"Printing a Document to a File" on page 90 for information about creating a print job that will be printed from a different computer.

Create a Print Job

1 Click the Start button, point to Settings, and choose Printers from the submenu.

2 Right-click the printer and, from the shortcut menu, choose Use Printer Offline for a network printer or Pause Printing for a local printer.

3 Print your document as usual.

4 Double-click the printer in the Printers folder to review the print jobs in the printer queue.

5 If your computer is not connected to the printer, shut down your system when you've finished, reconnect to the printer or the network, and start Windows.

6 If Windows tells you there are documents waiting to be printed, click Yes. Right-click the printer in the Printers folder and turn off the Work Offline option for a network printer or the Pause Printing option for a local printer to send all the print jobs to the printer.

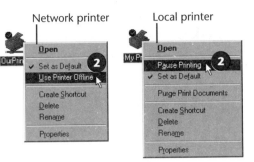

Network printer   Local printer

Windows gently reminds you that the printer is off line.

All the files you want to print are queued up, waiting until the printer is on line.

Controlling Your Printing

When you send your documents to be printed, each print job is *queued* in the order in which it's received. You can see the progress of your print job in the queue, and you can temporarily suspend printing of your document or even remove your document from the queue if you want. On a printer that's connected directly to your computer, or on a network computer for which you have administrative permission, you can suspend all printing and can even clear all documents from the printer queue.

TIP

Jumping the Queue. *The network administrator can set priorities for printing jobs on a network printer, so some print jobs might not be printed in the order in which they were received by the printer.*

View the Queue

1. Click the Start button, point to Settings, and choose Printers from the submenu.

2. Double-click the printer you're using to open a window showing all the documents in the printer queue.

You have full control of a local printer...

Documents in the printer queue

...but you can control only your own documents on a network printer.

Size of each document

Manage a Document

1 Right-click your document.

2 Choose the action you want from the shortcut menu:

◆ Pause Printing to stop your document from printing until you resume printing by choosing Pause Printing again

◆ Cancel Printing to delete the document from the print queue

Stop the Presses

1 From the Printer menu, choose Pause Printing to stop printing of all documents on that printer.

2 Choose the action you want from the Printer menu:

◆ Pause Printing (when checked) to resume printing the documents in the printer queue

◆ Purge Print Documents to delete all the print jobs in the printer queue

This document is being printed ahead of the paused document.

Choosing this command deletes all the print jobs in the queue.

6

Connecting to a Network Printer

When a printer is set up to be shared, you can easily connect to it, and you can configure your system for that printer. You need to set up the connection to the printer only once; thereafter, you can use the printer as if it were directly connected to your computer.

> **TIP**
>
> *Use the method described here even if you're connecting to the same printer that has been moved to a different location.*

> **TIP**
>
> *If you start dragging an icon but the window scrolls so fast that you lose your place, press the Esc key to cancel the drag-and-drop action before you release the mouse button.*

Get the Printer

1 Click the Start button, point to Settings, and choose Printers from the submenu.

2 Use Network Neighborhood, an Address toolbar, or Windows Explorer to locate the computer that has the printer, and open a window to that computer.

3 Select the printer you want to use.

4 Drag the printer and drop it on your Printers folder.

5 Complete the Add Printer Wizard.

Printing from MS-DOS to a Network Printer

Many MS-DOS–based programs are set to print to a printer that's connected to a standard printer port, such as LPT1 or COM1, and these programs can't normally print to a network printer. However, you *can* print to a network printer from an MS-DOS–based program. The trick is to have Windows reroute the program's output by "capturing" the network printer port. The MS-DOS–based program is fooled into thinking it's printing to a standard port, but its output is really being sent over the network.

TIP

When you run the Add Printer Wizard, select the option for printing from MS-DOS programs, and Windows will let you capture the port at that time.

Capture the Port

1 Click the Start button, point to Settings, and choose Printers from the submenu.

2 Right-click the printer you want to use and choose Properties from the shortcut menu.

3 On the Details tab, click the Capture Printer Port button.

4 Select the port that the MS-DOS program thinks the printer is connected to.

5 Type the path to the network printer if it's not already completed.

6 Turn on the Reconnect At Logon check box if you want this connection to be available every time you use your computer.

7 Click OK.

8 Click OK.

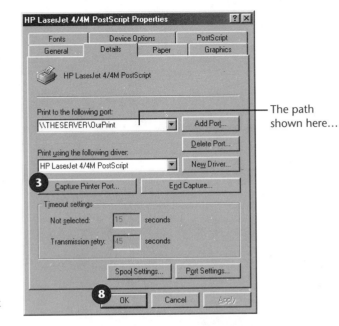

The path shown here...

...must be entered here.

6

Printing a Document to a File

If you don't have direct access to a specific printer, you can print a document to a file. The file contains all the special printer information from the program, so you don't need to start the program again to print—you simply send the file to the printer when the printer is available.

Create a Print File

1. Use the Add Printer Wizard in the Printers folder to install on your computer a printer that's connected to File instead of to a printer port. Be sure to specify the same manufacturer and model specifications for the printer to which you'll be sending the file.

2. Use your program to print a document to the new printer.

3. Type a name for the output file.

4. Click OK.

TIP

If you're going to hand off a print file to a service bureau, get all the relevant information about the correct target printer before you create your document. Many service bureaus are happy to provide you with their own preferred software when you're creating a print job on disk.

TRY THIS

Set the printer that's connected to File as your default printer, right-click a document file (such as a bitmap image), and choose Print. Type a filename for the output file. Start the command prompt, and send the file to the correct printer on the print server.

SEE ALSO

"Navigating Folders in MS-DOS" on page 133 for information about switching to a specific folder.

Send a Print File to a Printer

1 Click the Start button, point to Programs, and choose MS-DOS Prompt from the submenu.

2 Navigate to the folder that contains the print file.

3 At the prompt, type *copy filename printerdevice* (where *filename* specifies the print file and *printerdevice* identifies the location of the printer).

4 Press Enter.

Prints the file *mydoc.prn* using the printer connected to the LPT1 port.

Prints the file *mydoc.prn* using the network printer OurPrint on Theserver print server.

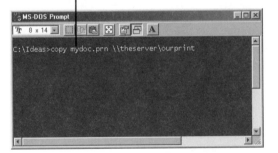

Sharing a Printer

You can set up your computer so that you can share your printer with other people in your workgroup. However, this situation requires a generous and even-tempered personality! When several people are using your printer, you'll find that your computer becomes quite sluggish.

TIP

Share Your Toys! *You must have print sharing set up for your computer before you can share your printer.*

SEE ALSO

"Sharing Your Computer" on page 72, "Sharing Folders Using Passwords" on page 74, and "Sharing Folders with Individuals" on page 76 for information about setting up sharing and specifying sharing permissions.

"Connecting to a Network Printer" on page 88 for information about setting up a network printer on your computer.

Share Your Printer

1. Click the Start button, point to Settings, and choose Printers from the submenu.

2. Right-click the printer you want to share and choose Sharing from the shortcut menu.

3. On the Sharing tab, turn on the Shared As option.

4. Type a name for the printer.

5. Type a comment if you want one.

6. Limit access to the printer:

   ◆ For Share-Level access, enter a password for use by those who may access the printer. Otherwise, leave the Password box blank.

   ◆ For User-Level access, click the Add button and specify the users.

7. Click OK.

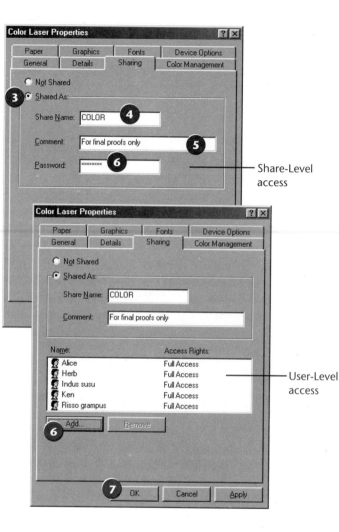

Share-Level access

User-Level access

7

Setting Up Your Desktop

Like everyone who works at a desk, you put papers here, reference materials there, perhaps a photograph or a plant in a spot where your elbow won't send it flying—in short, you design your work space so that it's as efficient and comfortable as possible. With Windows 98, you can extend your preferences to your computer's Desktop—in fact, you can change the look of the icons, the screen, and the Desktop itself so dramatically that your screen bears little resemblance to the standard Windows "look." Of course, if you're perfectly happy with Windows as is, you don't need to change a thing. It's your Desktop, and you can customize everything on it as often or as infrequently as you want.

Whatever your decision, in this section you'll learn how to make the most efficient use of your Desktop by placing on it the folders, documents, shortcuts, and any other items you use often so that you can access them right away. We'll show you how to create powerful toolbars that meet your individual needs, and we'll give you a quick introduction to the *Active Desktop*, which enables you to place a wealth of information at your fingertips with a single mouse-click. For complete details about the Active Desktop and information about adding Web content to your Desktop, you'll want to read Section 11, "Using the Net," which starts on page 171.

Customize
Your Environment

Windows 98 lets you customize your Desktop so that it functions the way you want it to. If you're a traditionalist, you can set your working environment to run with a double-click of an icon on your Desktop. If you like the look and feel of the Internet, you can set your icons to launch with a single click, and you can place all sorts

of jumps and HTML features right on your Desktop. Or perhaps you'd prefer to use toolbars to navigate and to run programs. No problem—you can arrange predefined toolbars, or new toolbars that you create, around the screen, and you can even have them disappear when you don't need them. If none of these options is exactly

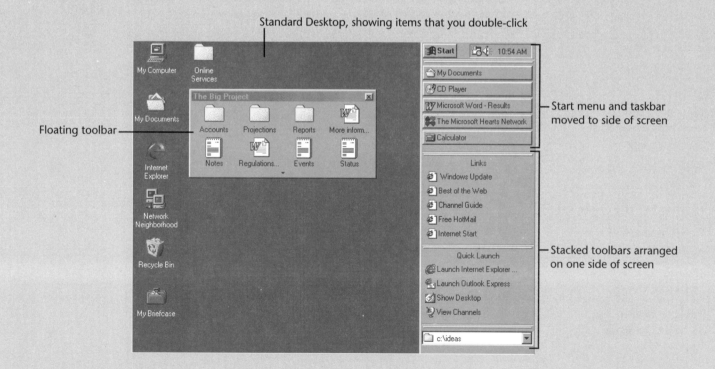

Standard Desktop, showing items that you double-click

Floating toolbar

Start menu and taskbar moved to side of screen

Stacked toolbars arranged on one side of screen

to your liking, you can mix and match them to create your own unique environment.

Much of the customization you can do is discussed in this section, but you'll find items that affect more than the Desktop discussed elsewhere. For information about using the Channel Bar, see "Viewing Channels" on page 178. For information about changing the way you click an icon—whether it's on the Desktop or in a folder window—see "Changing Your Click" on page 230.

Active Desktop, showing items
that need only a single click

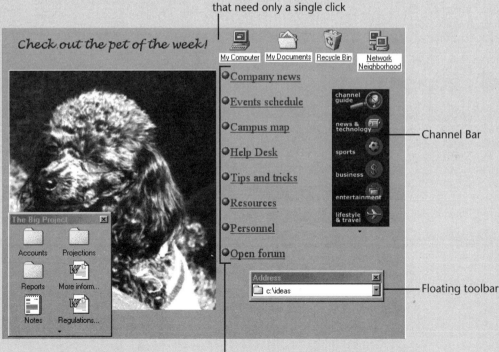

Channel Bar

Floating toolbar

Jumps to custom Web pages

Arranging Windows on the Desktop

When you have several windows open, your Desktop can become littered with overlapping windows. You can arrange the open windows for easy access, or you can minimize and store some or all of them on the taskbar to keep your Desktop neat and uncluttered.

TIP

If you want to access only one Desktop icon, use the Desktop toolbar. If you want full access to the Desktop, use the Desktop button on the Quick Launch toolbar to minimize all of your windows.

SEE ALSO

"Navigating with Toolbars" on page 98 for information about displaying the Quick Launch and Desktop toolbars.

Arrange Your Open Windows

1 Minimize any windows other than the ones you want displayed.

2 Point to a blank spot on the Windows taskbar and right-click.

3 Choose Cascade Windows, Tile Windows Horizontally, or Tile Windows Vertically to arrange all the open windows.

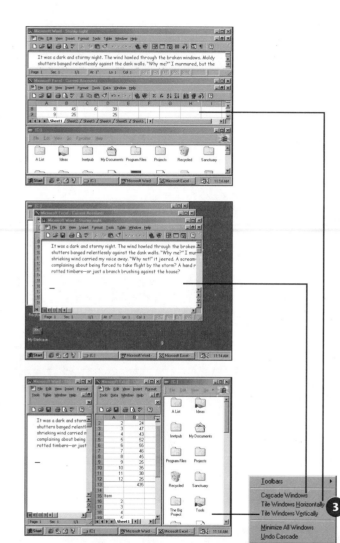

Controlling the Way Folder Windows Open

Depending on the view style you've selected, when you open a folder window from within its parent window, either a new window opens or the contents of the parent window are automatically replaced by the contents of the folder window you just opened. If you want, though, you can change the way a new window opens without changing any of your other view settings.

Use a Single Window or Multiple Windows

1 In any folder window, choose Folder Options from the View menu.

2 On the General tab, turn on the Custom option.

3 Click the Settings button.

4 Turn on an option:
- Open Each Folder In The Same Window if you want the parent folder's contents to be replaced by the contents of the opened folder
- Open Each Folder In Its Own Window if you want to open a new window for each folder you open

5 Click OK.

6 Click OK.

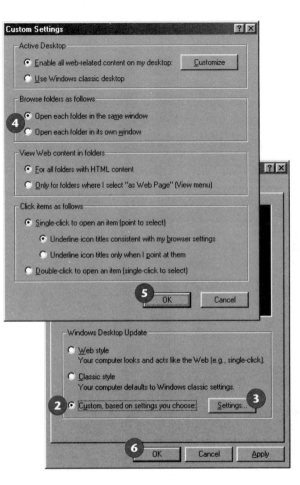

Navigating with Toolbars

Windows 98 provides you with four toolbars, which can give you access to almost anything you need: programs, folders, and documents, as well as Internet and intranet sites.

SEE ALSO

"Creating Your Own Toolbars" on the facing page for information about creating your own toolbars.

TRY THIS

Right-click a blank spot on the taskbar and use the Toolbars command on the shortcut menu to display several toolbars. Double-click the "raised" bar on a toolbar to expand the toolbar to full size (or to the maximum size it can attain). Double-click the raised bar again to shrink the toolbar to its minimum size. Place the pointer over the raised bar, drag to create a custom-size toolbar, and then drop the toolbar wherever you want it.

Display a Toolbar

1. Right-click a blank spot on the taskbar or on any toolbar.

2. Point to Toolbars on the shortcut menu and choose the toolbar you want to display. (A toolbar with a check mark next to its name is one that's already displayed.)

WINDOWS TOOLBARS	
Toolbar	**Function**
Address	Opens the item you specify when you type its full address or when you select the address of a previously visited location.
Links	Links you to the same Internet sites that are shown on the Links submenu of the Favorites menu.
Desktop	Provides quick access to the Desktop icons, files, folders, and shortcuts that are shown on your Windows Desktop.
Quick Launch	Launches Internet Explorer, Outlook Express, Channel Viewer, and Microsoft WebTV For Windows (if installed), or minimizes all windows on the Desktop.

See All the Buttons

1. If an entire toolbar or taskbar is not displayed, drag or double-click the small "raised" bar on the toolbar.

2. If all the buttons on a toolbar are still not visible, click the small left or right arrow (if present) to scroll through the items.

3. If all the buttons on the taskbar are still not visible, use the up or down arrow to scroll through all the items.

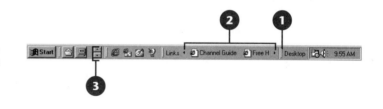

Creating Your Own Toolbars

The toolbars that come with Windows 98 are great, but if they don't meet your needs you can easily create your own customized toolbars by connecting to a folder in which you've placed all the items you want to appear on your toolbar.

TIP

If you no longer need a custom toolbar and want to delete it permanently, right-click it and choose Close from its shortcut menu. The toolbar will go away but the contents of the folder to which it was connected will be unchanged.

Create a Toolbar

1 Create a folder containing the documents, folders, and shortcuts that you want to appear on the toolbar.

2 Right-click a blank spot on a toolbar or on the taskbar, point to Toolbars on the shortcut menu, and choose New Toolbar.

3 In the New Toolbar dialog box, navigate to the folder you created, and select it.

4 Click OK.

5 Drag any documents, folders, or programs from other windows onto the toolbar to add a shortcut to the items. The shortcut to the added items is added to the folder that the toolbar is based on.

6 Use the new toolbar just as you use any other toolbar.

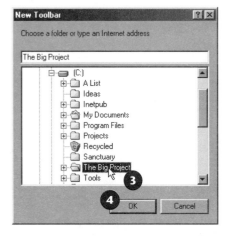

Folders and documents in The Big Project folder

Shortcuts created by dragging folders and documents from other folders onto the new toolbar

Hiding the Taskbar or a Toolbar

Toolbars—including the taskbar—are handy navigational devices, but they can sometimes get in your way. If you want to, you can hide any toolbar and have it appear only when you need it.

TIP

If you can't find the taskbar because it's hidden or because something else is on top of it, press the Ctrl+Esc key combination. This will display the taskbar with the Start menu open.

TIP

Any toolbar that's connected to the taskbar will be hidden when the taskbar is hidden and will be displayed when the taskbar is displayed.

Hide the Taskbar

1. Right-click a blank spot on the taskbar and choose Properties from the shortcut menu.

2. Turn on the Auto Hide option.

3. Turn on any other options you want.

4. Click OK.

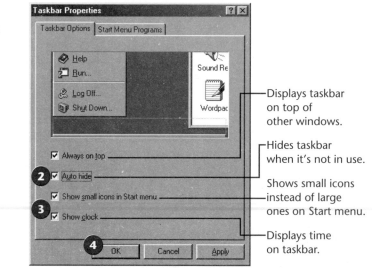

- Displays taskbar on top of other windows.
- Hides taskbar when it's not in use.
- Shows small icons instead of large ones on Start menu.
- Displays time on taskbar.

Hide a Toolbar

1. Move the toolbar to an edge of the screen that doesn't contain the taskbar.

2. Right-click a blank spot on the toolbar.

3. Choose Auto Hide.

4. Right-click a blank spot on the toolbar and choose Always On Top if the command doesn't already have a check mark next to it.

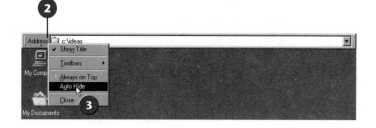

TIP

If you're working with two (or more) monitors attached to your computer, you can move the taskbar and any of the toolbars onto the part of the Desktop that is displayed on the second monitor. You can then dock the taskbar or toolbars at the edge of that monitor's screen.

SEE ALSO

"Rearranging the Taskbar and the Toolbars" on page 102 for information about moving a toolbar.

"Using Two Monitors" on page 252 for information about working with multiple monitors.

Display the Taskbar or a Toolbar

1 Move the mouse pointer to the edge of the screen where the taskbar or a toolbar is hidden. The taskbar or toolbar slides into view.

2 Use the taskbar or toolbar as you normally would: click buttons, type an address, or select an item from a drop-down list.

3 Move the mouse pointer off the taskbar or toolbar to hide the taskbar or toolbar again.

When the mouse pointer reaches the edge of the screen...

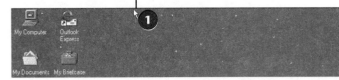

...the hidden toolbar appears.

Rearranging the Taskbar and the Toolbars

The taskbar and the toolbars are indispensable tools for working efficiently in Windows 98. If you want, you can rearrange them so that they're tailored even more closely to your working style. For example, you can change the size of a toolbar or the taskbar, and you can "dock" it at any of the four sides of your screen. You can also "float" the toolbars—but not the taskbar—anywhere on the Desktop.

Move Them

1 Point to a blank spot on the taskbar or to the small "raised" bar on a toolbar.

2 Do any of the following:

◆ Drag the taskbar or toolbar and drop it at the top, bottom, or either side of your screen to dock it.

◆ Drag a toolbar and float it by dropping it into an empty spot on the Desktop.

◆ Drag a floating toolbar to a side of the screen or onto a docked toolbar to dock the floating toolbar.

Floating toolbars created by dropping toolbars onto the Desktop

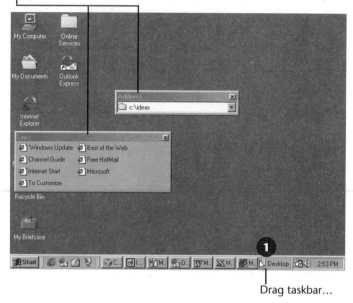

Drag taskbar...

...and drop it at the side of the screen.

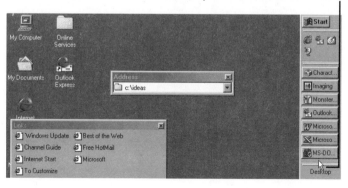

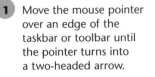

7

TRY THIS

Display several toolbars together with the taskbar on a single line along the bottom of the screen. Drag the top edge of the taskbar up. Observe that as you drag the taskbar up, the toolbars stack under each other. Keep dragging up until all the toolbars and the taskbar are on separate lines. Now set the taskbar and the toolbars to Auto Hide, and click the Desktop.

TIP

Customize Your Icons.
To change the size at which icons are displayed on a tool-bar, right-click a blank spot on the toolbar, point to View on the shortcut menu, and choose Large or Small. To include a text label to identify each icon, right-click the toolbar and choose Show Text from the shortcut menu. To include a text label to identify a docked toolbar, right-click the toolbar and choose Show Title from the shortcut menu.

Resize Them

1 Move the mouse pointer over an edge of the taskbar or toolbar until the pointer turns into a two-headed arrow.

2 Drag the border and drop it when the taskbar or toolbar is the size you want.

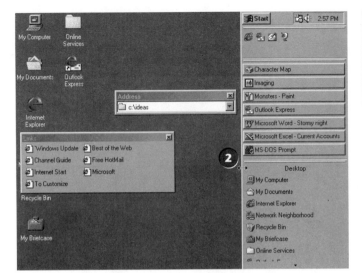

Stack Them

1 With the taskbar and the toolbars docked at the top or bottom of the Desktop, drag the inside edge of the taskbar.

2 Release the mouse button when the taskbar and the toolbars are stacked.

Adding Documents and Folders to the Desktop

The Windows 98 Desktop comes equipped with some icons that start programs or that lead you quickly to special locations. If there are documents or folders that you use regularly, you can place them on your Desktop to speed up your work.

SEE ALSO

"Navigating with Toolbars" on page 98 and "Creating Your Own Toolbars" on page 99 for information about accessing documents from a toolbar.

TIP

To use My Computer or Windows Explorer to work with the documents, shortcuts, and folders on the Desktop, open the Windows folder, the Profiles subfolder, the folder with your user name, and then the Desktop folder.

Add a Document

1. Double-click the My Computer icon.

2. Navigate through the folders to find the document you want.

3. Hold down the right mouse button, drag the document, and drop it on the Desktop.

4. From the shortcut menu, choose either to move or copy the document onto the Desktop, or to create a shortcut to the document.

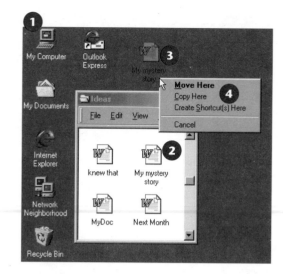

Add a Folder

1. Right-click a blank spot on the Desktop.

2. Point to New on the shortcut menu and choose Folder.

3. Type a name for the new folder, and press Enter.

7

TIP

If your computer is set up with different profiles for individual users, files saved to the Desktop might not be available to other users. If you want others to have easy access to a file, place the file in a common folder.

SEE ALSO

"Customizing a Computer for Different Users" on page 231 for information about creating user profiles.

TIP

If the program you're using doesn't support dragging and dropping, copy the selected text, right-click in a blank part of the Desktop, and choose Paste from the shortcut menu.

TRY THIS

Start WordPad and type some text. Select the text and drag it onto the Desktop. Start a new Word 6 document in WordPad, type some text, and then drag the WordPad scrap from the Desktop and drop it into the WordPad document.

Save a Document to the Desktop

1. Create a document in your program.

2. Choose Save from the File menu to display the Save As dialog box.

3. Select Desktop from the Save In drop-down list.

4. Type a name for the document.

5. Click the Save button.

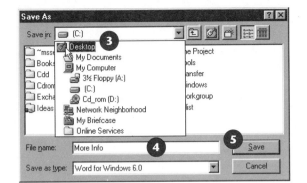

Save Part of a Document to the Desktop

1. Select the part of the document to be saved.

2. Drag the selection and drop it on the Desktop. (You'll notice that Windows puts a "scrap" icon on the Desktop.)

Drag content from here...   ...and drop it here.

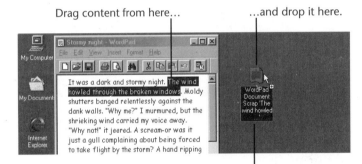

Content stored in scrap can be inserted into a document at a later time. Scraps can also be stored in folders, so you can organize them just as you can any other files.

Tidying Up the Desktop

If your Desktop becomes so cluttered with shortcuts, scraps of text, or overlapping icons that you can't find what you want at a glance, take a minute or two to do a little housekeeping.

TIP

The Auto Arrange command must be turned off before you can create your own arrangement of icons.

TIP

Icon-o-Blast! *If your Desktop is littered with a bunch of icons that you don't need any more, hold down the Ctrl key and click each icon. After you've selected all the icons to be deleted, press the Delete key, and confirm that you want to send the items to the Recycle Bin. If you want to delete the items permanently rather than send them to the Recycle Bin, hold down the Shift key when you press Delete.*

Arrange the Icons

1 Right-click a blank spot on the Desktop.

2 Point to Arrange Icons on the shortcut menu and choose the type of arrangement you want.

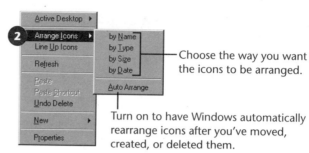

Choose the way you want the icons to be arranged.

Turn on to have Windows automatically rearrange icons after you've moved, created, or deleted them.

Create Your Own Arrangement

1 Drag the icons to the area of the Desktop where you want them.

2 Right-click a blank spot on the Desktop.

3 Choose Line Up Icons from the shortcut menu.

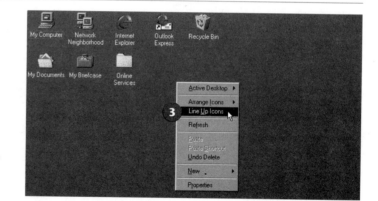

Making More Room on the Desktop

If you want to squeeze more items onto your Desktop, you can change the size of the Desktop...sort of. This is one of those "virtual" realities. You "enlarge" the available space by changing the scaling, which lets you fit more items on the Desktop even though its area on your screen doesn't get any larger. Your gain in "virtual" area does come at a cost, though—everything will be smaller and harder to read.

TIP

If Windows has the proper information about your monitor and graphics card, it will display valid settings only.

SEE ALSO

"Using Two Monitors" on page 252 for information about increasing the size of your Desktop by using more than one monitor.

Increase the Screen Area

1. Right-click a blank spot on the Desktop and choose Properties from the shortcut menu.

2. Click the Settings tab.

3. Drag and drop the slider to select a screen area.

4. Click the Advanced button.

5. Select a different font size if you want. (If you change the font size, you'll need to restart the computer when you resize the Desktop.)

6. Click OK.

7. Click OK or Close. (The OK button changes into a Close button when you change the font size.)

8. Click OK to confirm that you want to resize the Desktop.

9. After the Desktop has been resized, click Yes to accept the new settings or No to revert to the original settings. If you don't click Yes within 15 seconds, Windows restores the original settings.

Uses the same scaling on fonts that's used on all screen elements.

Enlarges font to increase readability of text.

Set your own font size.

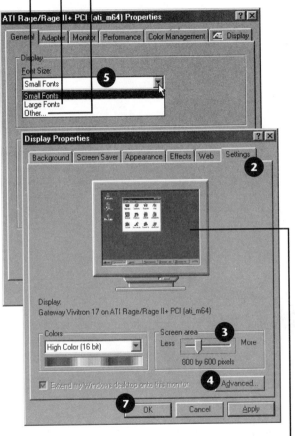

Preview the change in the Desktop area.

Changing the Look of the Desktop

Just as your physical desktop might be constructed from solid oak, printed plastic, or glass, your Windows Desktop can have a patterned surface. You can add a picture for even more interest, and you can have it occupy the entire Desktop surface or only part of it. You can even combine a picture with a patterned background. Keep experimenting until you find the look you like—it's a lot of fun!

SEE ALSO

"Putting a Web Page on Your Desktop" on page 110 for information about using an HTML document (a Web page) as the background for your Desktop.

Add a Pattern

1. Right-click a blank spot on the Desktop and choose Properties from the shortcut menu.

2. Click the Background tab if it's not already selected.

3. Click the Pattern button.

4. Select the pattern that you want to use from the Pattern list.

5. Click OK.

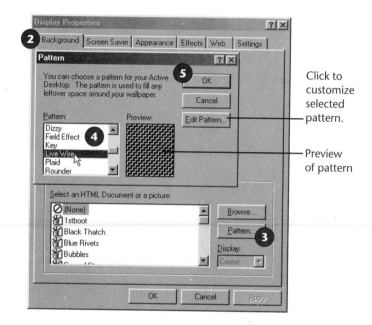

Click to customize selected pattern.

Preview of pattern

7

You can use only Paint-type bitmap pictures for Desktop patterns and pictures unless you turn on the Active Desktop. With the Active Desktop, you can use JPEG and GIF graphics formats that are designed for HTML documents.

When you use a Wallpaper picture, it's always on top of any pattern you select. You'll see the pattern only if the wall-paper picture is centered rather than tiled or stretched and if the picture is smaller than the whole screen. When you have the wallpaper and the pattern both set to (None) and the Active Desktop is deactivated, the Desktop will be the solid color that was set on the Appearance tab.

The background for the Desk-top icon text is set to the Desktop color that was speci-fied on the Appearance tab.

Add a Picture

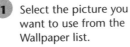

1 Select the picture you want to use from the Wallpaper list.

2 Click the Display option you want:

♦ Tile repeats the image to fill the Desktop.

♦ Center places a single copy of the picture in the center of the Desktop.

♦ Stretch extends the image to fill the Desktop. However, the image might be distorted or degraded.

3 Click OK.

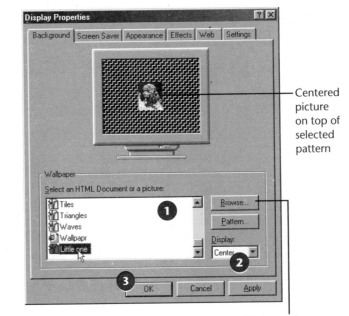

Centered picture on top of selected pattern

Click to use a bitmap file located outside your Windows folder.

Putting a Web Page on Your Desktop

The *Active Desktop* creates two layers on your Desktop. The top layer is the standard Desktop, which displays, among others, the Network Neighborhood and My Computer icons. The bottom layer is the Active Desktop, where you can place an HTML document (a Web page) for powerful formatting that can include hyperlinks to other locations and animated components.

SEE ALSO

"Viewing Channels" on page 178 for information about using the Channel Bar.

"Adding Web Content to the Desktop " on page 184 for information about placing active content on your Desktop.

TIP

Windows 98 comes with the FrontPage Express program, which lets you create your own HTML documents.

Turn On the Active Desktop

1. Right-click a blank spot on the Desktop.

2. Point to Active Desktop on the shortcut menu and choose View As Web Page if it's not already checked.

Get a Web Page

1. Right-click a blank spot on the Desktop, point to Active Desktop on the shortcut menu, and choose Customize My Desktop.

2. On the Background tab, specify the HTML document in one of two ways:

   ◆ Select a document from the list.

   ◆ Click the Browse button, and locate an HTML document on your computer or on your network.

3. Click OK.

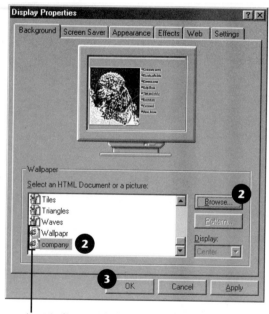

Icon indicates which items are HTML documents.

8

Working with Multimedia

Multimedia! Depending on what you use your computer for, multimedia can mean work or play—or a little or a lot of each. If your computer is set up to work with multimedia—if, that is, you have a sound card installed, speakers or a headset, a CD-ROM drive, and, optionally, a microphone—Windows is set to work with you.

You can play and create sounds, view video clips, and even play music CDs while you work. With the necessary equipment installed, you can also watch TV on your computer screen. You can associate sounds with events that take place on your computer: if you'd like to hear a duck quacking every time you receive new mail, or your child's voice babbling baby language when you shut down your computer, you can make it so.

You can insert music clips into your dissertation on Beethoven or Brubeck, and you can include video clips of your daughter's wedding in your e-mail to a far-off relative. Provided the person on the receiving end has a similarly equipped computer, the creative possibilities are endless. And, of course, multimedia opens up a whole new realm of wonderful educational and recreational tools—multimedia encyclopedias and other reference works; foreign-language courses; cooking and gardening programs; about a zillion exciting games…

Playing a Sound File

Windows 98 has built-in tools that run your multi-media files for you. What you need to play the media is the proper *hardware*—for example, a sound card and speakers—on your computer. Although most sound files are played as part of a program, and their playing is controlled by the program, you can play them directly yourself.

Play a Sound File

1 Open the folder or document containing the sound file.

2 Double-click the sound file. The sound starts to play.

Double-click to play a wave sound.

Double-click to play a MIDI sequence.

Title of file being played

Total playing time for entire file

Elapsed time from beginning of file

Play Part of a File

1 Right-click the sound file and choose Open from the shortcut menu.

2 Drag the slider and drop it where you want to start the play.

3 Click the Play button.

4 Use the Pause or Stop button or the slider to control your play. Use the Play button to replay the file.

5 Click the Close button when you've finished.

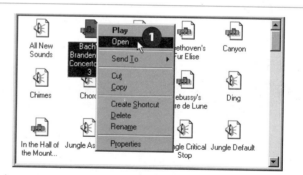

Controlling the Sound Volume

You can keep your music and other sounds muted so that you don't disturb other people, or, when you're the only person around, you can crank the sound level up and blast away! Although many programs have individual controls, you can use the volume control to set all your sound levels.

TIP

If the Volume icon doesn't appear on the taskbar, open Multimedia Properties from the Control Panel and, on the Audio tab, turn on the Show Volume Control On The Taskbar check box.

TIP

Many speakers have built-in volume controls. You can use these in conjunction with the volume control on the taskbar to fine-tune your sound levels.

Set the Master Volume Level

1. Click the Volume icon on the taskbar.

2. Drag the slider and drop it to adjust the volume.

3. Click outside the Volume icon to close it.

Set the Volume for Individual Devices

1. Double-click the Volume icon on the taskbar.

2. Adjust the settings for your devices.

Master control affects all devices.

Drag slider and drop to adjust balance.

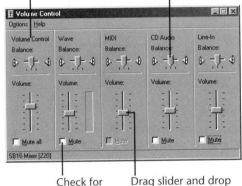

Check for no sound.

Drag slider and drop to change volume.

Playing a Video Clip

Most videos for your computer are controlled by a specific program—a game, for example, or a program such as DVD Player. Video *clips,* however, are often handled differently. These usually short video snippets can be included in a document or downloaded from a Web page. You can control both the play of the video clip and the way it's shown on your computer.

TIP

It's tempting to set your video to play in a full screen, but be aware that many videos are very grainy at that size. Experiment to find the best setting for a video on your display.

Set the Size of Video Playback

1. Click the Start button, point to Settings, and choose Control Panel from the submenu.

2. Double-click the Multimedia icon.

3. Click the Video tab.

4. Select the size of the playback.

5. Click OK.

Multimedia

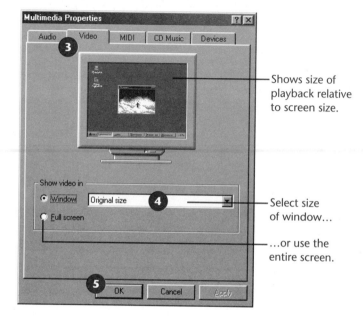

Shows size of playback relative to screen size.

Select size of window...

...or use the entire screen.

TIP

If you need greater playback control, start Media Player from the Start menu, and then open the video-clip file from Media Player.

TIP

What About DVDs?

Windows 98 supports some, but not all, DVD drives. Supported drives can be controlled using the DVD Player that comes with Windows. For unsupported drives, use the player software that came with your drive. Check Windows Update regularly to see whether Microsoft has added support for your drive.

SEE ALSO

"Controlling the Sound Volume" on page 113 for information about setting the sound volume for video.

"Watching Television" on page 120 for information about viewing direct-broadcast videos.

"Updating Your System" on page 268 for information about using Windows Update.

Play a Video Clip

1 Open the folder that contains the video file.

2 Double-click the video file. The video starts to play.

3 While the video is playing, click a control button to stop or pause the play, or use the slider to move to a different part of the file. If you're playing the video in Full Screen mode, click anywhere to return it into a window, and then use the controls.

4 If you adjusted the play, click the Close button when you've finished watching. (If you didn't adjust the play, the program will close automatically when it's finished.)

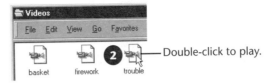

Double-click to play.

Video clip is the size you specified in the Multimedia Properties dialog box.

8

Creating a Sound File

If you have a microphone—also called an *external input device*—you can create your own sound files. Even without an external input device, you can create your own sound files by combining and editing your existing sound files.

Set Up a Sound File

1 Click the Start button, point your way through Programs, Accessories, and Entertainment, and then choose Sound Recorder from the submenu.

2 Choose Audio Properties from the Edit menu.

3 In the Audio Properties dialog box, choose the settings for your recording.

4 Click OK.

Audio Properties

Audio

Playback

Preferred device:
AudioPCI Wave Out

To select advanced options, click: Advanced Properties

3

Recording

Preferred device:
AudioPCI Wave In

To select advanced options, click: Advanced Properties

☐ Use only preferred devices.

☑ Show volume control on the taskbar.

4 OK   Cancel   Apply

Click to set recording volume and balance.

Select a recording device if your computer has more than one device.

Click if you want to adjust the sample-rate conversion quality to balance recording quality with playback performance.

Record Sounds

1. Click the Record button.

2. Speak, sing, whistle, or otherwise make sounds in front of the microphone.

3. Click Stop when you've finished.

4. Choose Save from the File menu.

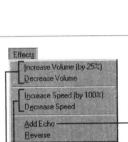

Add Sounds and Effects

1. Move the slider to the location in the sound file where you want to add an existing sound file.

2. From the Edit menu, choose

   ◆ Insert File to add a file and record over any existing sound.

   ◆ Mix With File to merge a file with the existing sound.

3. Locate the file and click Open.

4. Choose the type of effect you want to add from the Effects menu.

5. Save the file.

Click once for new echo.

Each click increases or decreases speed.

Each click increases or decreases volume.

Playing a Music CD

You can just drop a music CD into your disc drive and play it, or you can use CD Player to control how the CD is played—that is, to create a *play list* that specifies which tracks are played and the order they're played in. You can create a play list for each CD and save the list. Then, whenever that CD is loaded, Windows will use the play list.

Play a CD

1 Insert the CD into the disc drive.

2 Wait for Windows to start playing the disc.

3 Listen and enjoy!

4 Click the CD Player button on the taskbar.

5 Choose a play option from the Options menu:

◆ Random Order to have CD Player decide the order in which the tracks are played

◆ Multidisc Play if you have a multidisc CD player

◆ Continuous Play to resume playing the CD after the last track has been played

◆ Intro Play to play the first few seconds of each track; choose Preferences from the Options menu to specify how long each track is played

6 Click any control button, or choose a new option from the Artist or Track drop-down list box.

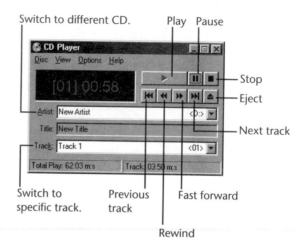

Switch to different CD. Play Pause
Stop
Eject
Next track
Switch to specific track. Previous track Fast forward
Rewind

SEE ALSO

"Controlling the Sound Volume" on page 113 for information about changing sound levels.

TIP

Every CD has a number that Windows uses as an identifier. Whenever you load the CD, Windows loads your play list.

TIP

It isn't necessary to name the CD, the artist, or the tracks, but doing so gives you maximum control. Instead, you can save time by simply arranging the tracks in the order you want them to play (for example, Track 1, Track 3).

TIP

Microsoft Plus! 98—an add-on to Windows 98—provides an enhanced CD Player, which, among other enhancements, can automatically download from the Internet the complete play list of a CD.

Create a Play List

1 Choose Edit Play List from the Disc menu.

2 Type the name of the recording artist and the title of the CD.

3 Click Clear All.

4 Select a track.

5 Type an identifying name for the track.

6 Click Set Name. Repeat steps 4, 5, and 6 for each track you want to use.

7 Select a track, or several tracks, from the Available Tracks list, and click Add.

8 Rearrange play order by dragging a track up or down in the Play List.

9 Click OK when you've finished.

All the tracks on the CD

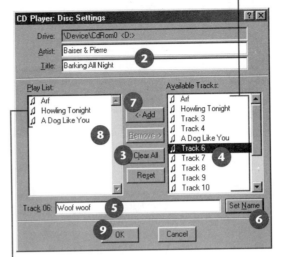

Tracks to be played, and the order in which they'll be played

Watching Television

Why work when you can watch TV? Okay, we're *joking!* But when it's time to take a little break or catch up on the news, you can use your computer to keep track of the TV schedule, and, if you have the correct hardware installed, you can view TV programs on your computer screen.

TIP

You can start WebTV from the Quick Launch toolbar or from the Start menu's Entertainment submenu.

TIP

If you have a TV tuner card installed and a cable or antenna connection, the WebTV program will scan and set up all your channels the first time you use it. You can then download program information from the Internet or have it extracted from the broadcast signal. After that, you can have the program information updated automatically.

Pick a Program

1. Start Microsoft WebTV For Windows if it's not already running. If the Program Guide isn't displayed, move the mouse to the top of the TV window (or press F10), and click the Guide button on the toolbar.

2. On the Guide tab, scroll through the listing to find the program you want to watch.

3. Click the program name.

4. Read the description of the program.

5. Click the appropriate button:

    ◆ Watch to view the program if it's currently being broadcast

    ◆ Remind to receive a reminder when the program is about to start

    ◆ Other Times to search for another time at which the same program is broadcast

Click to see additional information from the Internet about the selected channel.

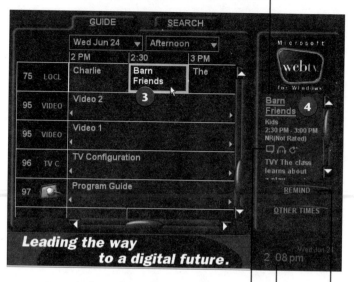

Icons indicate that program displays closed-captioning, is in stereo, and is a rerun.

Click to have Guide display listing for programs currently showing.

Remind button changes into Watch button when selected program is running.

Find a Program

1. If the Program Guide isn't displayed, move the mouse to the top of the TV window (or press F10), and click the Guide button on the toolbar.

2. Click the Search tab.

3. Specify what you want to find in the Categories list or in the Search For box.

4. Click the program name for more information.

5. Click the Watch or Remind button.

Click to specify the time period or the days for which you want program listings displayed.

Click to sort by title or time.

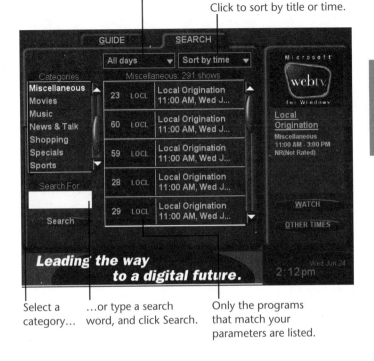

Select a category...   ...or type a search word, and click Search.   Only the programs that match your parameters are listed.

Customize the Viewer

1. With Microsoft WebTV For Windows running and a TV program displayed, move the mouse to the top of the TV window (or press F10).

2. When the toolbar appears, customize the viewer.

Click to scroll through the channels.

Click to specify which channels are displayed and whether closed-captioning is displayed.

Click to close WebTV.

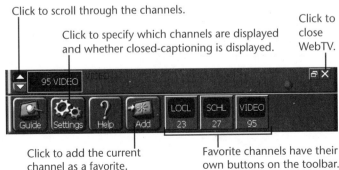

Click to add the current channel as a favorite.

Favorite channels have their own buttons on the toolbar.

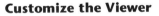

Associating a Sound with an Event

If you want audio cues for different events in Windows—closing a program or receiving new mail, for example—you can assign sounds to those events.

SEE ALSO

"Changing Your Input" on page 238 for information about assigning sounds to other events.

TIP

Put any sound files that you want to use for events into the Media folder (found in the Windows folder), and the sounds will immediately appear in the Name list.

Assign a Sound to an Event

1 Click the Start button, point to Settings, and choose Control Panel from the submenu.

2 Double-click the Sounds icon.

3 Select an event from the Events list.

4 Select a sound from the Name list, or use the Browse button to find a sound in another folder. Choose None from the list to remove a sound from an event.

5 Save the sound scheme.

6 Click OK when you've finished.

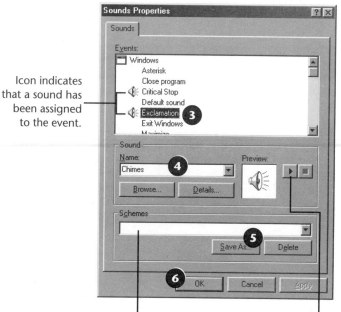

Icon indicates that a sound has been assigned to the event.

Click to hear the selected sound.

Select a scheme to assign sounds to several events at one time.

Running MS-DOS

Using Microsoft Windows 98 doesn't mean that you have to stop using MS-DOS commands or that you have to abandon your MS-DOS–based programs. Most of them run extremely well in Windows, some can be tricked into running in Windows, and many that don't work in Windows can be run in an exclusive MS-DOS mode.

MS-DOS is an integral part of the Windows operating system, giving you the best of both worlds. You can work at the MS-DOS prompt if that's the way you like to work. You can run all your old—and new—MS-DOS–based games. Or you can switch back and forth between MS-DOS and Windows as needed.

We'll cover some of the basic tasks here: starting MS-DOS–based programs, working from the command line, moving or copying text between Windows and MS-DOS, and generally making MS-DOS–based programs perform at their top level. We'll even show you a way to trick a bratty and selfish MS-DOS program into thinking that Windows isn't running and that it has the entire system to itself.

Our goal in this section is to help you get the most from your MS-DOS–based programs, whether you use them for work or for play.

Running MS-DOS Commands

When you need to work from the MS-DOS prompt, you can open an MS-DOS window and execute all your MS-DOS activities there, including using the basic MS-DOS commands, starting a program, and even starting a program in a new window.

TIP

Many MS-DOS commands have switches that allow the use of extra parameters, giving you greater control of the command.

TIP

Changes you make to the environment with commands such as Path and Prompt affect the current MS-DOS session only. To make the changes permanent, edit the Autoexec.bat file to include these settings.

Run an MS-DOS Command

1. Click the Start button, point to Programs, and choose MS-DOS Prompt.

2. At the prompt, type an MS-DOS command, including any switches and extra parameters, and press Enter.

3. Enter any additional commands you want to run.

—MS-DOS prompt

TOP 10 MS-DOS COMMANDS	
Command	**Use**
CD	Changes to the specified directory.
CLS	Clears the screen.
Copy	Copies the specified files or folders.
Dir	Shows contents of the current directory.
Drive:	Changes to the specified drive (type the drive letter and a colon).
Exit	Ends the MS-DOS session.
Mem	Displays memory configuration.
Path	Displays or sets the path MS-DOS searches.
Prompt	Changes the information displayed at the prompt.
Rename	Renames the specified file or files.

Repeat a Series of Commands

1 Type *doskey* and press Enter.

2 Type each command and press Enter.

3 Use the Up and Down arrow keys to scroll through the list of pre-viously used commands.

4 Use the Left and Right arrow keys to move the cursor within a command to edit it.

◆ Type over text that you want to replace.

◆ Press the Insert key to insert text at the cursor. Press the Insert key a second time to return to Overtype mode.

◆ Use the Delete key or the Backspace key to delete text.

5 Press Enter to execute the modified command or Esc to cancel the entire command line.

6 Type Exit to close the window when you've finished.

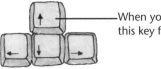

When you press this key four times...

...this command...

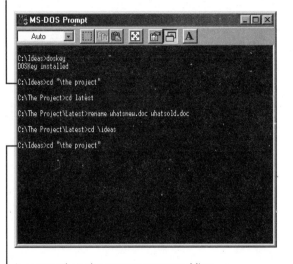

...is repeated on the current command line.

9

Exploring MS-DOS Commands

The version of MS-DOS that is part of Windows 98 provides a variety of useful commands. Those of you who are familiar with previous versions of MS-DOS will find that some commands in this version are new, some have been enhanced, and some have disappeared because Windows has made them obsolete.

TIP

The | used before the word "more" is known as a pipe, *and is usually typed by pressing Shift+\. This tells the system to send the output of the command through the MORE program, which displays the information one screenful at a time.*

Get Information on a Command

1. Open an MS-DOS Prompt window if one isn't already open.

2. Type an MS-DOS command followed by a space and /? and press Enter to get information about the command.

3. If the information scrolls off the screen, type the command and the /? Help switch (as in step 2), type a space followed by |*more*, and press Enter.

4. Read the information, and then press the Spacebar to see more information.

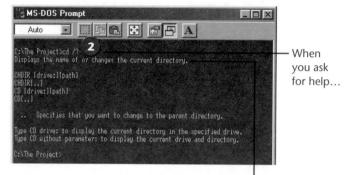

When you ask for help...

...the purpose and syntax of the command are displayed.

When you use the MORE command, the information is displayed one screenful at a time.

Renaming Files

One of the great features of MS-DOS is its ability to use wildcard characters to change several filenames at once. The two powerful wildcard characters are the question mark (?), which can represent any single character, and the asterisk (*), which can represent any number of characters.

Rename Files

1 Open an MS-DOS Prompt window if one isn't already open.

2 Navigate to the folder that contains the files you want to rename.

3 Type *rename* followed by the base of the filename (that is, the characters that are common among the files you're renaming), using wildcards to represent the characters that are different among the filenames.

4 Press Enter.

5 Type *dir* followed by the base of the renamed files, using wildcards, to confirm that the files were properly renamed.

This command will rename these files.

Neither command will rename this file.

This command will rename these files.

Customizing the MS-DOS Window

The MS-DOS environment has never been renowned for attractive screen text. The blocky, typewriter-style characters it usually displays work well with data or commands but don't have much aesthetic appeal. You can adjust the size of these characters or, if you really dislike the way they look, switch to a more attractive TrueType font designed specifically for the MS-DOS environment. You can also change the dimensions of the screen and use scroll bars to view text that doesn't fit into the window.

TIP

The MS-DOS Prompt window will automatically resize to accommodate the font size of your choice. However, because font sizes are measured in pixels, the size of both the font and the window will vary depending on the screen area you've set for your display.

Change the Font Size

1. If the toolbar isn't visible, click the MS-DOS icon and choose Toolbar from the menu.

2. Open the Font drop-down list and select a different font size. The window will resize to accommodate the new font size.

3. If the Font drop-down list doesn't display both bitmap and TrueType fonts, click the Properties button, and, on the Font tab, turn on the Both Font Types option. Click OK.

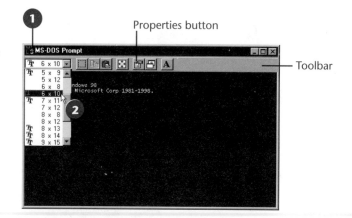

Properties button

Toolbar

SEE ALSO

"Making More Room on the Desktop" on page 107 for information about changing the screen area of your computer.

"Changing a Program's Appearance" on page 132 for information about making additional changes to the way the command prompt starts.

TIP

By default, the MS-DOS window is sized to display 80 characters on a line, with a total of 25 lines.

TIP

Choose the Full-Screen option to start the command prompt in full-screen mode; choose the Window option to start up in a window. If you choose the Window option, you can set the startup window size on the Program tab of the MS-DOS Prompt Properties dialog box. Note, however, that a maximized MS-DOS window doesn't always fill the entire screen— it takes up the area necessary to display the number of lines you've set in the font of your choice.

Change the Dimensions of the MS-DOS Window

1. Click the Properties button on the toolbar.

2. In the Initial Size box on the Screen tab, select the number of lines to be displayed.

3. Click OK.

4. Close the MS-DOS Prompt window, and then open a new MS-DOS Prompt window to display a window that contains the specified number of lines.

5. Do any of the following:

   ◆ Click the Full Screen button to make the window fill the entire screen. Hold down the Alt key and press Enter to return the window to its original size.

   ◆ Click the Maximize button to expand the window to its maximum size.

   ◆ Click the Restore button (if the window is maximized), and drag the window borders to resize the window.

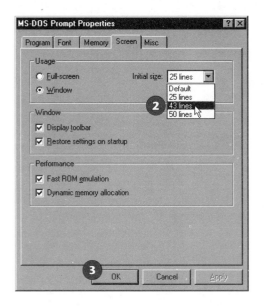

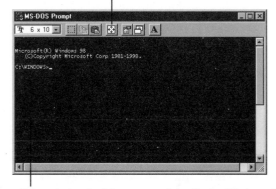

Full Screen button

If the window isn't large enough to display 80 characters across and/or the number of lines you specified, you can use the scroll bars that appear to view the entire contents of the window.

Starting a Program from the MS-DOS Prompt

Many MS-DOS programs are automatically added to the Start menu when they're installed, so they're just a click away. You can start others by clicking the appropriate icon in a folder window. If you're working from the command prompt, it's often easiest and quickest to start programs in the old-fashioned MS-DOS way. And if you want to merge the ease of use of Windows 98 with MS-DOS, you can do that too.

Start a Program

1. Open an MS-DOS Prompt window if one isn't already open.

2. Do either of the following:

   ◆ Type the program's path and filename, and press Enter to start the program in the current window.

   ◆ Type *start* followed by the path and filename, and press Enter to start the program in a new window.

3. When you've finished, use the program's menu to exit the program and return to the MS-DOS prompt.

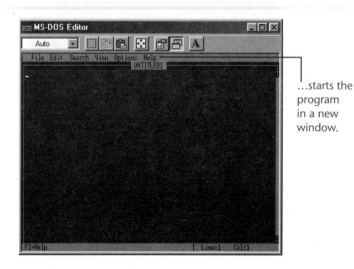

Current folder   Path to subfolder   Program filename

Typing this command starts the program in this window.

Typing this command...

...starts the program in a new window.

Find a Program to Run

1 Open an MS-DOS Prompt window if one isn't already open.

2 Type *start* followed by a space and a period, and press Enter. A window for the current folder opens.

3 Navigate through the folders to find the program you want.

4 Double-click the program to start it.

5 When you've finished, use the program's menu to exit the program and return to the MS-DOS prompt.

1 Typing this command...

...opens a window to the current folder.

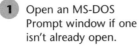

2 `C:\Ideas>start .`

Ideas

File Edit View Go Favorites Help

Competition Events Flood Frames Garden1

Garden1 Garden2 Hourly Image1 Image2

Image3 knew that Lilpdl Message Monster

40 object(s) (plus 1 hidden)   My Computer

Changing a Program's Appearance

You can customize some MS-DOS programs by adjusting the way they run in the MS-DOS window. Other MS-DOS programs use only their own internal settings and will ignore any properties settings you make. Use the procedure described here for the programs you can adjust; for the others, refer to the program documentation to change the way the program runs.

TIP

When you assign a shortcut key combination to a program, you can use the key combination to quickly switch to the running program.

TIP

To locate the program icon for a program that's listed on the Start menu's Programs submenu, right-click the program, choose Properties from the shortcut menu, and click the Find Target button.

Set the Properties

1 Right-click the program icon and choose Properties from the shortcut menu.

2 Click the Program tab.

3 Click in the Shortcut Key box and press a key combination.

4 Set the size of the window.

5 Click the Screen tab and set the size of the program.

6 Specify whether you want the toolbar to be displayed.

7 Make sure the Restore Settings On Startup box is checked to save settings.

8 Make any additional changes on the Font, Memory, and Misc tabs. Refer to the program documentation to assign optimum settings.

9 Click OK.

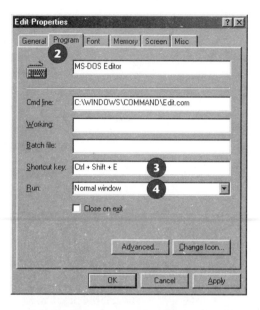

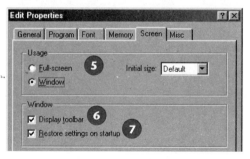

Navigating Folders in MS-DOS

Although working in MS-DOS usually means working with paths and using traditional MS-DOS filenames, Windows 98 makes your work a lot easier by using Windows folders and long filenames to help you navigate. Folders in MS-DOS have traditionally been called *directories*, but this distinction is becoming blurred as MS-DOS moves away from the traditional eight-character-plus-optional-three-character-extension naming limitations, and as MS-DOS and folder windows become more interactive.

TIP

To switch to a folder on a different drive, first switch to that drive by typing the drive letter followed by a colon at the command prompt, and press Enter. Then use the CD command to switch to the folder.

Switch Between Folders

Use any of the Change Directory (CD) commands shown in the table at the right. Substitute the actual paths and folder names for those shown here, and include the quotation marks where indicated.

MS-DOS COMMANDS FOR CHANGING FOLDERS	
Command	**Result**
CD ..	Moves up one folder (to parent folder).
CD ...	Moves up two folders.
CD	Moves up three folders.
CD *MS-DOS directory name*	Moves to specified subfolder.
CD *path\MS-DOS directory name*	Moves to specified folder.
CD *"long folder name"*	Moves to specified subfolder.
CD *"\path\long folder name"*	Moves to specified folder.

Use a Folder Window

1 Type *cd*

2 Switch to the folder window.

3 Drag the folder and drop it at the command prompt.

4 Click in the MS-DOS Prompt window to activate it.

5 Press Enter.

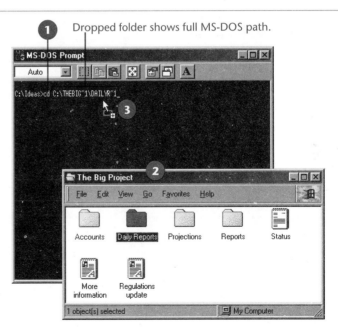

Dropped folder shows full MS-DOS path.

Copying Text in MS-DOS

Among the many ways in which Windows 98 and MS-DOS work well together is the ability they give you to share text between your MS-DOS output, the MS-DOS command line, your MS-DOS–based programs, and even your Windows-based programs.

SEE ALSO

"Copying Material Between Documents" on page 46 for information about copying and pasting text.

"Running MS-DOS Commands" on page 124 for information about working at the MS-DOS prompt.

TIP

In a word processing program, set the text from MS-DOS to a monospace font such as Courier New for proper alignment of columnar data.

Copy MS-DOS Output

1. Run your MS-DOS command in an MS-DOS window.

2. If the toolbar isn't visible, click the MS-DOS icon and choose Toolbar from the menu.

3. Click the Mark button.

4. Click to position the mouse pointer where you want to start the selection.

5. Hold down the left mouse button, drag over the area to be copied, and release the mouse button.

6. Click the Copy button.

```
C:\WINDOWS>mem

Memory Type        Total      Used       Free

Conventional       640K       35K        605K
Upper              0K         0K         0K
Reserved           384K       384K       0K
Extended (XMS)     48,128K    160K       47,968K

Total memory       49,152K    579K       48,573K

Total under 1 MB   640K       35K        605K

Total Expanded (EMS)              48M (49,840,128 bytes)
Free Expanded (EMS)               16M (16,777,216 bytes)

Largest executable program size      605K (619,008 bytes)
Largest free upper memory block      0K      (0 bytes)
MS-DOS is resident in the high memory area.

C:\WINDOWS>
```

Paste Text into a Windows-Based Program

1. Switch to the Windows-based program.

2. Choose Paste from the Edit menu.

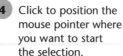

```
Untitled - Notepad
File  Edit  Search  Help

Here's the information you requested:

Memory Type        Total      Used       Free
----------------   --------   --------   --------
Conventional       640K       35K        605K
Upper              0K         0K         0K
Reserved           384K       384K       0K
Extended (XMS)     48,128K    160K       47,968K
----------------   --------   --------   --------
Total memory       49,152K    579K       48,573K
```

Text from the MS-DOS window

MS-DOS Quick Reference.
Create a document in WordPad listing the MS-DOS commands that you use frequently. Next to each command add an explanation of what it does. Save the document. When you're working in MS-DOS and can't remember the command you need, open the document, copy the command, switch back to your MS-DOS window, and paste the command into the command line.

If you want to copy something from a Windows program that doesn't have a Copy command, try selecting the item and then pressing Ctrl+C to copy it. If you want to paste something into a Windows program that doesn't have a Paste command, try pressing Ctrl+V. This technique doesn't work for all programs, but it does work especially well if you are copying or pasting information to or from a Windows dialog box.

You can't copy text from or paste text into the MS-DOS command prompt when it's running in full screen.

Copy Text from Windows into MS-DOS

1 Copy text from the Windows document.

2 Switch to the MS-DOS window.

3 Click the Paste button.

4 Edit the inserted text as you'd edit any MS-DOS command.

5 Press Enter to carry out the command.

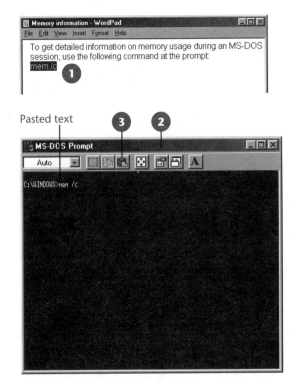

Pasted text

9

Sending MS-DOS Output to a File

Many MS-DOS commands and programs send a great deal of information to your screen. You can redirect the information and save it in a text file for further reference.

Redirect the Output

1. Open an MS-DOS Prompt window if one isn't already open.

2. Type the command, type a space followed by > *filename* (where *filename* is the name of the file you want the information sent to). If you want to store the output file in a folder other than the active folder, include the full path in the filename.

3. Press Enter.

4. Type *notepad filename* (where *filename* is the name of the file), and include the path if the file isn't in the active folder.

5. Press Enter.

6. Examine the output.

7. Close Notepad when you've finished.

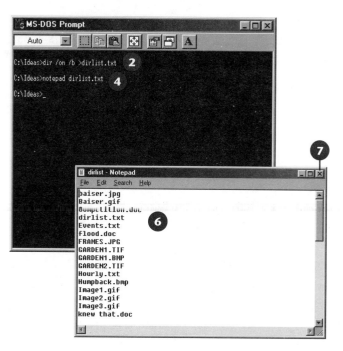

Running in MS-DOS Mode Only

Despite the usefulness of today's powerful operating systems, there are often situations in which all you need is MS-DOS. In fact, there are times when the sophisticated configurations, drivers, and resources of Windows might actually interfere with your work. You can start MS-DOS without starting Windows, or, if Windows is running, you can exit Windows and restart the computer in MS-DOS mode.

SEE ALSO

"Running MS-DOS Commands" on page 124 for information about working at the MS-DOS prompt.

Start MS-DOS Without Starting Windows

1. Start your computer, and hold down the Ctrl key.

2. When the Windows 98 Startup menu appears, choose a startup option, as shown in the table at the right, by typing the option number shown on your screen. Press Enter.

3. Run your MS-DOS–based program.

4. Exit the program, and turn your computer off. Turn your computer back on to start Windows.

End a Windows Session and Work in MS-DOS

1. Click the Start button, and choose Shut Down.

2. Turn on the Restart In MS-DOS Mode option.

3. Click OK.

4. Work from the MS-DOS command line. When you've finished, type *exit* to restart Windows.

WINDOWS 98 STARTUP OPTIONS	
Option	Usage
Command prompt only	Loads any startup files (Autoexec.bat and Config.sys) and displays the MS-DOS prompt.
Safe Mode command prompt only	Bypasses the startup files and displays the MS-DOS prompt.
Previous version of MS-DOS	Loads any startup files and runs the version of MS-DOS that was installed before Windows 98 was installed (provided you chose to keep the previous MS-DOS version during Windows Setup).

9

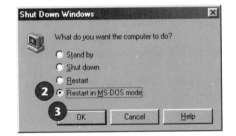

Getting an MS-DOS Program to Run

If an MS-DOS program won't run, you can adjust your system's settings to accommodate the program's needs. Some MS-DOS programs are unfriendly and refuse to run when Windows is running. Some are greedy and want a huge chunk of your computer's resources; others are just plain selfish and want the entire system to themselves. You might need to experiment a bit to find the right technique for your program.

Change the Available Memory

1 Right-click the program icon and choose Properties from the shortcut menu.

2 Click the Memory tab and try new memory settings.

3 Click OK to close the program's Properties dialog box.

Set to program specifications.

Keep Auto setting unless program specification is different.

Turn on if program causes sporadic errors to system.

Set to program specification. If no specification, try the Auto or the 8192 setting.

Keep Auto setting unless program specification is different.

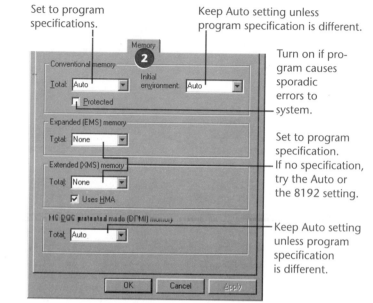

Pretend That Windows Isn't Running

1 Right-click the program icon and choose Properties. On the Program tab, click the Advanced button.

2 Turn on Prevent MS-DOS–Based Programs From Detecting Windows.

3 Click OK to close Advanced Program Settings, and click OK to close the program's Properties dialog box.

Turn on to make your program think that Windows isn't running.

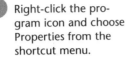
Run in MS-DOS Mode Only

1. Right-click the program icon and choose Properties from the shortcut menu.

2. On the Program tab, click the Advanced button.

3. Turn on the MS-DOS Mode check box.

4. Change other settings as needed.

5. Click OK to close the Advanced Program Settings dialog box.

6. Click OK to close the program's Properties dialog box.

Closes all programs and runs only in MS-DOS mode.

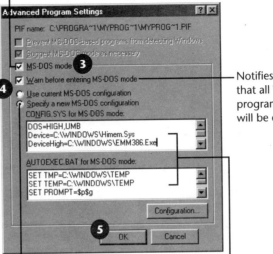

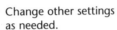

Notifies you that all Windows programs will be closed.

Select only if program specification requires special Config.sys and Autoexec.bat settings...

...and make the changes here. Click the Configuration button to automatically add commands to the files.

9

10

Sending and Receiving E-Mail and News

For many people, the ability the computer affords them to communicate, either for business or for pleasure, is one of its most used and most valued features. If you work on a computer in a large business office, you probably use a dedicated mail system that handles all your mail through a network mail server. However, if your computer isn't set up with a powerful Internet or intranet e-mail tool, or if what you have doesn't work with your Internet browser, doesn't support HTML formatting, or doesn't have a good news reader, then Outlook Express is the tool for you!

Like its more powerful sibling, Microsoft Outlook (which comes with Microsoft Office), Outlook Express helps you organize incoming and outgoing messages and lets you customize their appearance. It even does some of your work for you—for example, based on names in your Address Book, it will complete an address when you type only the first couple of letters, and it can automatically add your signature to your messages. You can send enclosures, or *attachments,* with your e-mail: documents, pictures, even sound and video clips. You can format messages with fonts, colors, and even Web components by using the HTML format. And Outlook Express does double duty as an e-mail program *and* a news reader, so you need to learn how to do most things only once.

Adding E-Mail and News Accounts

You can set up Outlook Express with one or more mail accounts and one or more news servers. When you set up a service such as The Microsoft Network (MSN), or any of the services you'll find listed in the Online Services folder on the Windows Desktop, some of the accounts will probably be added automatically to Outlook Express. You can, however, add more accounts yourself.

Specify Your Mail Service

1. Double-click the Outlook Express icon on the Desktop.

2. Choose Accounts from the Tools menu.

3. On the Mail tab of the Internet Accounts dialog box, check to see whether the account you want has already been set up.

4. If the account isn't listed, click the Add button, and choose Mail from the menu that appears.

5. Complete the steps of the Internet Connection Wizard to specify your mail account.

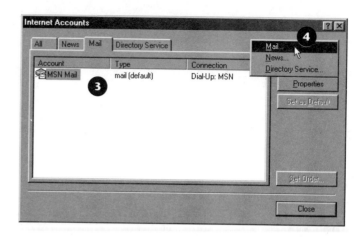

WHAT YOU NEED TO SPECIFY A MAIL ACCOUNT	
Information	**Example**
Internet e-mail address	DuskyC@MyISP.com
Type of incoming mail server	POP3
Incoming mail server name	email.MyISP.com
Outgoing mail server name	smtp.email.MyISP.com
Your Internet mail logon name	DuskyC
Your Internet mail password	MailPassword
A name for the account	My ISP Internet mail
Connection method	Connect using my phone line

Specify Your News Server

1 On the News tab of the Internet Accounts dialog box, check to see whether the account you want has already been set up.

2 If the account isn't listed, click the Add button, and choose News from the menu that appears.

3 Complete the steps of the Internet Connection Wizard to specify your news account.

4 Click Close when you've finished.

WHAT YOU NEED TO SPECIFY A NEWS ACCOUNT

Information	Example
Internet e-mail address	DuskyC@MyISP.com
Internet news server name	News.microsoft.com
News server logon name (if required)	DuskyC
News server password (if required)	NewsPassword
A name for the account	Microsoft newsgroups
Connection method	Connect using my phone line

10

Sending E-Mail

You don't have to write an envelope, lick a stamp, or trek to the mailbox on a cold, rainy day. All you do is select a name, create a message, and click a Send button. Outlook Express and your mail server do the rest.

SEE ALSO

"Adding an Address to the Address Book" on page 164 for information about using your Address Book.

TIP

You can customize Outlook Express so that it displays information in various ways. For example, you can display the Outlook Bar, the Folder List, or the Folder Bar to switch to different folders and services.

SEE ALSO

"Customizing Outlook Express" on page 166 for information about hiding or displaying the Outlook Bar or the Folder List.

Address a Message

1 On the Outlook Bar or in the Folder List, click Inbox if it's not the currently active folder.

2 Click the Compose Message button.

3 Start typing the recipient's name. Press Enter when Outlook Express completes the name, or continue typing if the proposed name is incorrect. Add more names as required, making sure that names are separated by semicolons.

4 Press the Tab key to move to the CC or BCC field, and type the names of the people who are to receive a copy of the message. (The names in the CC field are included in all copies of the message; the names in the BCC—blind copy— field are not included in the messages sent to the people listed in the To and CC fields.)

The Outlook Bar

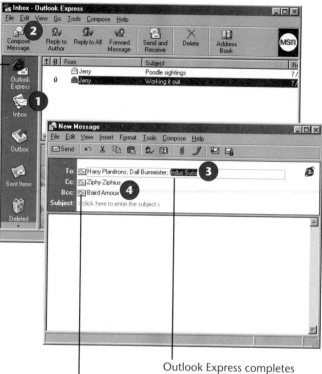

Outlook Express completes the name automatically, based on names in your Address Book.

Click any of the address icons to find e-mail names in your Address Book if you can't remember them.

TIP

When you're composing a long message, it's a good idea to frequently choose Save from the File menu to save a copy of the message in the Drafts folder.

TIP

To economize on connection and phone charges, compose your messages off line. Each time you click Send, the message will be stored in your Outbox until the connection is made.

SEE ALSO

"Adding a Signature to a Message " on page 157 for information about adding your signature to outgoing messages.

"Sending a Formatted Message" on page 160 for information about using HTML formatting in your messages.

"Sending and Receiving Secure Messages" on page 168 for information about digitally signing and encrypting your messages.

Compose a Message

1. Click in the Subject box, type a subject for your message, and press Tab to move into the message area.

2. Type your message.

3. Use any of the following send options:

   ◆ Click the Insert Signature button to add a predefined text closing.

   ◆ Click the Digitally Sign Message button to include digital identification.

   ◆ Click the Encrypt Message button to scramble the message for security.

   ◆ Point to Set Priority on the Tools menu to mark the message with a high- or low-priority tag.

4. Click the Send button to send the document.

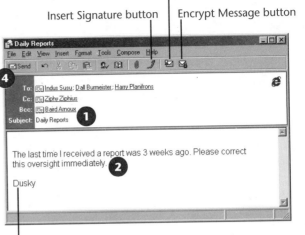

Digitally Sign Message button

Insert Signature button   Encrypt Message button

Signature inserted using the Insert Signature button

Reading E-Mail

Outlook Express lets you specify how frequently you want it to check for incoming mail, and it notifies you when you receive new mail. You can check your Inbox and see at a glance which messages have and haven't been read, or you can set the view to list unread messages only.

TIP

I Need It Now! *To receive mail immediately when you don't want to wait for your system to check your mailbox for you, click the Send And Receive button.*

Set the Delivery Options

1. Choose Options from the Tools menu to display the Options dialog box.

2. On the General tab, turn on the check box to check for new mail, and specify how often you want the mail to be checked.

3. Turn on the check box to play a sound if you want to be alerted by an audible signal.

4. Click OK.

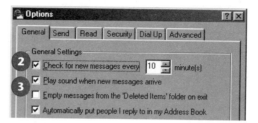

Set the View

On the View menu, point to Current View and choose

- ◆ All Messages to see all messages, whether read or unread. (When all messages are displayed, the unread messages are shown in bold type.)

- ◆ Unread Messages to see only the messages you haven't yet read.

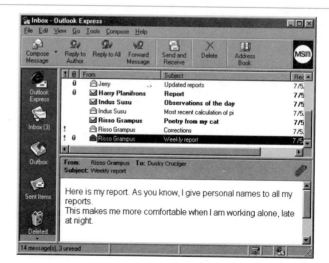

SEE ALSO

"Filing Messages in Different Folders" on page 150 for information about receiving messages in a folder other than your Inbox.

"Organizing Your Messages" on page 162 for information about accessing and managing your messages.

TIP

To change the order in which your messages are listed, point to Sort By on the View menu and select the column by which the messages are to be sorted. To view a message in a separate window, or to display a message if the preview pane isn't displayed, double-click the message header. To hide or display the preview pane, or to display it next to the message, choose Layout from the View menu.

TIP

Be Cautious! *If you receive an attachment from an unknown or a possibly untrustworthy location, save the attachment to disk and use a virus-scan program to inspect the file.*

Read Your Messages

1 Switch to the Inbox if it's not the currently active folder.

2 Click the header of an unread message.

3 Read the message.

4 Click the Attachment icon to list the name of the attached file or files.

5 Click the file to open it.

6 Specify whether you want to open the enclosure or save it to disk, and click OK.

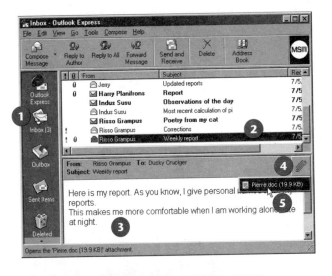

Replying to E-Mail

When you receive an e-mail message that needs a reply, all it takes is a click of a button to create a reply that's already addressed for you. But be careful when you use the Reply To All button! If the original message contained alias names for groups, you could be replying to the entire company instead of to one or two people.

TIP

If a message has a long string of replies, consider deleting some of the older ones if you feel they're not really relevant any more. It's good e-mail etiquette, however, to note in your message that you've deleted some previous messages.

Reply to a Message

1 Select the message you want to respond to.

2 Click the appropriate reply button:

- ◆ Reply To Author to send your reply to the writer of the message only

- ◆ Reply To All to send your reply to the writer of the message and to everyone listed in the original message's To and CC lines

3 Add names to or delete names from the To and CC lines. Make sure that individual names are separated by a semicolon and that no semicolons are left behind if you delete a name.

4 Type your reply.

5 Click the Send button.

The reply message is addressed automatically.

The original subject line is included. *RE* indicates that this is a reply.

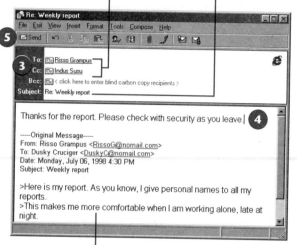

The original header information and message text are included. If any attachments were sent with the original message, they are not included in the reply.

Forwarding E-Mail

Message forwarding is a great convenience: you can forward any e-mail message that you've received to one person or to many people. Or, if you've sent an original message to several people and then you realize that you've left someone out, you can forward that message to the person you forgot—with your apologies, of course.

Forward a Message

1. Click the message you want to forward.

2. Click the Forward button.

3. Insert the recipients' names in the To and CC lines.

4. Type your message.

5. Click the Send button.

Forward Several Messages

1. Select the messages to be forwarded, and click the Forward button.

2. Insert the recipients' names in the To and CC lines of the new message window.

3. Type a subject.

4. Type your message.

5. Click the Send button.

FW tells you that a message is being forwarded.

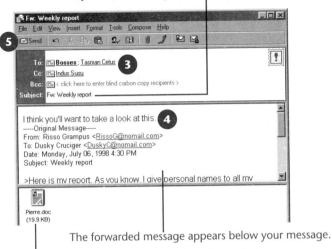

The forwarded message appears below your message.

Any attachments in the original file are forwarded.

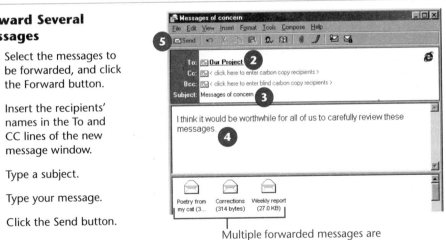

Multiple forwarded messages are included as attachments in one message.

10

Filing Messages in Different Folders

If you use several mail services, if more than one person uses your computer and mail, or if you want to categorize your incoming mail, you can tell Outlook Express to place your mail in the appropriate folder.

TRY THIS

If you receive unsolicited or junk mail from one specific source, use the Inbox Assistant to move all the messages from that source into your Deleted folder. If you're so annoyed that you want revenge, you can automatically return the offending mail to the sender or, if replies aren't accepted, have the junk forwarded to the Post-master at the originating server.

SEE ALSO

"Organizing Your Messages" on page 162 for information about accessing and managing your messages.

Specify the Rules

1. On the Outlook Bar or in the Folder List, click Inbox if it's not the currently active folder.

2. Choose Inbox Assistant from the Tools menu.

3. Click Add.

4. Specify the identifying criteria.

5. Turn on the Move To check box.

6. Click the Folder button and specify where you want the message stored. Click OK.

7. Click OK.

8. Click OK.

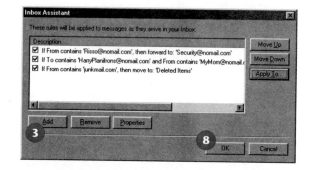

Creating an Out-of-Office Message

When you'll be away from your computer for one or more days and you want anyone who e-mails you to know that you're not ignoring their messages, you can have Outlook Express reply for you with an automatic out-of-office notification. You can also have all your messages forwarded to a different account or to another person.

TIP

If you normally work off line and connect manually to a mail server, don't forget to set your computer to work on line, and to periodically connect to the server. Otherwise, all your messages will remain on the mail server, and the Inbox Assistant won't be able to download and respond to any messages until you connect and check your mail.

Set Up Your Message

1 Compose your out-of-office message, leaving the address blank but including a subject.

2 Choose Save As from the File menu, and save the message in a folder. Close the New Message window.

3 Choose Inbox Assistant from the Tools menu, and click the Add button.

4 Turn on the All Messages check box.

5 To have your messages forwarded, turn on the Forward To check box and specify a recipient.

6 Turn on the Reply With check box, and use the Browse button to locate and specify the message you saved.

7 Click OK in the Properties dialog box and again in the Inbox Assistant dialog box.

8 To disable your out-of-office message, choose Inbox Assistant from the Tools menu, turn off the option for the message, and click OK.

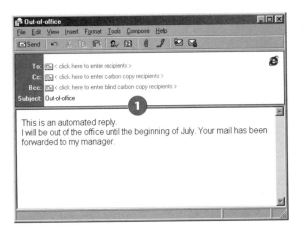

Subscribing to Newsgroups

With so many newsgroups available, you'll probably want to be selective about the ones you review. You can do so by *subscribing* to the newsgroups you like. Subscribed newsgroups appear in the Message pane when you select the news server and on the Folder Bar, if it's displayed, when you expand the listing for a news server.

SEE ALSO

"Adding E-Mail and News Accounts" on page 142 for information about setting up your news servers.

TIP

To display the Folder Bar, choose Layout from the View menu, and turn on the Folder List option.

Select Your Newsgroups

1 With Outlook Express connected on line and a news server selected on the Outlook Bar or in the Folder List, click the News Groups button.

2 If you have more than one news server, select the one you want to use.

3 Search for the newsgroups you want to access.

4 Double-click a newsgroup to subscribe to it.

5 Repeat steps 2 through 4 to subscribe to other news servers.

6 Click OK.

Limit the newsgroups to be displayed, or leave blank to view all newsgroups.

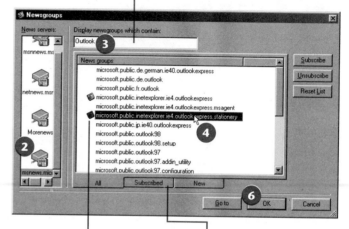

The newspaper icon shows you've subscribed to that newsgroup.

Only the newsgroups you've subscribed to are listed on the Subscribed tab.

Reading the News On Line

Reading the news—or the gossip, tirades, and misinformation that often pass for news in Internet newsgroups—is as simple as reading your mail. All you need to do is select the newsgroup, select the message, and read it.

TIP

A "thread" is a series of messages in which one person posts a message and other readers reply to the message and/or to the replies.

TIP

Regardless of how you set the view, your system downloads all your message headers. Switching views only adjusts what is filtered out in the display. To fine-tune what is downloaded, use the Newsgroup Filters command on the Tools menu to define your own filters.

Select a Message

1 On the Outlook Bar or in the Folder List, click the news server.

2 Double-click the newsgroup.

3 On the View menu, point to Current View and choose the view you want:

◆ All Messages to see everything

◆ Unread Messages to display only those messages you haven't read

◆ Downloaded Messages to see the messages you previously downloaded

◆ Replies To My Posts to see responses to your messages

4 Read the message headers.

5 Click to open a message.

6 Read the message.

Click the Folder Bar to display all the newsgroups you've subscribed to.

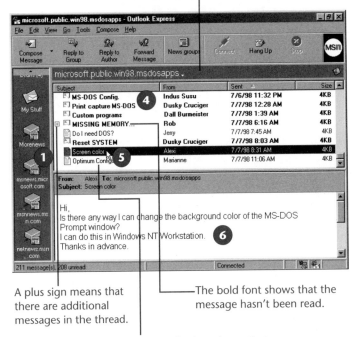

A plus sign means that there are additional messages in the thread.

The bold font shows that the message hasn't been read.

The regular font shows that the message has been read.

10

Reading
the News
Off Line

When you're exploring newsgroups on line, Outlook Express normally downloads and stores only the headers (titles) of your messages; the messages themselves remain on the news server until you ask to read them. When you select a message header, the body of the message is then downloaded. To view messages later, when you're not connected, you can tell Outlook Express to download and store the messages.

Read Selected News Off Line

1 Working either on line or off line, select one or more messages from a newsgroup.

2 Point to Mark For Retrieval on the Tools menu and choose any of the following:

◆ Mark Message to mark the selected message for retrieval

◆ Mark Thread to mark all messages in that thread for retrieval (not available if multiple messages are selected)

◆ Mark All Messages to mark all messages in the newsgroup for retrieval

3 Choose Download All from the Tools menu, and connect to your server if you're not already connected.

4 Disconnect from the news server.

5 Read the news.

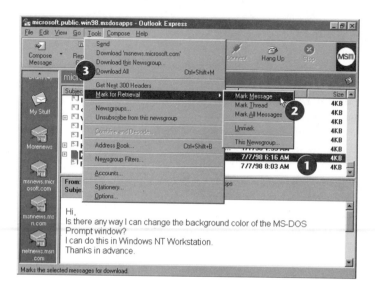

Get All the News

1 Click the news server to display all the Subscribed newsgroups.

2 Click a newsgroup.

3 Choose Properties from the File menu.

4 On the Download tab, turn on the option to retrieve messages.

5 Turn on a download option.

6 Click OK.

7 Repeat steps 2 through 6 for each newsgroup you want to download.

8 Choose Download All from the Tools menu to connect and download all the marked newsgroups.

9 Read the news.

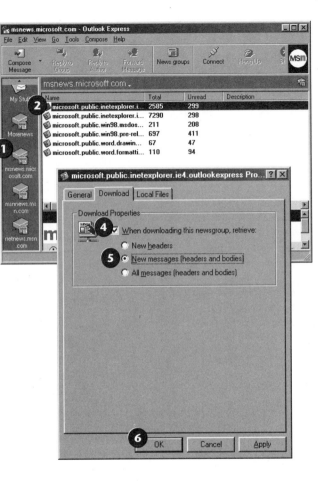

Adding to the News

Most newsgroups are inter-active—that is, you can post your own messages and reply to other people's mes-sages. You can compose your messages on line or off line. When you're off line, the message is saved and will be posted to the newsgroup the next time you connect.

TIP

Looking for Answers?
To find the replies to your messages, point to Current View on the View menu and choose Replies To My Posts.

SEE ALSO

"Sending a Formatted Message" on page 160 for in-formation about using HTML formatting to send your mes-sage with full formatting.

Create a Message

1 Open the newsgroup in which you want to post your message.

2 Select the type of message you want to post:

◆ Click Compose Message to create a new message in the newsgroup.

◆ Select a message, and click Reply To Group to place your reply in the newsgroup as part of the original message's thread.

◆ Select a message, and click Reply To Author to send an e-mail reply to the author of the message only.

3 Type a subject, and press Tab.

4 Type your message.

5 Click Post if you're creating a newsgroup message; click Send if you're creating an e-mail message.

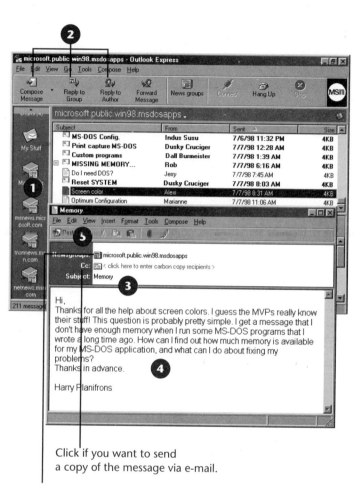

Click if you want to send a copy of the message via e-mail.

Click if you want to address the message to more than one newsgroup.

Adding a Signature to a Message

Outlook Express can speed up your work by inserting your signature automatically for you at the end of your messages. You can tell Outlook Express to add the information at the end of every message you send, or to insert it in selected messages when you click a button.

SEE ALSO

"Sending E-Mail" on page 144, "Replying to E-Mail" on page 148, and "Forwarding E-Mail" on page 149 for information about sending your messages.

TIP

If your message is in HTML format, your signature file can be an HTML document too. If you enjoy experimenting with HTML, you can create anything, from an attractive or ornate signature to a humorous or truly obnoxious one.

Define Your Signature

1 Choose Stationery from the Tools menu.

2 On either the Mail or News tab, click the Signature button.

3 Type the signature you want to use, or specify the text or HTML document that contains the signature.

4 Specify whether you want the signature added automatically to all outgoing messages.

5 Specify whether you want the signature added automatically to replies and forwarded messages.

6 Click OK, and click OK again to close the Stationery dialog box.

7 Create a message. Click the Insert Signature button if you chose not to automatically include the signature in all messages.

Type your signature text here...

...or specify a text document or an HTML document.

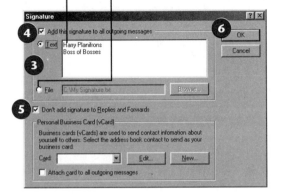

Your signature either appears automatically in the document...

...or appears when you click the Insert Signature button.

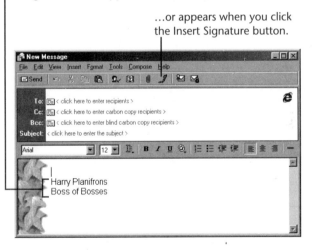

Harry Planifrons
Boss of Bosses

10

Adding a File to a Message

You can easily place text from an existing file directly into the body of a mail or newsgroup message. You can also send an entire file—a Word document, a sound file, or a text file, for example—by including it in a message as an *attachment*. When you send the message, the attached file is sent as an object and is usually shown as an icon in your message. If the file is too big for the server you're using, you can have Outlook Express break the file into pieces, and the server should subsequently reassemble the pieces into a complete file.

Include the Contents of a File in a Message

1 Click in the message where you want the text to be inserted.

2 Choose Text From File from the Insert menu.

3 Use the Insert Text File dialog box to find and select the file to be included.

4 Click Open. The text appears in your message.

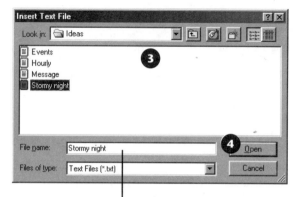

The contents of the text file...

...are inserted into the message.

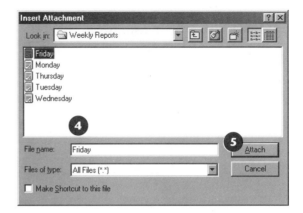

TRY THIS

If you've sent a file and the recipient can't read it, try sending the message and the file in a different format. If your message is in HTML format, try sending the message as text. Then send two messages, one in UUENCODE format and the other in MIME format. To specify text format, choose Options from the Tools menu, and, on the Send tab, choose the Plain Text format. To specify the encoding, click the Settings button. Make sure you note which format you used, and check with the recipient or the newsgroup to see which format worked.

TIP

Breaking Up Isn't Hard to Do! *If a server rejects an attached file because it's too big, you can still send the file by breaking it into smaller components that will later be reassembled into a single file. To do so, choose Accounts from the Tools menu, select the server, click Properties, and, on the Advanced tab, specify the maximum file size the server will accept.*

Attach a File to a Message

1 Create and address a message.

2 Type the message text.

3 Click the Insert File button.

4 Use the Insert Attachment dialog box to find and select the file to be included.

5 Click Attach. The file's icon appears in your message. Repeat steps 3 and 4 to include additional files, and click Attach.

6 Send the message as you would any other message.

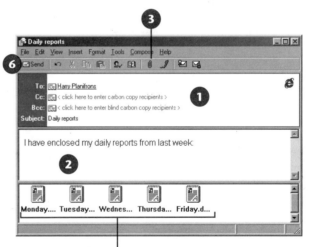

You can include one or more files in your message.

10

Sending a Formatted Message

If you're tired of plain old boring text, you can jazz up your messages with formatting based on HTML, the language that's used in Web pages. Although you can achieve spectacular results using HTML, only those recipients who have e-mail or news readers that support HTML (such as Outlook Express) will be able to see the formatting. Others will probably receive a garbled message.

TIP

If you receive complaints from individuals who can't read your HTML-formatted documents, select their names in your Address Book, click Properties, and, on the Personal tab, turn on the Send E-Mail Using Plain Text Only option.

Enable HTML Formatting

1. In Outlook Express, choose Options from the Tools menu.

2. On the Send tab, turn on the HTML formatting option for the service (e-mail or news) that you want to use.

3. Click OK.

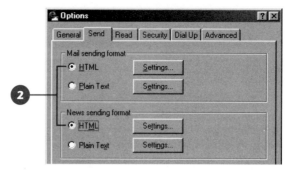

Set Your Default Stationery

1. In Outlook Express, choose Stationery from the Tools menu.

2. On either the Mail or News tab, turn on the This Stationery option.

3. Click the Select button.

4. Select the stationery design you want to use.

5. Click OK.

6. Click OK in the Stationery dialog box.

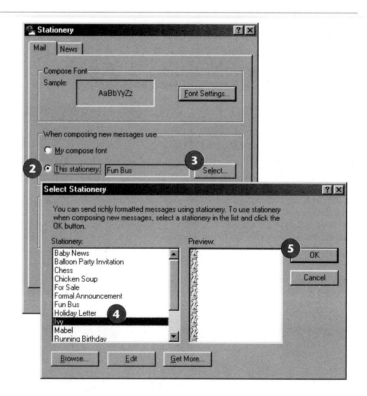

SEE ALSO

"Sending E-Mail" on page 144, "Replying to E-Mail" on page 148, and "Forwarding E-Mail" on page 149 for information about sending your messages.

TIP

To switch quickly between plain text and formatted text after you start composing your message, open the Format menu and choose Rich Text (HTML) or Plain Text.

TIP

If you want to add cool elements and formatting to your message, create the content in FrontPage Express, copy it, and paste it into your message.

TRY THIS

If you don't like any of the stationery designs, you can use a background color or a picture instead. To do so, choose No Stationery from the Compose Message list, and, in the New Message window, specify a background color or a picture by choosing Background from the Format menu. (You must have enabled HTML formatting for this technique to work.)

Format a Message

1 Do either of the following to start a message:

◆ Click the Compose Message button to use the default stationery.

◆ Click the down arrow at the right of the Compose Message button, and select the stationery you want from the list.

2 Address your message.

3 Type your text.

4 Use the tools on the Formatting toolbar to format the message or to add lines, graphics, and hyperlinks.

5 Click Send when you've finished.

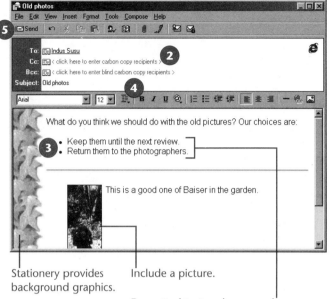

Stationery provides background graphics.

Include a picture.

Formatted text and paragraphs

10

Organizing Your Messages

Outlook Express comes with a folder system that is useful for managing and accessing your e-mail and newsgroup messages. You can also create as many folders and subfolders as you need to organize and store your messages. You can customize each folder by changing the number of columns that are displayed in the window, the order in which the columns appear, and their width.

SEE ALSO

"Filing Messages in Different Folders" on page 150 for information about categorizing your messages if you use more than one mail server or if several people use your mail system.

Create a Folder System

1. If the Folder List isn't displayed, choose Layout from the View menu, turn on the Folder List option, turn off the Outlook Bar option if you want, and click OK.

2. Right-click a folder and choose New Folder from the shortcut menu.

3. Click the folder in which you want to create a new folder.

4. Type a name for the new folder.

5. Click OK.

6. Repeat steps 2 through 5 to create additional new folders.

7. To organize your messages, drag message headers from the right pane into the appropriate folders in the Folder List.

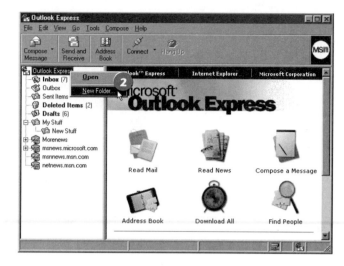

Create a folder in the Outlook Express folder to have the new folder appear on the Outlook Bar...

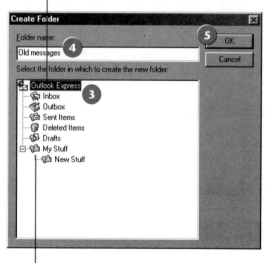

...or create a folder within another folder if you want the subfolder to be visible only in the Folder List.

Customize a Folder

1. Click the folder to be customized.

2. Choose Columns from the View menu.

3. Add the columns you want displayed, or remove those you don't need.

4. Select a column and use the Move Up or Move Down button to re-order the columns.

5. Click OK.

6. Drag the border between columns to change the column widths.

Add columns from here.   Delete columns from here.

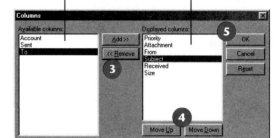

Columns appear in the arrangement you specify.   Drag a border to resize a column.

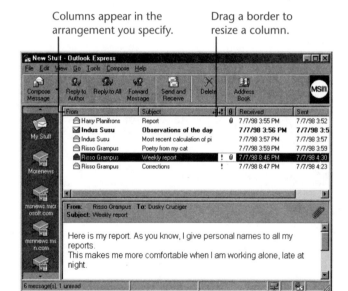

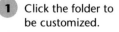

Adding an Address to the Address Book

When you use e-mail, you don't need to type an address every time you send a message; you can retrieve addresses from the Address Book. If you frequently send one message to the same group of people, you can gather their addresses into a *group*, and then all you need to find is that one address item. How convenient!

TIP

Additional information, such as phone numbers or office numbers, might be displayed next to names in the Address Book. To see all the information that's listed, point to a name and wait for the information to pop up.

SEE ALSO

"Sending a Business Card" on page 167 for information about exchanging detailed Address Book information.

Create a New Address

1. With Outlook Express or any mail folder selected, click the Address Book button on the toolbar if the Address Book isn't already open.

2. Click the New Contact button on the Address Book toolbar.

3. Fill in the information you want to record on the different tabs of the Properties dialog box.

4. Click OK.

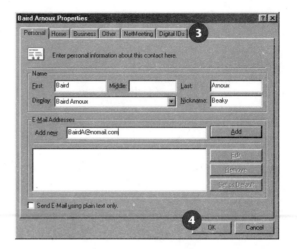

Add an Address from a Message

1. In the Inbox, double-click the message to open it in a separate window.

2. In the message header, right-click the name you want to add.

3. Choose Add To Address Book from the shortcut menu.

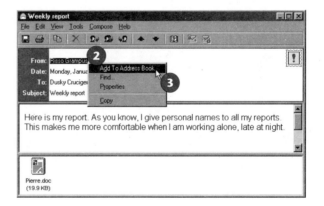

Create a Group

1 On the Address Book toolbar, click the New Group button.

2 Type a descriptive name, or *alias*, for the group.

3 Click Select Members.

4 Select from your Address Book the names of the people you want to include in the group.

5 Click Select.

6 When the list is complete, click OK.

7 Click OK.

8 In a new message, type the name of the group in the To, CC, or BCC line.

9 Send the message. Everyone in the group will receive the message.

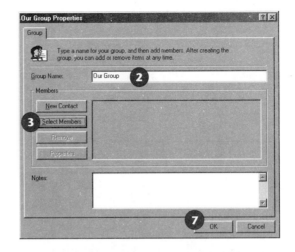

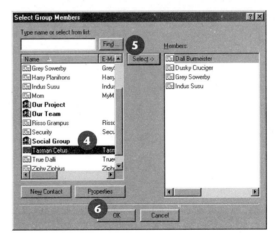

10

Customizing Outlook Express

Outlook Express doesn't have to look the same all the time; you can customize it to fit your individual working style. You can use the tools it provides to specify exactly how you want to navigate through your mail and news folders, and you can change the layout of the different parts of the window.

TIP

To change the font and font size of the messages you receive, choose Options from the Tools menu, and click the Fonts button on the Read tab.

TIP

If the preview pane isn't displayed, double-click the message header to open the message in a separate window.

Change the Layout

1 Choose Layout from the View menu to display the Window Layout Properties dialog box.

2 In the Basic section, turn on the navigation tools you want to use.

3 In the Toolbar section, specify where you want the toolbar to be located and whether you want text labels to identify the toolbar buttons.

4 In the Preview Pane section, specify whether you want to use the preview pane and, if so, where you want it to be located and whether you want the message header to be shown in the preview pane.

5 Click OK.

Outlook Bar   Folder Bar—click to temporarily display folders.

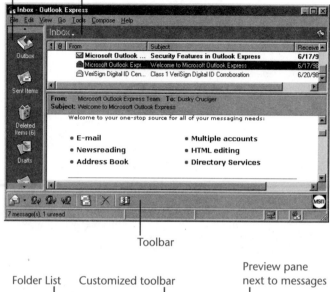

Toolbar

Folder List   Customized toolbar   Preview pane next to messages

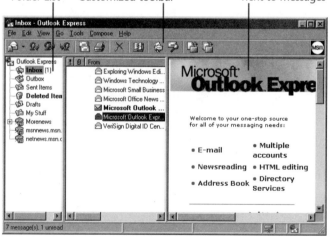

Sending a Business Card

You can send an electronic business card, or *v-card*, with your messages. This "virtual" card includes all the information that's found in an Address Book entry, so—as well as your name, address, phone, and e-mail information—you can include your Web-page address, NetMeeting connection information, digital IDs, and any other information you want.

SEE ALSO

"Read Your Messages" on page 147 for information about opening an attachment.

Send Your Card

1 Choose Stationery from the Tools menu.

2 On the Mail tab, click the Signature button.

3 Select your name from the Card list (it's listed if you've already completed an Address Book entry).

4 If your name isn't listed, click New, complete the information, and click OK.

5 Specify whether you want the card automatically attached to all outgoing messages.

6 Click OK, and click OK again to close the Stationery dialog box.

7 Create a message. Choose Business Card from the Insert menu if you chose not to automatically attach the business card to all messages.

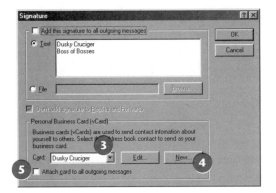

When recipients open the business card, they see all the information you've provided...

...and can easily add it to their Address Books.

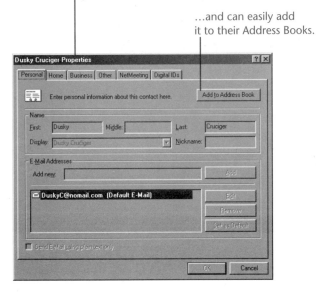

Sending and Receiving Secure Messages

If you're worried about prying eyes on the Internet, you can protect your mail messages by encrypting them so that only people with the correct digital ID can read them. You can also digitally sign your messages to authenticate their origin. You obtain your digital ID from a security provider, and then you exchange digital IDs with your intended recipients. You cannot send out an encrypted message without knowing your recipient's digital ID.

Set Up Your Security

1. Choose Options from the Tools menu, and click the Security tab.

2. Specify whether you want to digitally sign and encrypt all outgoing messages.

3. Click Get Digital ID.

4. Follow the instructions provided to install the ID. Click OK to close the Options dialog box when you've finished.

5. Choose Accounts from the Tools menu.

6. On the Mail tab, select your mail service, and click Properties.

7. On the Security tab, turn on the check box to use a digital ID.

8. Click the Digital ID button, select the certificate, and click OK.

9. Click OK to close the Properties dialog box, and click Close to close the Accounts dialog box.

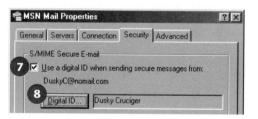

Click to see detailed information about obtaining and using a digital ID.

TIP

The first time you receive a digitally signed or encrypted message, you'll probably see a Help message instead of the message itself. Turn on the Don't Show Me This Help Screen check box, and click the Continue button.

TIP

You can also exchange digital IDs using electronic business cards or an e-mail locator service.

TRY THIS

Click the Start button, point to Find, and choose People from the submenu. Select a directory service in the Look In box, type the name and/or e-mail address of a person to whom you want to send an encrypted message, and click Find Now. Locate and select the person in the list, and click Properties to verify the person's identity and that a digital ID is listed. Click Add To Address Book in the Find People dialog box.

SEE ALSO

"Sending a Business Card" on page 167 for information about sending an electronic business card containing your digital ID.

Exchange Digital IDs

1 Create a message, click the Digitally Sign Message button, and send the message. Have someone send you a digitally signed message.

2 In a digitally signed message you've received, click the Digital Signature button, and choose View Security Properties from the menu that appears.

3 On the Security tab, click Add Digital ID To Address Book, and click OK. Click OK again to close the Security Properties dialog box.

Click to access the digital ID of the sender.

Send an Encrypted Message

1 Address a message to someone whose digital ID is listed in your Address Book.

2 Click the Encrypt Message button if you chose not to automatically encrypt all messages.

3 Send the message.

Icon indicates message has been encrypted.

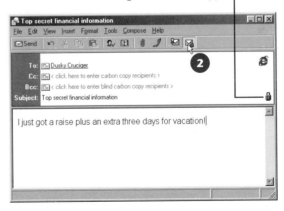

10

11

Using the Net

Despite all the hype, the Internet—or its corporate cousin, your company's *intranet*—is simply a communications medium. What can the net do for you? More than we can possibly describe here—but we *can* help you explore some of the ways Windows helps you communicate on the Internet.

Microsoft Windows 98 has advanced beyond the use of specific tools and has integrated direct connections to the Internet onto your Desktop so that all the Internet's resources are always available to you. Powerful and useful...yes. Dazzling and confusing...possibly. Fortunately, like most Windows features, your connections and settings can be customized so that you allow onto your Desktop only *what* you want to see *when* you want to see it.

Using Internet Explorer and all its tools is a subject for an entire book. Our purpose here is to get you comfortable with basic operations and confident enough to go out and enjoy your explorations.

We assume you're already connected, either through your company network or through an Internet Service Provider (ISP). If you're not connected, use the Setup programs in the Online Services folder on your Desktop, use the Internet Connection Wizard, or contact an ISP to obtain setup software.

Going to a Web Page

To Internet Explorer, the only differences between the Internet and a company intranet are the connection and the type of address you use to connect. In either case, you can go directly to a specific site—provided you have its address or a shortcut to it—or you can "surf" the net to find the site.

Jump to a Site

1. Start Internet Explorer, and connect to the Internet if you're not already connected.

2. If a toolbar you want isn't displayed, point to Toolbars on the View menu, and choose the toolbar you want from the submenu.

3. Drag the Links toolbar if it's not fully displayed.

4. Click a button to go to a site.

Use an Address

1. Double-click the Address toolbar to expand it.

2. Click the current address to select it, and insert the address you want to go to. (Internet Explorer will help by inserting part of the address—*http://*, for example—as you type, or by displaying the entire address of a site you've visited before.)

3. Press Enter.

Drag to display the hidden Links toolbar.

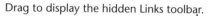

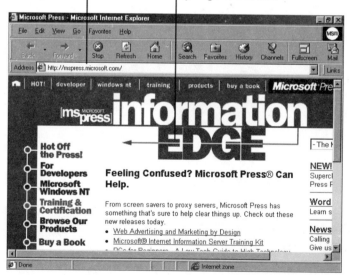

The Links toolbar contains links to several locations.

When you enter this address... ...you go to this site.

TIP

When Internet Explorer starts, it automatically goes to your home page. However, many Internet services change your home page to their main page when you install the service. Fortunately, you can easily switch back to your original home page.

SEE ALSO ·

"Changing Internet Explorer Links" on page 174 for information about changing the home page.

TIP

Many mail and newsgroup messages contain hyperlinks to Web pages. When you click one of those links, Internet Explorer will start automatically if it's not already running, and it will go to the specified address.

TIP

Windows temporarily stores Web pages, so if you want to read pages but economize on connection charges, connect to the pages, wait for each page to download, and then disconnect (but leave Internet Explorer running). Use the Forward and Back buttons to browse through the pages you've downloaded.

Surf the Net

1 From your current page, do any of the following:

◆ Click the Search button, and use a service to locate a site by name or location.

◆ Click a relevant jump on the page to go to a new site.

◆ Click the Back button to return to a previous site.

◆ Click the Forward button to return to a site you left using the Back button.

◆ Open the Address list on the Address toolbar to select and jump to a previously visited site.

◆ Click the Stop button to stop downloading a page, and then jump to a different location.

2 If you get lost, click the Home button to return to your home page, or use the Search Explorer Bar to conduct another search.

Move backward and forward through sites you've already visited.

When the mouse pointer changes into a tiny hand, it's pointing to a jump that will take you to a different location.

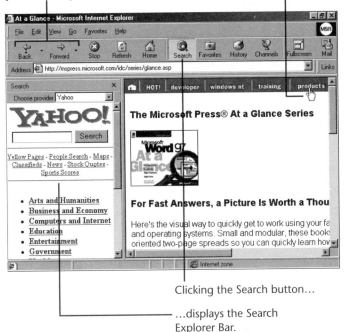

Clicking the Search button...

...displays the Search Explorer Bar.

Changing Internet Explorer Links

When you first start Microsoft Internet Explorer, it has a preinstalled home page and it already contains some links to other pages. Depending on your needs, you might want to have a different Internet home page. If you're using an intranet, you might want to set the home page to the main intranet page. And by customizing the other links, you can create quick and easy access to other pages with a click of a button.

SEE ALSO

"Going to a Web Page" on page 172 for information about jumping to a site.

Set a New Home Page

1. Navigate to the page you want to use as your home page.

2. Choose Internet Options from the View menu, and click the General tab in the Internet Options dialog box.

3. Click the Use Current button.

4. Click OK.

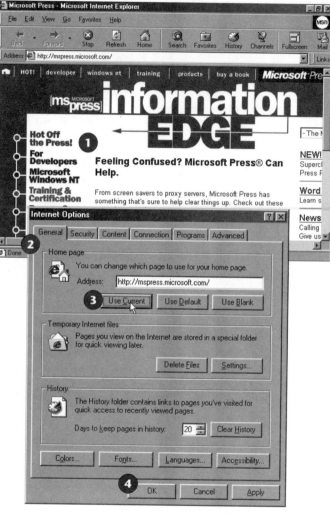

TIP

You can also drag a link and drop it at a different location on the Links toolbar, or you can drop it in the Favorites Explorer Bar, on the Desktop, on the Quick Start toolbar, or on any custom toolbar.

SEE ALSO

"Restore an Item from the Recycle Bin" on page 34 for information about restoring a deleted link.

"Rearranging the Taskbar and the Toolbars" on page 102 for information about arranging toolbars.

TRY THIS

Quick Links. *While you're connected to the Internet, double-click the icon at the right edge of the menu bar, and see where you end up. Now switch to any folder window or to Windows Explorer, and double-click the Windows flag icon on the menu bar. Yes, that's the Internet outside of Internet Explorer!*

Add a Link

1 Navigate to the page you want to use as a link.

2 Display both the Address and the Links toolbars.

3 Drag the address of the current site from the Address toolbar and drop it in an empty spot on the Links toolbar.

4 Rearrange items on the Links toolbar by doing either of the following:

◆ Drag a button and drop it at a new location on the Links toolbar.

◆ Right-click a button and choose Delete from the shortcut menu to remove that button from the Links toolbar.

Drag an address…

…to the Links toolbar…

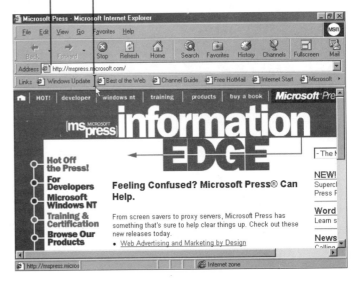

…and drop it to create a new link.

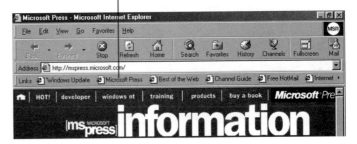

Returning to Your Favorite Sites

When you find a good source of information or entertainment, you don't need to waste a lot of time searching for that site the next time you want to visit it. You can simply add the site to your Favorites list, and Internet Explorer obligingly creates a shortcut to the site for you.

TIP

If you'll be storing many different favorite locations, click the Create In button in the Add Favorite dialog box, and create a folder structure for your pages.

TIP

To return to a site that you didn't save, click the History button on the Standard Buttons toolbar, and locate and click the site in the History Explorer Bar.

Save a Location

1. Navigate to the site whose location you want to save.

2. Choose Add To Favorites from the Favorites menu.

3. Specify whether and how you want to subscribe to the site. (Select the first of the three options if you want to create a link to the site without going through the process of subscribing to the site.)

4. Type a name for the site, or use the proposed name.

5. Click OK.

Return to a Location

1. Click the Favorites button on the Standard Buttons toolbar.

2. In the Favorites Explorer Bar, click the name of the site you want to return to. If the site is contained in a folder, click the name of the folder and then the name of the site.

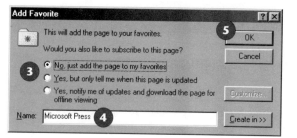

Sharing a Site

Don't keep all the good sites to yourself! You can share a great site with friends and colleagues by sending them the Web page or a shortcut to the site. If you prefer, you can save the shortcut to a page and include it in your mail or insert it into a document at a later date.

SEE ALSO

"Going to a Web Page" on page 172 for information about jumping to a site.

Send It

1 Navigate to the site you want to share with someone.

2 On the File menu, point to Send.

3 From the submenu, choose

- ◆ Page By E-Mail to send the entire page to someone.

- ◆ Link By E-Mail to send the address and a shortcut to the page.

- ◆ Shortcut To Desktop to store a shortcut to the page on your Desktop.

4 Address your message. If you stored the shortcut on your Desktop, drag the shortcut into your message.

5 Send the message.

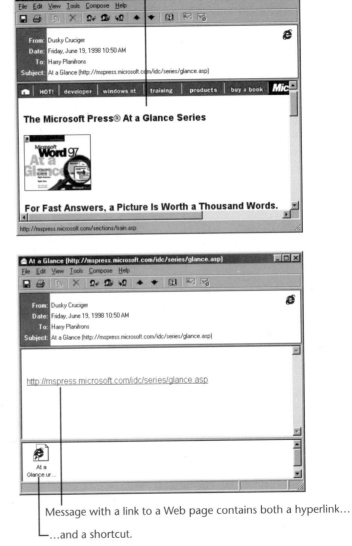

Message with a Web page

Message with a link to a Web page contains both a hyperlink...

...and a shortcut.

Viewing Channels

Windows 98 provides you with a bunch of *channels*. But what *are* channels? They're simply links between your computer and certain specially designed Internet sites. With a click of your mouse, you can jump to an Internet site, decide whether you want to subscribe to it, and then customize the way you want the information to be displayed and sent to you.

TIP

If the Channel Bar isn't visible on your Desktop, click the View Channels button on the Quick Start toolbar or the Channels button on the Standard Buttons toolbar in Internet Explorer.

SEE ALSO

"Controlling the Channel Bar" on page 183 for information about displaying the Channel Bar.

Set Up a Channel

1. Click a channel category on the Channel Bar on the Desktop. The Channel Viewer appears.

2. Click the channel whose content you want to view.

3. Follow the instructions on the page.

4. Click the Add Active Channel button on the subscription Web page.

5. Specify whether and how you want to subscribe to the site.

6. Click OK.

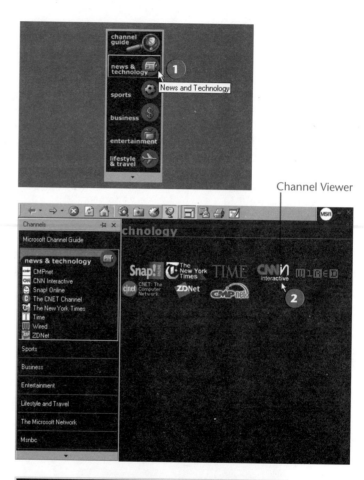

Channel Viewer

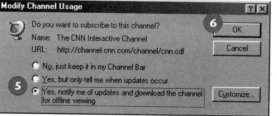

View a Channel

1 Move your mouse to the left until the Channel Bar slides into view.

2 Click the channel you want to view. If necessary, click a category to expand it and list the channels, and then click the channel you want.

3 Click to turn on the pushpin icon if you want the Channel Bar to remain on your screen and the Web page to resize. Turn off the pushpin and move the mouse to the right until the Channel Bar slides off the screen if you want to view the Web page in the full window.

4 Review the information.

5 Switch to another channel, or close the window when you've finished.

Modifying Channels

As your interests or priorities change, or as you add more channels to the Channel Bar, you might want to modify the type of information you receive and how or when it's downloaded.

TIP

When you subscribe to a site, you usually let the publisher of the site determine both the schedule for downloading and which pages are downloaded. However, you can take control of both these items by customizing your subscription. For example, you might want to download some pages less frequently, or not to download some of the larger items, such as videos. You can even decide not to have anything automatically downloaded and instead to be informed whenever the content of the site has changed.

Change What's Sent

1. With the Channel Viewer open, click the Full Screen button to display the channels in a standard Internet Explorer window.

2. Choose Manage Subscriptions from the Favorites menu.

3. Right-click the subscription you want to modify, and choose Properties from the shortcut menu.

4. On the Receiving tab, select a subscription type.

5. Click the Advanced button if you want to change the content to be sent, and click OK.

6. Turn on the check box if you want to receive an e-mail message whenever the site is updated.

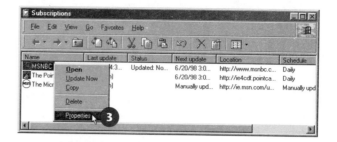

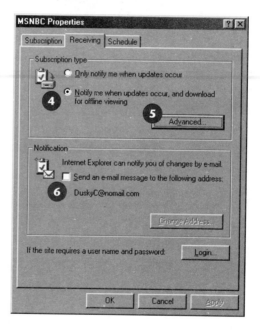

To update information between scheduled updates, or if you have set the subscription update to be done manually, right-click the channel and choose Update Now from the shortcut menu. To update all your subscriptions manually, choose Update All Subscriptions from the Favorites menu of Internet Explorer, Windows Explorer, or a folder window.

"Removing Channels" on page 182 for information about deleting or unsubscribing from channels.

If you're concerned about the time it takes to download a site but you still want to download most of its content, click the Advanced button, and turn off some of the large items that aren't always necessary, such as sound and video. As a safeguard, turn on the Never Download More Than check box, and specify the largest download size you'll allow from the site.

Change When It's Sent

1 Click the Schedule tab.

2 Do either of the following:

 ◆ With the Scheduled option selected, open the Scheduled drop-down list and select a predefined schedule, or click New and define your own schedule. If you previously created a custom schedule, select it from the list, and click Edit.

 ◆ Select the Manually option.

3 Click OK.

Turn on to schedule updates for times when you're not using the computer.

Turn on to have the computer connect automatically via modem to update the information.

11

Removing Channels

We all know that you *can* have too much of a good thing! Perhaps you've decided to get rid of some of the channels you've set up on the Channel Bar. Or perhaps you want to keep certain channels without receiving automatic updates. It's a snap to do either or both.

SEE ALSO

"Modifying Channels" on page 180 for information about deactivating automatic downloading.

TIP

When you delete an item from the Channel Bar, you can recover the item from the Recycle Bin if you want. When you unsubscribe from a channel, however, you must reconnect to the Web site and resubscribe if you want to restore the subscription.

Delete a Channel

1 With the Channel Viewer open, display the Channel Bar and navigate to the channel you want to delete.

2 Right-click the channel and choose Delete from the shortcut menu.

3 Click Yes to confirm the deletion.

Unsubscribe from a Channel

1 On the Channel Bar of the Channel Viewer, right-click the channel to be modified, and choose Properties from the shortcut menu.

2 On the Subscription tab, click Unsubscribe.

3 Click Yes to confirm the subscription deletion.

4 Click OK.

5 Close the Channel Viewer.

Controlling the Channel Bar

The Channel Bar can be a useful tool, but if you find that it's in your way, or if you simply don't use it, you can move it out of your way, reshape it, or just turn it off.

TIP

If you're working with the Active Desktop not displayed as a Web page, and if the Channel Bar doesn't appear when you start Windows, right-click the Internet Explorer icon on the Desktop, choose Properties from the shortcut menu, click the Advanced tab, and turn on the Show Channel Bar At Startup check box.

TIP

If the Internet Explorer Channel Bar isn't listed on the Web tab of the Display Properties dialog box, click the Reset All button.

Move, Resize, or Close the Channel Bar

1. If you're using the Active Desktop, point to the Channel Bar on your Desktop to make its borders appear.

2. Do any of the following:

    ◆ Drag the top border and drop the Channel Bar at a new location.

    ◆ Move the pointer over a border, and drag and drop the border to resize the Channel Bar.

    ◆ Click Close.

Drag to resize.   Drag to move.   Click to close.

Display the Channel Bar

1. Right-click a blank spot on the Desktop, point to Active Desktop on the shortcut menu, and choose Customize My Desktop.

2. On the Web tab of the Display Properties dialog box, turn on the Internet Explorer Channel Bar check box.

3. Click OK.

11

Adding Web Content to the Desktop

Adding Web components to your Active Desktop provides you with windows to updated information without the clutter of a full Web page. A Web component can be almost anything, from a clock to a database search engine. Many Desktop components are updated automatically from a Web site; others contain links to one or more Web sites.

TIP

When you subscribe to a Web site, you are often given the option of adding components to your Desktop.

SEE ALSO

"Viewing Channels" on page 178 for information about subscribing to a Web site.

Add a Component

1. Right-click a blank spot on the Desktop.

2. Point to Active Desktop on the shortcut menu, and choose Customize My Desktop.

3. If you're not viewing the Desktop as a Web page, turn on the View My Active Desktop As A Web Page check box.

4. Click the New button.

5. If the New Active Desktop Item dialog box appears, click Yes to use the Microsoft Active Desktop Gallery, or click No to specify a different Web page.

6. Use the Active Desktop Gallery Web page or the Web page you specified to add components to your Desktop.

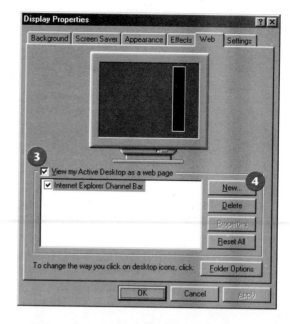

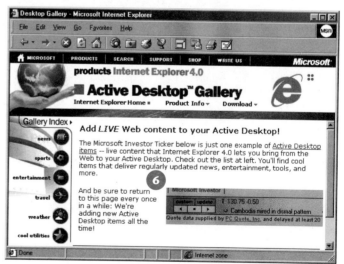

Customizing the Channel Screen Saver

Some of the channels you'll subscribe to contain components that become part of the screen saver. You can control which components you want displayed and for what length of time they're visible, whether or not they're accompanied by music, and the way you want to deactivate the screen saver.

TIP

If the screen saver doesn't go away when you press a key, or if the Close box doesn't appear, click the screen saver and try again.

SEE ALSO

"Viewing Channels" on page 178 for information about subscribing to channels.

"Using a Screen Saver" on page 222 for information about selecting a screen saver.

Customize the Screen Saver

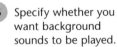 Right-click a blank spot on the Desktop and choose Properties from the shortcut menu.

② On the Screen Saver tab, select Channel Screen Saver from the Screen Saver list if it's not already selected.

③ Click the Settings button.

④ Turn check boxes on or off to specify which channels are to be included. (Only the channels you've subscribed to that supply screen-saver components are listed.)

⑤ Specify the length of time each channel is to be displayed.

⑥ Specify whether you want background sounds to be played.

⑦ Specify the way you want the screen saver to be closed.

⑧ Click OK.

⑨ Click OK to close the Display Properties dialog box.

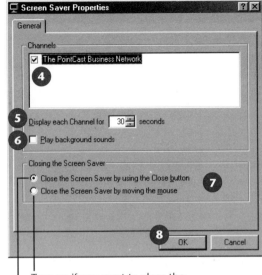

Turn on if you want to close the screen saver by moving the mouse.

Turn on if you want to close the screen saver by clicking it and then clicking the Close button. This enables you to click the hyperlinks of the active channel.

11

Hosting a Web Site

If your company has an intranet, you can use the Microsoft Personal Web Server to set up your computer to host your own Web site. With the Personal Web Server installed, you can create your home page (the opening page of your Web site), and you can then publish documents on your site that will be accessible to your intranet colleagues.

TIP

The Personal Web Server isn't automatically installed with Windows. The first time you try to run it from the Start menu, you'll see instructions for installing it from the Add-Ons folder of the Windows 98 CD.

TIP

Sneak Preview. *Even if you aren't connected to a company intranet, you can use the Personal Web Server to preview any Web pages you create before you post them to the ISP who will be hosting your Web site.*

Create a Home Page

1. Double-click the Personal Web Server icon on the taskbar.

2. Review and then close the Tips window if it appears.

3. Click Web Site.

4. Complete the steps of the Home Page Wizard.

5. Complete the information you want to be included on your home page.

6. Click the Enter New Changes button.

7. Review your page.

8. E-mail the location of your Web site to your colleagues.

The address of your home page

The root directory for your documents

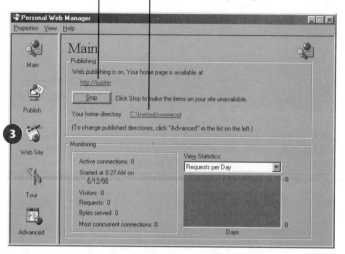

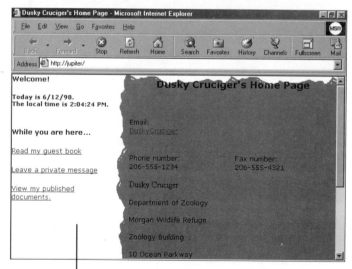

The Home Page Wizard produces a simple but useful home page.

Publish a Document

1. Drag the document and drop it on top of the Publish shortcut icon on the Desktop. The Personal Web Manager appears.

2. Type a description of the document.

3. Click the Add button.

4. Use the Browse button to locate any other documents to be published, add a description for each document, and click Add.

5. Click the >> button to complete the wizard.

6. Use the Address toolbar in Internet Explorer or on the taskbar to go to your home page.

7. Use the links on your home page to view the published documents.

8. Click the Close button to close the Personal Web Manager window. (The Personal Web Server will continue to run.)

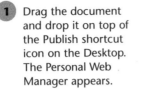

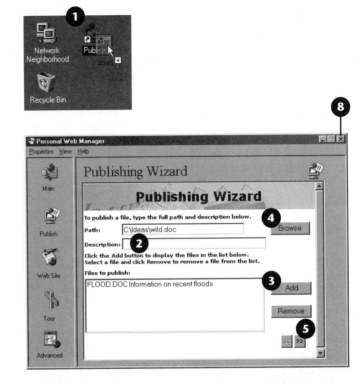

Type the name of your computer to view your Web page as others will see it.

11

Talking on the Net

With Microsoft NetMeeting, you can use the Internet or your company's intranet to hold voice and video conversations or text conversations (chats). The first time you run NetMeeting, a wizard walks you through the setup and asks you to provide the necessary information. After that, you can use a directory service to connect on the Internet, or you can call colleagues on your intranet.

TIP

To start NetMeeting from Internet Explorer or Outlook Express, choose Internet Call from the Go menu. You can also start NetMeeting from the Start menu.

TIP

Microsoft maintains several directory servers that are available for your use. You can connect to any of them, or to other directory servers, when you start NetMeeting.

Get Listed on the Internet

1. With NetMeeting running and your computer connected to the Internet, choose Options from the Tools menu.

2. On the Calling tab, turn on the options you want, and specify the directory server you want to be listed on.

3. Click OK.

4. Click Yes if you're asked to log on to the server.

5. Select the directory service you logged on to.

6. Verify that you're listed.

Turn on to log on automatically to the directory server.

Select a server.

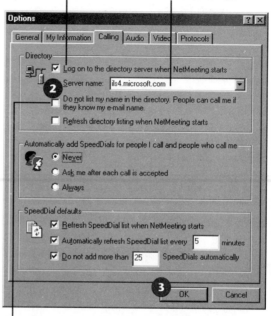

Turn on to enable others to connect to you using this server and to keep your name off the directory listing.

Verify that the correct category and server are listed.

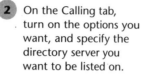

Your listing is based on the entries on the My Information tab of the Options dialog box.

*"Sending a Business Card"
on page 167 for information
about sharing your contact
information, including your
NetMeeting contact address.*

SEE ALSO

TIP

Nyet Meeting. *If you're
troubled by incoming telephone
calls when NetMeeting is running, choose Do Not Disturb
from the File menu to ignore
all incoming calls until you
choose Do Not Disturb again.*

TIP

*To connect to a computer on
your network, type the computer's name in the Address
box and set Call Using to Automatic. Your network must be
using the TCP/IP network protocol to run NetMeeting.*

TIP

*Always establish voice and/or
video connections before having
any other computers connect
when you're hosting a meeting.*

TIP

*To call someone you've previ-
ously called, use Speed Dial or
the History listing of calls.*

Make a Call

1 If you're using a locator
server, select the server
and category, and click
the name of the person
you want to call.

2 Click the Call button on
the NetMeeting toolbar.

3 If it isn't already shown
in the Address box,
type the address.

4 Click the Call button.

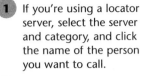

Calling using
Microsoft's
directory server

Receive a Call

Do either of the following:

◆ Choose Options from
the Tools menu, turn
on the Automatically
Accept Incoming
Calls check box on the
General tab, and click
OK to answer incom-
ing calls automatically.

◆ Click the Accept
or Ignore button to
answer incoming calls
manually.

If you don't want to accept all calls automatically,
you can choose which ones to answer.

11

Conferring on the Net

When you're part of a NetMeeting, you can sit back and be an observer, or you can be an active participant by displaying items on the Whiteboard and working with shared programs. When you do participate, whatever you contribute is viewed by everyone participating in the conference.

TIP

The Whiteboard can have multiple pages; use the buttons at the bottom right of the window to move among the pages and to add new pages.

TRY THIS

Be Prepared. *Before you connect to a meeting, add a page to the Whiteboard, move to that page, and add the elements you want to present at the meeting. When you connect, that Whiteboard page will be available for your presentation.*

Brainstorm on the Whiteboard

1 Click the Whiteboard button on the NetMeeting toolbar.

2 Use any of the following tools to convey information:

♦ The Pen, Line, or any shape tool to draw on the Whiteboard

♦ The Text tool to type text

♦ The Eraser tool to select and remove an element

♦ The Remote Pointer or the Highlighter to emphasize an area

♦ The Selection tool to select and drag elements to new locations

3 Use any of the following methods to insert additional information:

♦ The Select Area or Select Window tool to select and paste part of the screen or a whole window

♦ The Paste command to copy material from the Clipboard

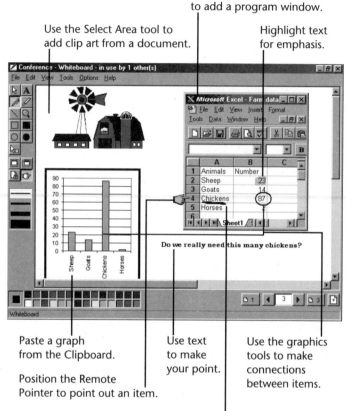

Use the Select Area tool to add clip art from a document.

Use the Select Window tool to add a program window.

Highlight text for emphasis.

Paste a graph from the Clipboard.

Position the Remote Pointer to point out an item.

Use text to make your point.

Use the graphics tools to make connections between items.

Use the Pen tool for freehand drawing.

SEE ALSO

"Talking on the Net" on page 188 for information about connecting to a meeting.

TIP

To pass on information in text format, use the Chat feature of NetMeeting. You can save the contents of the Chat and Whiteboard windows for later review by choosing Save from the File menu.

TIP

The person who is running the program "owns" it, so he or she can take control of the program or stop sharing it at any time. When this happens, the Collaborate button changes its appearance and becomes the Stop Collaborating button.

TIP

When someone else is in control of a shared program, the mouse pointer displays that person's initials.

Share a Program

1. Start the program.

2. Click the down arrow on the Share button.

3. Click the name of the program to be shared.

4. To allow others to modify the contents of the program, click Collaborate.

5. On another computer in the meeting, click Collaborate, click in the shared program, and make any changes to the content.

6. On the computer that owns the program, click the mouse to regain control, and do either of the following:

   ◆ Click the Stop Collaborating button to continue to display the program but prevent others from modifying it.

   ◆ Click the down arrow on the Share button, and click the shared program to work on it by yourself without displaying it on other computers.

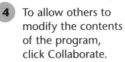

Tab shows who owns the program.

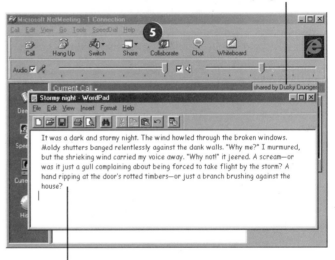

Shared program is viewed by all, but only one person at a time can work on it.

Getting Information Without Using the Internet

You don't have to use the Internet to download up-to-the-minute information. If you have a TV tuner card installed on your computer and you can receive a PBS TV station (in the U.S. and Canada only), you can use the WaveTop program to collect information from the TV signal and store it on your computer. Then you can view the information just as you would view any Web page.

> **TIP**
>
> *The information is embedded in a hidden part of the broadcast signal, so you can receive it using a cable or antenna connection.*

View the Information

1 Click the Start button, point to Programs and then Accessories, and choose WaveTop from the submenu. (The first time you use WaveTop, you'll need to run a setup and registration procedure.)

2 Click the category you want to view.

3 Click the item you want to view.

4 Review the information.

Click for access to Help.

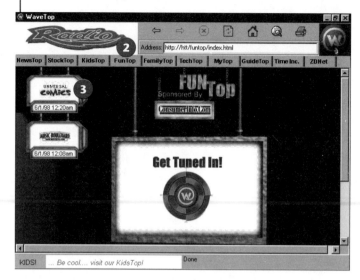

Select What's Stored

1 Click the MyTop button.

2 Click the category you want to customize.

3 Turn check boxes on or off, depending on the services you want.

4 Wait for the channel information to be downloaded and stored.

5 Switch to the category and view the information.

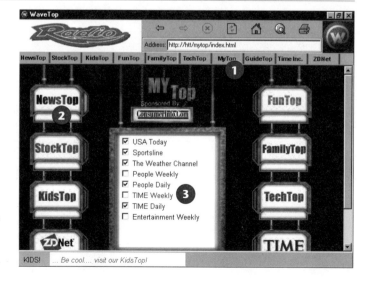

12

Staying in Touch

If your work involves traveling, read this section before you take off! If you use different computers at different locations, or if you have a desktop computer at work and you travel with a notebook computer, this section of the book will help you avoid the pesky problems that can occur when you're working long distance.

You'll find out how to create one or more virtual Briefcases, into which you can stuff a bunch of files from your main computer. You can work on the files on the road, and then update them back at the office on your main computer with a mouse-click or two. Alternatively, you can easily connect to your own computer, to a corporate network, or to an online service from wherever your travels take you, and then you can work on your files just as if you were in the office. If you have a modem, you can set up a HyperTerminal so that you can connect to bulletin boards or other types of terminal services, and you can transfer files between computers. You can also transfer files between computers that aren't normally connected—to download files from a laptop computer onto your main computer, for example—by creating a temporary network connection between the two computers with a cable. And, for the ultimate in convenience, you can use your modem with the Phone Dialer accessory program to place telephone calls for you.

Using the Briefcase to Manage Files

When your work travels with you, whether it's from your office to your home or to the other side of the world, you often need to take copies of files from your main desktop computer and use them on a different computer. If you've done this a lot, and you're aware of how difficult it can be to keep track of the most recently changed version of a file, you'll like the Briefcase. Okay, so it's not made of fine Corinthian leather. You won't care when you see how easily you can synchronize the changes you make in your traveling files with the originals on your main computer.

Copy the Briefcase onto a Floppy Disk

1 Right-click a blank spot on the Desktop, point to New, and choose Briefcase from the shortcut menu. Give the new Briefcase a descriptive name.

2 Open a folder window, and drag a file or folder onto the new Briefcase icon.

3 If a welcome screen appears the first time you use the Briefcase, click the Finish button.

4 On the Desktop, right-click the Briefcase and send it to a floppy disk.

Dragging a file onto the Briefcase icon copies the file into the Briefcase.

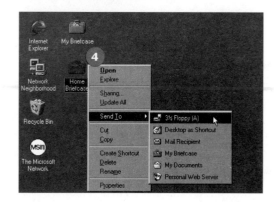

Use the Briefcase Files

1 Insert the floppy disk into your other computer, drag the Briefcase from the disk onto the Desktop, and double-click the Briefcase icon.

2 Double-click a file to use it, and save the file to the Briefcase. When you've finished, drag the Briefcase from the Desktop to the floppy disk.

Update the Files

1 Insert the disk into your main computer.

2 Open My Computer, open a window for the disk, and drag the Briefcase onto the Desktop.

3 Double-click the Briefcase icon.

4 To update

◆ A single file, select the file and choose Update Selection from the toolbar.

◆ All files, choose Update All.

5 Click Update to confirm the updating.

The Briefcase records the location of the original files...

...and tracks which files have been changed.

Connecting from Different Locations

If you travel around a lot—breakfast in New York, lunch in Chicago, and dinner in Seattle, perhaps—and you dial in to your corporate network or online service from your computer from each location, you need to tell Windows where you're calling from so that it can use the correct dialing properties for that location.

TIP

Most modem-based services, such as Outlook Express and HyperTerminal, have buttons or menu commands that take you directly to the Dialing Properties dialog box.

TIP

Once a dialing location has been set up, you can select it in the Dialing From list.

Create a New Location

1 Double-click My Computer, and open the Dial-Up Networking folder.

2 Double-click the connection you want to use.

3 In the Connect To dialog box, click the Dialing Properties button.

4 In the Dialing Properties dialog box, click the New button, and type a name for the location.

5 Specify the location you're calling from. Click the Area Code Rules button if you need to dial an area code without first dialing 1.

6 Specify any special prefix-dialing requirements.

7 If you want to use a calling card, turn on the For Long Distance Calls, Use This Calling Card check box, click the Calling Card button, and specify the card and number.

8 Click OK.

9 Click Connect to connect or Cancel to connect later.

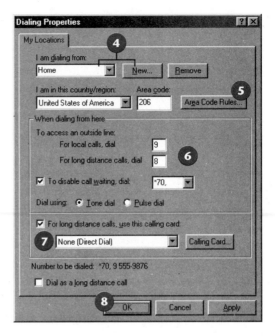

Calling to Your Computer

If you want to connect to your computer from another computer, or give access to others to facilitate file transfer between computers, you can turn your computer into a dial-up server. You control who can gain access to your computer by using a password, and you can limit access to folders by setting sharing properties for the folders.

SEE ALSO

"Sharing Your Computer" on page 72 for information about sharing folders.

"Connecting to Your Network from a Remote Location" on page 198 for information about dial-up networking.

"Adding or Removing Windows Components" on page 256 for information about installing Dial-Up Server and Dial-Up Networking if they're not already installed.

Create a Server

1 Double-click My Computer, and then double-click Dial-Up Networking.

2 Choose Dial-Up Server from the Connections menu.

3 Turn on the Allow Caller Access option.

4 Click Change Password, type a new password, confirm it, and click OK.

5 Click Server Type.

6 Select the type of server, and click OK.

7 Click OK to start the server.

8 Provide the access number, server type, and password to the people who need the information.

9 To disable the server, double-click the Dial-Up Server icon on the taskbar, turn on the No Caller Access option, and click OK.

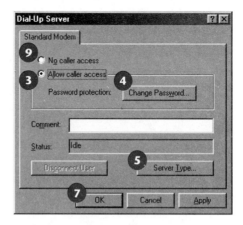

12

Connecting to Your Network from a Remote Location

If your network has dial-up network services, and you have permission to connect from a remote location, you can establish a dial-up connection and connect to your network by phone. Once you're connected, you can access the network just as if you were in the office.

TIP

The network administrator can restrict your access to a single folder or computer when you dial in, or can give you full access to the entire network.

SEE ALSO

"Adding or Removing Windows Components" on page 256 for information about installing Dial-Up Networking if it isn't already installed.

Set Up Your Computer

1. If you're using a computer that isn't normally connected to the network, configure it exactly as if it were connected to the network, using the same network protocols, computer name, workgroup name, and domain name if any, and your logon passwords.

2. Open My Computer and double-click Dial-Up Networking.

3. Double-click Make New Connection.

4. Step through the Make New Connection Wizard, typing a name for the connection and a phone number for the computer.

Use a descriptive name for the connection.

Type the number of the direct line to the server's modem.

Connect to the Network

1. If you haven't already logged on to your computer as if you were connecting to the network, restart Windows and log on.

2. In the Dial-Up Networking folder, double-click the connection you created.

3. Type your password to connect to the dial-in server, and verify the phone number and your dialing location.

4. Click Connect.

5. Wait for the connection to be made, and provide any passwords required.

6. Work on the network as usual. When you've finished, log off from the network if required.

7. Double-click the Dial-Up Networking icon.

8. Click the Disconnect button.

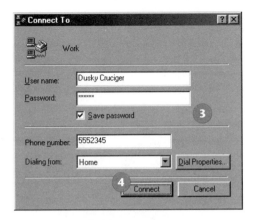

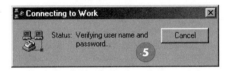

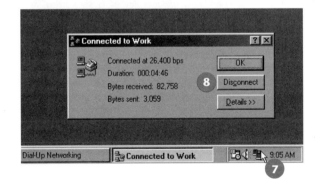

Connecting with a Terminal

When you need to connect by modem with a terminal—a bulletin board, for example—you can do so using HyperTerminal. HyperTerminal is a program provided by Windows 98 that lets your computer function as a terminal. And if you have problems connecting or communicating, you can modify the settings to improve the connection.

TIP

HyperTerminal comes with some preconfigured setups for various popular services. To use one of these setups, double-click its icon, and confirm and/or modify the connection information, if necessary.

SEE ALSO

"Adding or Removing Windows Components" on page 256 for information about installing HyperTerminal if it isn't already installed.

Set Up Your Terminal

1 Click the Start button, point your way through Programs, Accessories, and Communications, and choose Hyper-Terminal from the submenu.

2 Double-click the Hypertrm icon in the HyperTerminal folder window.

3 Type an identifying name for the connection, select an icon, and click OK.

4 Enter your phone information, and click OK.

5 Click the Dial button.

6 Use the sign-on information you've been assigned, and verify that the information is being displayed correctly.

7 Sign off, and click the Disconnect button.

Scroll up to see text that has scrolled off the window. Text from previous sessions is also shown.

Click to disconnect.

Follow the directions of the host terminal.

Modify the Connection

1 Click the Properties button on the HyperTerminal toolbar.

2 On the Settings tab, click the ASCII Setup button.

3 Modify the settings as shown in the table, below right.

4 Click OK.

5 Click OK in the Properties dialog box.

6 Choose Save from the File menu.

7 Try your connection again.

ASCII Setup

ASCII Sending
☐ Send line ends with line feeds
☐ Echo typed characters locally
Line delay: 0 milliseconds.
Character delay: 0 milliseconds.

ASCII Receiving
☐ Append line feeds to incoming line ends
☐ Force incoming data to 7-bit ASCII
☑ Wrap lines that exceed terminal width

OK   Cancel

CONNECTION-SETTING TROUBLESHOOTING	
If you have this problem	**Make this setting**
Text you send is in one long line.	Turn on the Send Line Ends With Line Feeds check box.
You don't see what you send.	Turn on the Echo Typed Characters Locally check box.
Some of the text you send isn't received.	Enter *1* for Line Delay. Increase the value if necessary.
Some of the characters you send drop out.	Enter *1* for Character Delay. Increase the value if necessary.
Text you receive is in one long line.	Turn on the Append Line Feeds To Incoming Line Ends check box.
Text you receive is garbled.	Turn on the Force Incoming Data To 7-Bit ASCII check box.
The ends of lines are not visible.	Turn on the Wrap Lines That Exceed Terminal Width check box.

12

Transferring Files by Modem

If you want to transfer files directly between computers via modem, you can transfer them the old-fashioned way—that is, from terminal to terminal. There is no limitation on file size, and you'll probably get the maximum speed from your modem. You can even use this method to transfer data between different types of computers, including mainframes and computers that aren't running Windows, provided the other computer has a modem and communications software. However, the procedure described here assumes that both computers are using HyperTerminal.

SEE ALSO

"Connecting with a Terminal" on page 200 for information about setting up a Hyper-Terminal connection.

Set Up the Terminals

1. On the host computer, double-click the Hypertrm icon.

2. Click the Cancel button instead of dialing.

3. Click the Properties button on the toolbar, and click the ASCII Setup button on the Settings tab.

4. If they're not already turned on, turn on the Send Line Ends With Line Feeds and Echo Typed Characters Locally check boxes.

5. Click OK.

6. Click OK.

7. On the calling computer, set up HyperTerminal to dial the host computer, using the same ASCII Setup settings on both computers.

8. On each computer, choose Save from the File menu to save the settings.

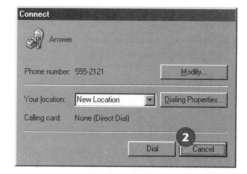

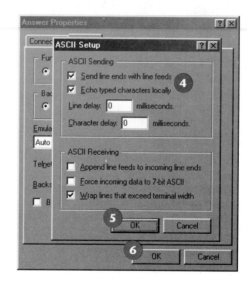

TIP

If the transmission is very slow, verify that the modem or the COM port is set to work at its maximum speed. If you're getting too many errors, reduce the transmission speed. To adjust the speed, choose Properties from the File menu, and click the Configure button on the Connect To tab.

SEE ALSO

"Attach a File to a Message" on page 159 for information about transferring a file by attaching it to an e-mail message.

"Conferring on the Net" on page 190 for information about transferring a file over the Internet using NetMeeting.

"Calling to Your Computer" on page 197 for information about making a network connection to your computer via modem.

"Connecting to Your Network from a Remote Location" on page 198 for information about connecting to your network via modem.

Connect the Computers

1. On the answering computer, choose Wait For Call from the Call menu.

2. On the calling computer, click the Connect button and then the Dial button.

3. Type messages to each other to coordinate the transfer.

4. On the computer that will receive the file, click the Receive button on the HyperTerminal toolbar, specify the folder and protocol for the file, and click Close.

5. On the computer that's sending the file, click the Send button on the HyperTerminal toolbar, locate the file, and click Send.

6. Wait for the file to be sent.

7. Click the Disconnect button when you've finished.

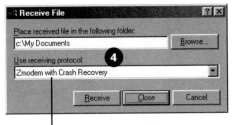

Use the same protocol on both computers.

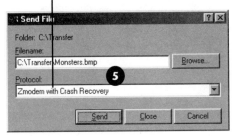

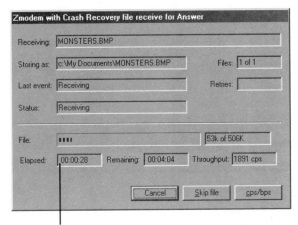

The status of the file transfer is displayed.
Both computers receive the status information.

12

Connecting Two Computers with a Cable

To transfer information between two computers that aren't normally connected— a notebook computer and a desktop computer, for example—you connect them with a cable that links their serial or parallel ports. The cable creates a network connection between the two computers, with one computer *hosting* the other.

TIP

If both computers are equipped with infrared communication ports, you can use these ports instead of using a cable from a serial or parallel port.

SEE ALSO

"Sharing Folders Using Passwords" on page 74 and "Sharing Folders with Individuals" on page 76 for information about sharing folders.

Connect the Computers

1 Configure the computer that will be the guest to have at least one of the same network protocols as the host computer.

2 Connect the cables.

3 On each computer, click the Start button, point to Programs and then Accessories, and choose Direct Cable Connection from the submenu.

4 On each computer, step through the Direct Cable Connection Wizard. Specify the port to which the cable is connected on each computer.

5 Complete the steps of the wizard, and wait for the connection to be established.

Designate your main computer as the host.   Designate the other computer as the guest.

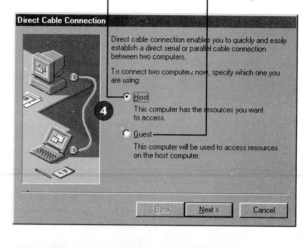

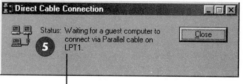

After you've completed the steps of the wizard, the host computer listens and waits for the guest computer to connect.

Exchange Information

1 Use standard techniques to navigate through folders, and to move, copy, or delete folders or files. (Note that when you connect two computers, you have access to the other computer's shared folders only.)

◆ Open any of the shared folders from the host computer.

◆ Explore any network connections to which the guest computer is granted access through the host computer.

◆ Use the host computer's Network Neighborhood to explore any shared folders on the guest computer.

2 On the guest computer, click Direct Cable Connection on the taskbar, and click Close to disconnect.

3 On the host computer, click Direct Cable Connection on the taskbar, and click Close to end the direct cable connection session.

When the guest computer connects...

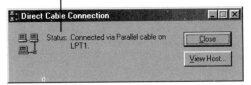

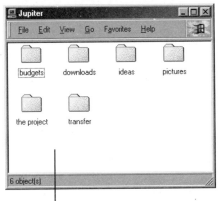

...the host computer's shared folders are displayed on the guest computer.

12

Making a Phone Call

If you have a telephone connected to your modem, you can use a Windows accessory program called Phone Dialer to place a telephone call for you. You can automate the process even further by using Speed Dial buttons.

TIP

If Phone Dialer isn't listed on the Communications sub-menu of the Start menu's Accessories submenu, you'll need to install it.

SEE ALSO

"Adding or Removing Windows Components" on page 256 for information about installing Windows components.

TRY THIS

Make a series of calls using Phone Dialer. Then choose Show Log from the Tools menu. Voilà—details of all your completed calls!

Dial a Number

1. Click the Start button, point your way through Programs, Accessories, and Communications, and choose Phone Dialer from the submenu.

2. Type the phone number or click the buttons to enter the number.

3. Click Dial.

4. Enter a name for the log record if desired.

5. Once the number has been dialed, pick up the phone and click the Talk button.

6. When the conversation is over, hang up the phone.

The number that you type or enter by clicking the number buttons is shown here.

Speed It Up

1. Click a blank Speed Dial button.

2. Type a name for the button.

3. Enter the phone number.

4. Click Save.

5. Repeat steps 1 through 4 to add or change speed-dial numbers.

6. Click a Speed Dial button to call that number.

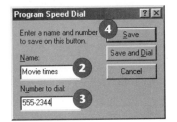

12

13

Changing
the Look
of Your
Computer

Most of us tend to choose our clothes, our furniture, and the various other trappings of our daily lives based on personal preferences that include style, size, color, comfort, and efficiency. You love your old car because you're tall and it has enough headroom; I love my blue suede shoes because they're...blue. These preferences are part of our personalities—they might change radically over time but, for better or worse, we always have at least a few of them.

Now that computers are a part of so many people's daily lives, we want our computers to reflect our personalities, too. Whether it's your computer or your employer's, you can customize it so that it looks and works exactly the way you want it to. You can keep the standard "Windows" look, you can change the look to that of a Web page, or you can design your own look that includes elements from both styles. You can customize your folder windows with colors and pictures, and you can change the size and color of almost everything. You can use the handy Magnifier to enlarge anything on your screen, you can choose among screen savers and colorful Desktop Themes, and you can try different mouse pointers.

It's easy and fun to customize the look of your computer, whether you do it one time only or once a month.

Windows 98 Views

The addition to Windows of a Web-style view opens up a whole new world of customization options. You can set Windows 98 to look and feel as if it's part of the Web, you can make it look and work as if you were still using Windows 95, or you can customize it so that it has a little of both styles and is uniquely your own. The table below lists the various Windows 98 elements and their customization options and results, and the facing page shows the two basic views of Windows.

	WINDOWS 98 VIEWS		
Element	**Classic view**	**Web view**	**Custom**
Icon	Icons are not underlined; click to select, double-click to open.	Icons are underlined; point to select, click to open.	Single-click setting: icons are underlined, or are underlined only when selected. Double-click setting: icons are not underlined.
Window	Windows are viewed without Web-page content or background picture. Individual windows can be set to be viewed as Web pages.	Windows with HTML content are viewed as Web pages, and can include background picture.	All windows or selected windows only can be viewed as Web pages.
Desktop	Desktop has no HTML content.	Active Desktop can contain Web-page elements.	Desktop can display or hide Web-related content.
Subfolder	Subfolders open in new window.	Subfolders open in same window as parent folder.	Subfolders can open in same window or in new window.

Classic View

Web View

Standard Desktop

Folder viewed as Web page

Active Desktop has active components.

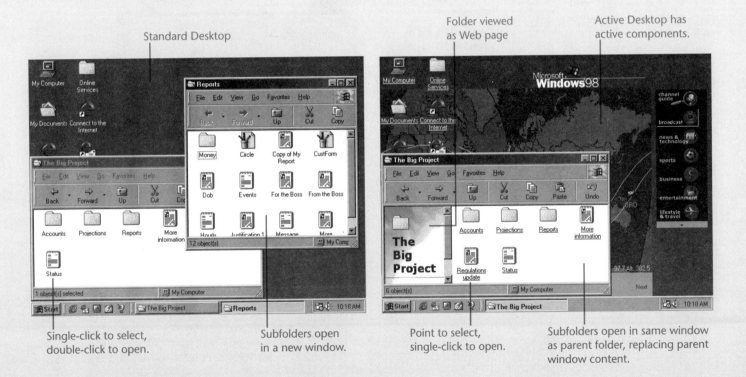

Single-click to select, double-click to open.

Subfolders open in a new window.

Point to select, single-click to open.

Subfolders open in same window as parent folder, replacing parent window content.

Switching Views

Windows 98 provides you with two main views, or *styles,* which affect the look of your interface: Web style and Classic style. You can switch between the two styles, or you can create your own custom-blended look. Whatever your customization plans, you need to decide on your main style before you can start making changes.

SEE ALSO

"The Views Go On" on page 42 and "Windows 98 Views" on pages 210–211 for information about the effects of using the different views on the way you work.

Set the Main Style

1 Point to Settings on the Start menu, and choose Folder Options from the submenu.

2 On the General tab, select

   ◆ Web Style for a Web browser–style interface.

   ◆ Classic Style for a Windows 95–style interface.

   ◆ Custom to specify a mix of Web and Classic styles.

3 Click OK.

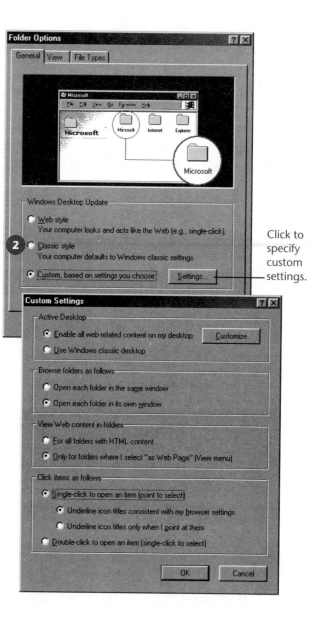

Click to specify custom settings.

Hiding Desktop Icons

If you're working in Web view, and your information is displayed on your Desktop as Web components or as a Web page with links, you might find that the standard Windows icons serve little purpose other than to clutter up your workspace. No problem—you can easily hide those icons.

TIP

Now You See 'Em, Now You Don't. *Desktop icons are hidden only when you're viewing the Active Desktop as a Web page. To quickly make your icons visible again, right-click the Desktop, point to Active Desktop, and choose View As Web Page from the shortcut menu.*

SEE ALSO

"Putting a Web Page on Your Desktop" on page 110 for information about using an HTML document as a background for your Desktop.

Hide the Icons

1. Right-click a blank spot on the Desktop and choose Properties from the shortcut menu.

2. On the Effects tab, turn on the Hide Icons When The Desktop Is Viewed As A Web Page check box.

3. On the Web tab, verify that the View My Active Desktop As A Web Page check box is turned on and that the Web components you want displayed on your Desktop are checked.

4. On the Background tab, verify that the HTML document that contains your links is selected.

5. Click OK.

Web (HTML) document contains links to information.

Desktop with icons hidden

Web components provide access to information.

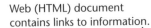

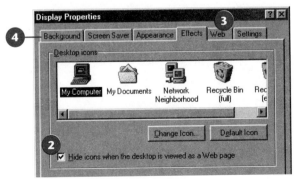

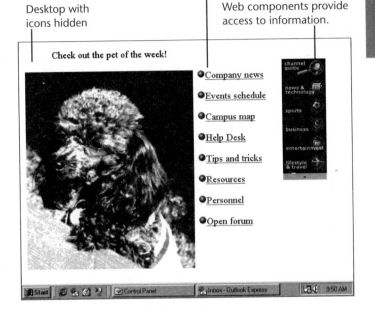

13

Customizing a Folder Window

When you're looking at pages in Web view, you can customize all your folder windows to your liking. When viewed as a Web page (an HTML document), a folder window contains many more components than it does when viewed as a regular folder window: separate sections for information that changes as you select topics, for example, or links to other locations.

TIP

If you're viewing a page in Web view but you can't see all the information, try widening or maximizing the window.

TIP

When you set the view to Web style, all windows that contain HTML elements will be displayed as Web pages.

Display or Hide a Web Page

1 Open the folder window you want to modify.

2 Choose As Web Page from the View menu. If there's already a check mark next to the command, choosing the command will turn off the Web Page view.

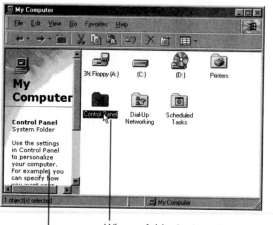

When a folder is viewed as a Web page...

...items display additional information when selected.

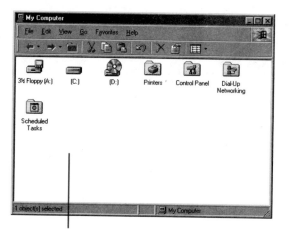

When a folder is not viewed as a Web page, items display less information but take up less space in the window.

Add a Picture

1 Choose Customize This Folder from the View menu.

2 In the Customize This Folder Wizard, turn on the Choose A Background Picture option.

3 Click Next.

4 Select a picture from the list, or click the Browse button to locate and open a picture.

5 Click to select an icon text color if the default color won't show up against the picture.

6 Specify whether you want a color as a background for the text, and, if so, which color.

7 Click Next.

8 Click Finish to complete the wizard.

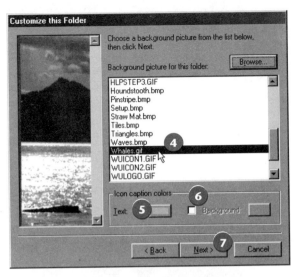

Selected picture is the background for the folder window.

Making All Windows Look the Same

Individuality, while generally a good quality, can sometimes be distracting and confusing. Consistency has its merits too, but can often be boring and predictable. However, by customizing a single window and applying the customization to all your windows, you can create the best of both worlds: individuality combined with consistency.

TIP

Back to the Drawing Board! *Click the Reset All Folders button on the View tab of the Folder Options dialog box if you want to remove all customization for all folders and return the view to the Windows default settings.*

Customize All Windows

1 From My Computer, open the window you want to customize.

2 Experiment, using the View menu commands, to customize

- ◆ The type of icons to be displayed.
- ◆ Whether the folder is to be viewed as a Web page.
- ◆ The options you want on the View tab of the Folder Options dialog box.

3 Choose Folder Options from the View menu.

4 On the View tab of the Folder Options dialog box, click the Like Current Folder button.

5 Click Yes when asked to confirm that you want to set all folders to match the current folder.

6 Click OK to close the Folder Options dialog box.

This folder window is the template...

...for the customization of your other folder windows.

Displaying Paths, Extensions, and Hidden Files

If you're a computer traditionalist who loves to know exactly where you are in the computer's directory tree, or if you'd rather see a file's full name, including its extension, than the type of file or the program with which the file is associated, Windows is ready to accommodate your preferences.

TIP

To obtain a description of each item in the Advanced Settings list, click the Help button in the upper right corner of the Folder Options dialog box, and then click the option in the list.

Display the File Information

1 Point to Settings on the Start menu, and choose Folder Options from the submenu.

2 Click the View tab.

3 Turn on the check boxes you want.

4 Click OK.

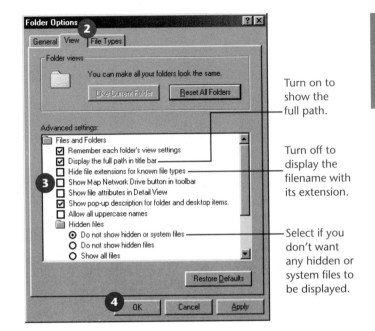

Turn on to show the full path.

Turn off to display the filename with its extension.

Select if you don't want any hidden or system files to be displayed.

Improving the Look of Your Screen

You can turn on several enhancements to improve the look of your screen, especially if you are running at a high resolution and in High Color or True Color.

Turn on the Enhancements

1 Right-click a blank spot on the Desktop and choose Properties from the shortcut menu.

2 Click the Effects tab.

3 Turn on the options you want.

4 Click OK.

Animates menus, windows, and drop-down lists so that they slide out when you open them and slide back when you close them.

Removes "dithering" from icons when system is set to High Color or True Color.

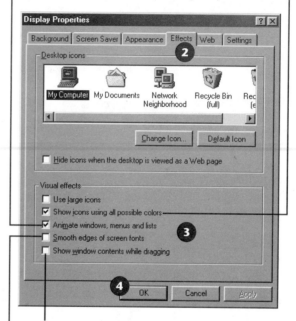

Moves the window itself when it's being dragged, instead of showing a placeholder rectangle.

Places shading around screen fonts to reduce their jagged look on the screen, but doesn't affect printed fonts.

Changing Screen Colors

If you're tired of looking at the same old colors, you can brighten up—or tone down—the colors on your screen. You can select a predefined color scheme or define your own color scheme.

TIP

Disappearing Act! *Change your colors with caution, and be sure to keep enough contrast between a text color and its background. If, for example, you change the menu font color to the same color as the menu itself, you won't be able to see the menu items until you select them.*

TRY THIS

Two-Tone Title Bar. *In the preview area, click the title bar of the active window. The words "Active Title Bar" will appear in the Item list. Select a color in the Color box and a second color in the Color 2 box. The setting will produce a title bar with graduated colors—that is, the first color will fade into the second color.*

Select a Color Scheme

1. Right-click a blank spot on the Desktop and choose Properties from the shortcut menu.

2. Click the Appearance tab.

3. Select a color scheme. (The High Contrast and the Large and Extra Large schemes provide settings that make the Windows components more easily visible on your screen.)

4. Preview the scheme.

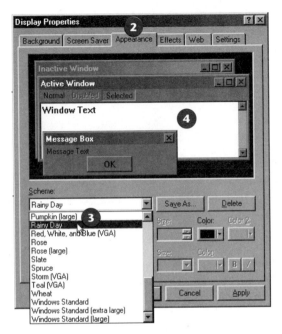

Modify the Scheme

1. Select an item from the Item list.

2. Change the color.

3. Change the color of any other items.

4. Click the Save As button, type a name for your color scheme, and click OK.

5. Click OK to apply the changes.

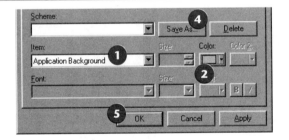

Making Everything More Colorful

Most computers can display different levels of color, from a simple 16-color or 256-color palette that's fine for displaying colors in dialog boxes to a more complex true-color palette that produces photographic-quality colors. The higher levels of color use up a lot of memory, so—depending on the capabilities of your computer—you might have to work with reduced screen resolution if you need to use the highest color settings.

SEE ALSO

"Making More Room on the Desktop" on page 107 for information about setting the screen resolution.

Change the Color Palette

1 Right-click a blank spot on the Desktop and choose Properties from the shortcut menu.

2 Click the Settings tab.

3 Select a setting in the Colors drop-down list. (The colors available depend on your computer system.)

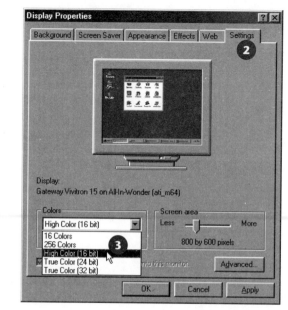

Set the Compatibility Options

1 Click the Advanced button.

2 On the General tab, specify whether you want your computer to restart automatically, to ask you if it should restart, or not to restart when you change the color settings.

3 Click OK, and then click OK to close the Display Properties dialog box.

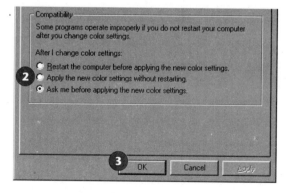

Enlarging the View

You can increase the size of many Windows elements, but some items can still be too small to view comfortably. If you'd like to enlarge *everything*, the Magnifier is the answer. With it, you can increase the size of anything on your screen, whether it's a Windows component or a program you've installed.

TIP

The Accessibility Tools must be installed before you can use the Magnifier.

SEE ALSO

"Adding or Removing Windows Components" on page 256 for information about installing the Accessibility Tools.

TIP

The Invert Colors option affects only the Magnifier. The Use High Contrast Scheme option changes the color scheme for all Windows elements.

Set Up the Magnifier

1 Click the Start button, point your way through Programs, Accessories, and Accessibility, and choose Magnifier from the submenu.

2 Set the magnification level you want.

3 Turn on the check boxes to specify how you want the Magnifier to follow your actions.

4 Specify whether you want to use higher-visibility colors in the Magnifier.

5 Click OK.

Use the Magnifier

1 Depending on the options selected, move the mouse, type text, or select an item to display your actions.

2 Observe your actions in the Magnifier.

3 When you've finished, right-click in the Magnifier and choose Exit from the shortcut menu.

The Magnifier follows the movements of the mouse.

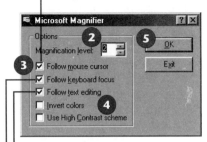

Centers on the insertion point when you're editing text.

Shows the element that has *focus*—that is, the selected item.

What you do here... ...is shown here.

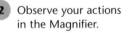

Using a Screen Saver

If you work at a computer for hours every day, it's good for your eyes—and for your mental health—to take a break and look at something different once in a while. If you work in an office with other people, you might not want your colleagues to be able to read your screen—albeit unintentionally—any time you're away from your desk for a few minutes. What you need is a screen saver to provide a nice little respite from your work as well as some privacy. If you want to add some security you can use the password option, but then you'll need to enter your password to use the computer when the screen saver is running.

TIP

Microsoft Plus! 98—an add-on to Windows 98 that's available separately—contains many additional screen savers.

Choose a Screen Saver

1. Right-click a blank spot on the Desktop and choose Properties from the shortcut menu.

2. Click the Screen Saver tab.

3. Select a screen saver.

4. Click Settings to set options for the screen saver.

5. Set the length of time you want your computer to be inactive before the screen saver starts.

6. Click Preview to see the screen saver in full screen. Move your mouse to end the preview.

Preview of screen-saver selection

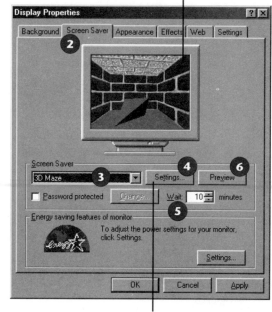

Settings are different for each screen saver.

SEE ALSO

"Starting Up" on page 8 for information about starting Windows with a password, and "Changing Your Passwords" on page 78 for information about changing or disabling your password.

"Customizing the Channel Screen Saver" on page 185 for information about using the channel screen saver.

TIP

What do you do if you forget your password? Pay the price! Turn off your computer, wait a few seconds, and turn it back on. Return to the Screen Saver tab and change the password to one you'll remember. You'll lose any unsaved work, but at least you'll be able to use your computer again.

Add a Screen-Saver Password

1 Turn on the Password Protected check box.

2 Click the Change button.

3 Enter your password twice.

4 Click OK.

5 Click OK.

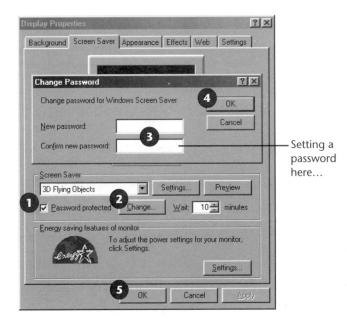

Setting a password here...

...requires entering the same password to remove the screen saver and return to your work.

Changing the Look with Desktop Themes

You can change the entire appearance of your computer with Desktop Themes. Using one of the themes, you can change not only the background picture and your screen saver but the mouse pointers, sounds, icons, colors, and fonts—all at the same time.

SEE ALSO

"Adding or Removing Windows Components" on page 256 for information about installing Desktop Themes.

TIP

Microsoft Plus! 98—an add-on to Windows 98 that's available separately—contains many additional (and exciting) Desktop Themes.

Switch Themes

1. Click the Start button, point to Settings, and choose Control Panel from the submenu.

2. Double-click the Desktop Themes icon.

3. Select a theme from the Theme drop-down list.

4. Select the items to which you want to apply the changes. (Items that aren't checked will use the current settings.)

5. Click the Screen Saver button to preview the screen saver.

6. Click the Pointers, Sounds, Etc. button to preview the mouse pointers, sound, and visual-elements schemes.

7. Make sure you like the settings before you put them into effect.

8. Click OK.

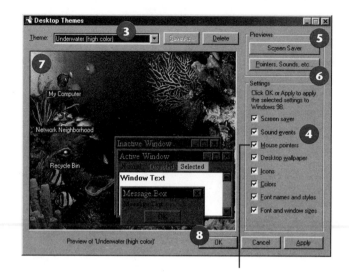

SEE ALSO

"Changing the Look of the Desktop" on page 108 and *"Changing Screen Colors"* on page 219 for information about changing the appearance of your Desktop.

"Associating a Sound with an Event" on page 122 for information about changing sounds.

"Using a Screen Saver" on page 222 for information about changing the screen saver.

"Changing the Mouse Pointers" on page 226 for information about changing mouse pointers.

TRY THIS

Select the Desktop Theme you want to use as your basis, and leave all the options checked. Click Apply. Choose a different theme, and turn off all but the one or two features you want to apply from this theme. Click Apply. Choose another theme, apply one or two features, and click OK to close the dialog box. Open the Display dialog box and use the Effects tab to change an icon. Make any other changes using the Display, Mouse, and Sounds dialog boxes. Open the Desktop Themes dialog box and save the theme.

Customize Your Settings

1. In the Control Panel, double-click Desktop Themes, apply a Desktop Theme, select the items you want from that theme, and click Apply.

2. Repeat step 1 to add the elements you want from other themes. Click OK.

3. In the Control Panel, double-click Display, and customize the display by changing the wallpaper, screen saver, color of elements, and any individual icons. Click OK.

4. In the Control Panel, make any changes you want to the mouse pointers or sounds.

5. In the Control Panel, double-click Desktop Themes.

6. With Current Windows Settings shown in the list, click Save As, type a name for the theme, and click Save.

7. Click OK.

Icons from the Nature theme

Wallpaper from the Underwater theme

Mouse pointer from The 60's USA theme

Font from the Travel theme

Windows colors customized on the Appearance tab

Individual icon changed on the Effects tab of the Display Properties dialog box

13

Changing the Mouse Pointers

Would you like something more exciting than an arrow as a mouse pointer? Do you sometimes have difficulty finding the pointer on the screen? You can make your work more interesting or a little easier by using different pointers for the standard Windows events shown on the Pointers tab of the Mouse Properties dialog box. Your choices are varied, from three-dimensional pointers to oversized black pointers that are impossible to miss!

Change the Pointer Scheme

1 Click the Start button, point to Settings, and choose Control Panel from the submenu.

2 Double-click the Mouse icon.

3 Click the Pointers tab.

4 Select a new scheme from the Scheme drop-down list.

Mouse Properties

Buttons | Pointers | Motion

Scheme

Animated Hourglasses

(None)
Animated Hourglasses
Windows Black
Windows Black (extra large)
Windows Black (large)
Windows Inverted
Windows Inverted (extra large)
Windows Inverted (large)
Windows Standard
Windows Standard (extra large)
Windows Standard (large)

Busy

Precision Select

Text Select

Use Default | Browse...

OK | Cancel | Apply

SEE ALSO

"Adding or Removing Windows Components" on page 256 for information about adding the Mouse Pointers component.

TIP

If you have Desktop Themes installed, you can "borrow" mouse pointers from those themes. Use the Browse button to find the icons in the Themes subfolder of the Plus! folder, which is usually in the Program Files folder.

SEE ALSO

"Switch Themes" on page 224 for information about changing all your mouse pointers in one fell swoop.

"Adjusting Mouse Actions" on pages 248–249 for information about customizing your mouse's performance.

"Wheeling Around with Your Mouse" on page 250 for information about using an IntelliMouse.

Customize the Pointers

1 Select the event and pointer you want to change.

2 Click the Browse button.

3 Click the pointer you want for the selected event.

4 Click Open.

5 Repeat steps 1 through 4 to change other individual pointers.

6 Save the modified scheme with a new name.

7 Click OK.

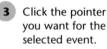

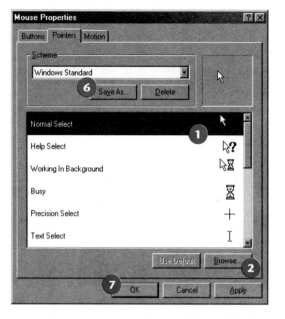

14

Changing the Way Your Computer Works

As time goes by, you'll probably want to make some changes to your system. If you always start your work day using one particular program, you can put that program in the StartUp folder so that it starts automatically when you start Windows 98. You can make all sorts of changes to the mouse, including specifying the way you want it to respond to your clicks, changing its speed, and reconfiguring the buttons for left-handed use. If you share a computer with other people, each of you can customize the computer to reflect your own preferences and working style.

You can add items to or delete them from the Start menu, or completely redesign it. If you like the speed and convenience of the Documents menu, you can wipe it clean when you start a new project. You can change the date, the time, and even the basic setup of your computer so that you can use it in another region or country. If you have any problems with your vision, hearing, or manual dexterity, Windows provides several solutions—you can press key combinations one key at a time, use high-contrast color schemes for better visibility, control mouse movements with the numeric keypad, and so on.

And, if your Desktop isn't big enough for you, you can attach two—or more—monitors to your computer and actually spread your Desktop out over those screens!

Changing Your Click

Windows 98 comes with two basic "looks": Classic style, which keeps everything on your computer screen looking and working just the way it did in Windows 95, and Web style, in which everything looks and works as if you were using a Web browser. One of the biggest differences between the two styles, or views, is the way Windows responds to your mouse movements and clicks. Fortunately, you don't have to limit yourself to one style or the other if neither exactly suits *your* working style; you can create your own custom mix so that the mouse works in the way that's most comfortable for you.

SEE ALSO

"Windows 98 Views" on page 210 for information about the effects you'll get when you choose Web or Classic style.

Set the Style

1. Click the Start button, point to Settings, and choose Folder Options from the submenu.

2. On the General tab, turn on the Custom option.

3. Click the Settings button.

4. Specify the way you want to use the mouse.

5. Click OK.

6. Click OK to close the Folder Options dialog box.

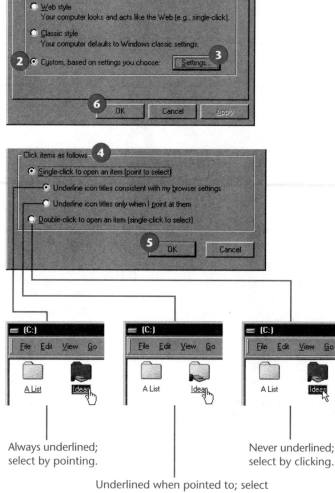

Always underlined; select by pointing.

Underlined when pointed to; select by pointing to for a few moments.

Never underlined; select by clicking.

Customizing a Computer for Different Users

Windows remembers. If you share your computer with other people, each of you can tell Windows how you want the computer set up. Then, every time you log on, Windows will set up your preferences (also called your *user profile*).

TIP

When you work on a network, you can log on to any computer on your network that's running Windows 98, and your preferences will be set up on that computer. If your personalized settings aren't available on another network computer, check with your network administrator. Some networks don't support this feature.

Run the Wizard

1. Click the Start button, point to Settings, choose Control Panel from the submenu, and double-click the Users icon.

2. Click Next in the Enable Multi-User Settings window.

3. Type your user name, and click Next.

4. Type and confirm your password, and click Next.

5. Turn on the check boxes for the items you want to personalize.

6. Specify whether you want to start with a copy of the existing items or create new ones, and click Next.

7. Click Finish to create the settings and restart your computer.

8. Log on as a new user, and customize your settings.

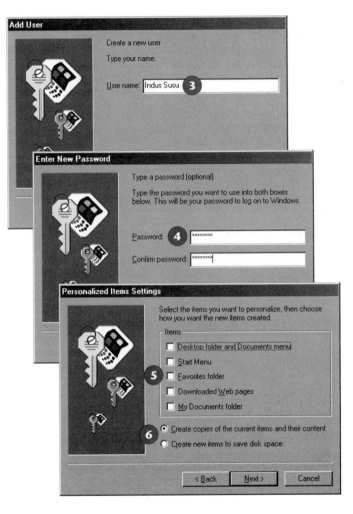

14

Changing the Start Menu

The Start menu is a great resource for organizing and starting your programs and associated documents. You can customize the Start menu by adding and deleting programs, or moving programs around to create an arrangement that's logical and convenient for the way you work.

TIP

Programs listed on the Start menu are not the programs themselves but shortcuts to the programs. When you add, move, or delete an item whose name appears on the Start menu, you're affecting only the shortcut to the program, not the program itself.

Add an Item

1 Use Windows Explorer or My Computer to locate the item you want to add.

2 Drag the item to the Start button, and, without releasing the mouse button, hold the item there until the Start menu opens.

3 Do either of the following:

◆ Drag the item to the top of the menu and drop it.

◆ Drag the item, point to Programs, drag the item onto the Programs submenu, and either drop it or continue dragging and pointing to submenus until you reach the desired location, and then drop the item.

Drop the program at the top of the Start menu…

…or place it on a submenu.

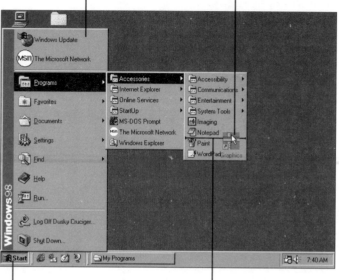

The bar shows the location at which the program will appear on the submenu.

After you drop the program, it becomes part of the submenu.

Rename an Item. *Open the Start menu and locate the item you want to rename. Drag the item off the menu and drop it on your Desktop. Rename the shortcut, drag it back onto the Start menu, and drop it at its original location.*

"Redesigning the Start Menu" on page 234 for information about adding your own submenus.

"Changing the Way a Program Starts" on page 236 for information about modifying the way a program starts from the shortcut menu.

"Starting a Program When Windows Starts" on page 237 for information about adding items to the StartUp folder.

Move an Item

1 Open the Start menu, and the submenus if necessary, and locate the item you want to move.

2 Drag the item and drop it in the new location.

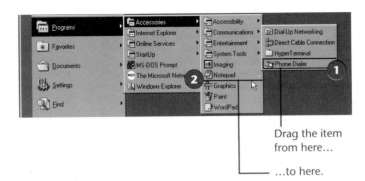

Drag the item from here...

...to here.

14

Delete an Item

1 Open the Start menu, and the submenus if necessary, and locate the item you want to delete.

2 Right-click the item and choose Delete from the shortcut menu.

3 Confirm that you want to delete the item.

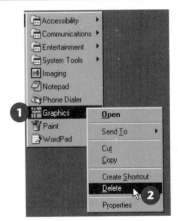

Redesigning the Start Menu

The beauty of Windows 98 is the flexibility it gives you to change things around. For example, if you'd like to reorganize the Start menu so that it works more logically for you, you can restructure it by creating or deleting submenus. Windows uses folders to organize the Start menu, so you have to create a subfolder to be able to create a submenu.

TIP

That Item Is No Longer on the Menu. *You delete a subfolder the same way you delete any Start-menu item—right-click it and choose Delete from the shortcut menu.*

SEE ALSO

"Renaming or Deleting a File or Folder" on page 32 for information about renaming a folder.

Add a Submenu

1. Click the Start button, point to Settings, and choose Taskbar & Start Menu from the submenu.

2. On the Start Menu Programs tab, click the Advanced button.

3. In the Windows Explorer window that appears, select the folder (and thereby the Start menu submenu) in which you want to create a submenu.

4. Right-click a blank spot in the right pane, point to New, and choose Folder from the shortcut menu. Rename the folder, using the name you want to appear on the submenu. Close Windows Explorer.

5. Click OK in the Taskbar Properties dialog box.

6. Open the Start menu, and drag your program or document onto the new submenu.

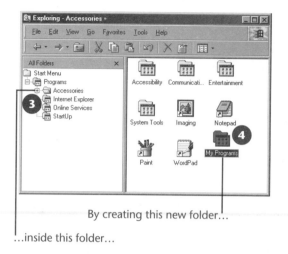

By creating this new folder...

...inside this folder...

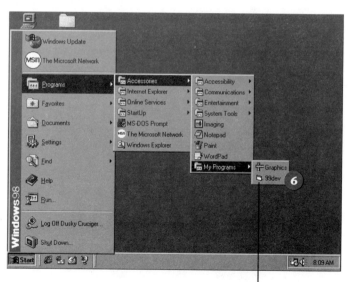

...you create this new submenu.

Removing the Contents of the Documents Menu

Using the Documents menu is a quick and handy way to access your most recently used documents. But some-times—when you start a new project, for example—you don't want to sort through a menu of docu-ments that are unrelated to your current project. You can start with a clean slate by resetting the Documents menu.

> **TIP**
>
> *Removing the documents from the Documents menu deletes only the shortcuts to the docu-ments, not the documents themselves.*

> **TIP**
>
> *To remove a single item, right-click it and choose Delete from the shortcut menu.*

Reset the Documents Menu

1. Click the Start button, point to Settings, and choose Taskbar & Start Menu from the submenu.

2. On the Start Menu Programs tab, click the Clear button.

3. Click OK. The contents of the Documents menu, as well as some other recent history lists (such as the one con-tained in the drop-down list of the Address tool-bar on the taskbar), are cleared.

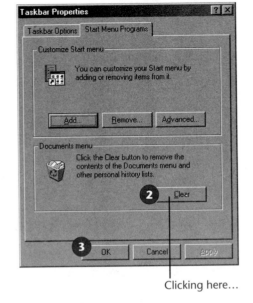

Clicking here…

…gives you a fresh start.

Changing the Way a Program Starts

Many programs have special command switches that you can use to start the program or to modify how it starts or runs. You can add these commands to the shortcut that starts the program, as well as specify the size of the window and even a key combination that quickly switches to the program.

Modify the Shortcut

1 Open the Properties dialog box for the shortcut as follows:

◆ For a shortcut on the Desktop or in a folder, right-click the shortcut and choose Properties from the shortcut menu.

◆ For a Start-menu item, click the Start button, point your way through the submenus until you locate the item, right-click it, and choose Properties from the shortcut menu.

2 Click the Shortcut tab.

3 Change the settings.

4 Click OK.

Specify the folder that contains the required related files if the program can't find them.

Add command switches.

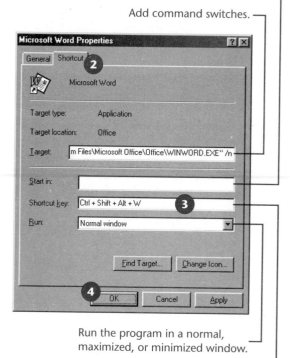

Run the program in a normal, maximized, or minimized window.

Press a key combination to assign a keyboard shortcut that switches to the running program.

Starting a Program When Windows Starts

If you always start your work day using the same program, you can have that program start when Windows starts. And if you use the same document each day, you can have it start automatically in the program. Windows will take a little longer to load, but your program will be ready for you right away.

TIP

To restart a program you closed that starts automatically when Windows starts, don't restart Windows. Open the StartUp submenu and choose the program.

SEE ALSO

"Specifying Which Program Opens a Document" on page 244 for information about the association between documents and programs.

Add a Program to Windows StartUp

1. Locate the program on the Programs submenu of the Start menu.

2. Drag the program onto the StartUp item on the Programs submenu.

3. When the StartUp submenu opens, drop the program onto the submenu.

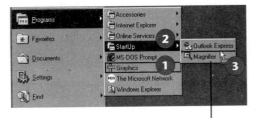

All items on the StartUp submenu will start when Windows starts.

Add a Document to Windows StartUp

1. Use Windows Explorer or My Computer to locate the document.

2. Drag the document onto the Start button, and, without releasing the mouse button, hold the document there until the Start menu opens.

3. Drag the document to the Programs submenu and then to the StartUp item.

4. Drop the document onto the StartUp submenu.

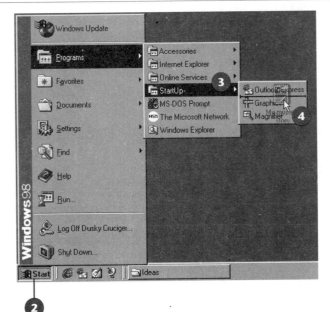

14

Changing Your Input

If you find it difficult to press key combinations; if you sometimes repeat characters accidentally; or if you often turn on the Caps Lock, Num Lock, or Scroll Lock key accidentally, you can customize the way Windows responds to your keystrokes. If you have problems using the mouse, you can switch its functions to your keyboard's numeric keypad. And if you have problems hearing the sounds your computer makes, you can use visual cues instead.

TIP

If you don't see the Accessibility Options icon in the Control Panel, you must install the Accessibility component.

SEE ALSO

"Adding or Removing Windows Components" on page 256 for information about installing Windows components.

Set the Options

1. Click the Start button, point to Settings, and choose Control Panel from the submenu.

2. Double-click the Accessibility Options icon.

3. In the Accessibility Properties dialog box, turn on the options you want to use, as shown in the table at the right.

4. Click the Settings button for the option you selected, and specify how you want the option to function. Click OK.

5. Repeat steps 3 and 4 to set all the options you want to use.

6. On the General tab, specify whether you want the features you selected to be turned off after the computer has been idle for a set period of time.

7. Click OK to close the dialog box.

ALTERNATIVE INPUT OPTIONS	
Feature	**What it does**
StickyKeys	Sets key combinations with Alt, Ctrl, and Shift keys to be pressable one key at a time.
FilterKeys	Ignores repeated characters or too-rapid key presses.
ToggleKeys	Makes unique sounds when you turn the Caps Lock, Num Lock, or Scroll Lock key on or off.
SoundSentry	Flashes a specified screen component when the system beeps.
ShowSounds	Sets programs to display text instead of sounds. Programs must be designed to support this.
MouseKeys	Sets numeric keyboard to control mouse movements.
High Contrast	Changes the Windows color scheme to provide better readability.
SerialKey devices	Provides support for alternative input devices.

Adjusting the Date and Time

If you take a laptop computer with you when you travel, or if your computer's battery has run down, you'll need to adjust the computer's clock to the correct time zone. If you've had your computer repaired, you'll probably need to correct the date and time.

TIP

If the Date/Time icon isn't shown on the taskbar, right-click a blank spot on the taskbar, choose Properties from the shortcut menu, and, on the Taskbar Options tab, turn on the Show Clock option. To adjust the date or time without displaying the clock, double-click the Date/Time icon in the Control Panel.

Adjust the Time Zone

1 Double-click the time on the taskbar.

2 Click the Time Zone tab.

3 Select your time zone from the list.

4 Specify whether you want the clock to adjust automatically for daylight-saving time changes.

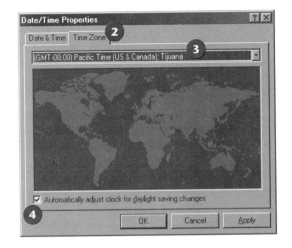

Adjust the Date and Time

1 Click the Date & Time tab.

2 Select the current month from the drop-down list.

3 Select the current year.

4 Click today's date.

5 Click the hour, minute, second, and AM or PM to be adjusted.

6 Click the arrows to adjust the time.

7 Verify the time on the clock face.

8 Click OK.

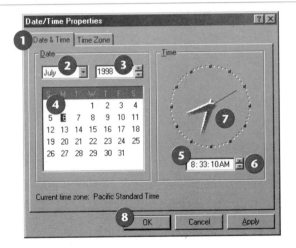

Changing the Date and Time Format

Windows uses the most commonly accepted ways to display date and time, but you can change the display to the format you prefer.

DATE FORMATS
7/5/98
or
07/05/1998
or
July 5, 1998

TIME FORMATS
3:05:30 P
or
03:05:30 PM
or
15:05:30

TIP

To see whether the date is correct, point to the time on the taskbar and hold the mouse steady until the date appears.

Change the Date Format

1. Click the Start button, point to Settings, and choose Control Panel from the submenu.

2. Double-click the Regional Settings icon.

3. Click the Date tab.

4. Select or type a different format for the short date. See the table at the right for valid codes.

5. Click Apply, and inspect the date in the Short Date Sample box.

6. Select or type a different separator for the short date.

7. Click Apply, and inspect the date in the Short Date Sample box.

8. Select or type a different format for the long date.

9. Click Apply, and inspect the date in the Long Date Sample box.

CODES FOR DATE FORMATS	
Code	**Result**
M	Month number
MM	Month number, always two digits
MMM	Three-letter month abbreviation
MMMM	Full month name
d	Day number
dd	Day number, always two digits
ddd	Three-letter day abbreviation
dddd	Full day name
yy	Year number, last two digits only
yyyy	Full year number

SEE ALSO

"Adjusting International Settings" on page 242 for information about changing settings for a different region or country and language.

TIP

Many programs format the date and time using their own code; such programs might not utilize the settings shown in our tables. If the date and time appear in a different format in one of your programs, consult the program's Help for formatting details.

TRY THIS

On the Date tab, set the long-date format to ddd, MMM d, YY, and click Apply. On the Time tab, set the time format to HH:mm:sst, and click OK. Take a look at the time on the taskbar, and then point to the time to see the date.

Change the Time Format

1. Click the Time tab.

2. Select or type a different format for the time. See the table at the right for valid codes.

3. Click Apply, and inspect the time in the Time Sample box.

4. Select or type a different separator for the time.

5. Click Apply, and inspect the time in the Time Sample box.

6. Select or type a different AM symbol.

7. Click Apply, and inspect the time in the Time Sample box.

8. Select or type a different PM symbol.

9. Click Apply, and inspect the time in the Time Sample box.

CODES FOR TIME FORMATS

Code	Result
h	Hour in 12-hour format
hh	Hour in 12-hour format, always two digits
H	Hour in 24-hour format
HH	Hour in 24-hour format, always two digits
m	Minute
mm	Minute, always two digits
s	Second
ss	Second, always two digits
t	AM or PM symbol, first character only
tt	AM or PM symbol, all characters

14

Adjusting International Settings

If you are working in, or producing documents for use in, a region or country other than the one for which your computer was originally configured, you can change the default region and have Windows automatically adjust the numbering, currency, time, and date schemes used by your programs. If you are working with a different language, you can also switch the layout of your keyboard to conform to that language.

Change the Default Region

1. Click the Start button, point to Settings, and choose Control Panel from the submenu.

2. Double-click the Regional Settings icon.

3. On the Regional Settings tab, select a language and, if necessary, the associated country.

4. Click OK.

5. Click Yes when prompted to restart the computer.

6. Double-click the Regional Settings icon in the Control Panel again. Use the Number, Currency, Time, and Date tabs to make any other adjustments to the settings.

7. Click OK.

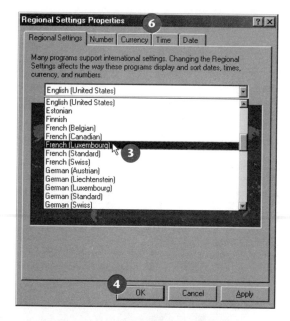

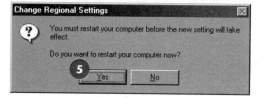

Change the Keyboard

1. Click the Start button, point to Settings, and choose Control Panel from the submenu.

2. Double-click the Keyboard icon.

3. On the Language tab of the Keyboard Properties dialog box, click the Add button. In the Add Language dialog box, select a language and, if necessary, the country, and click OK.

4. Turn on the Enable Indicator On Taskbar check box.

5. Click OK.

6. If prompted, insert the Windows CD and click OK.

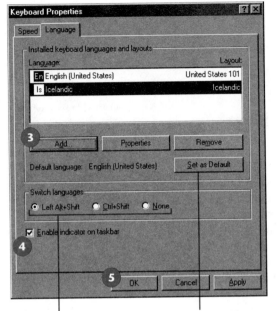

Select key combinations to switch quickly between languages.

Click to always start up in the selected language.

Switch Layouts

1. Click the keyboard layout abbreviation on the taskbar.

2. Select the keyboard layout you want.

14

Specifying Which Program Opens a Document

When you double-click a document, it usually opens in its associated program— a Microsoft Excel document opens in Microsoft Excel, a bitmap image opens in Paint, and so on. Sometimes, however, you might want one type of document to open in a different program—perhaps you want text documents to open in WordPad instead of in Notepad, for example. You can make this happen by associating the file type with a program.

TIP

The types of files listed on the File Types tab depend on the programs you have installed.

Select the File Type

1 Click the Start button, point to Settings, and choose Folder Options.

2 Click the File Types tab.

3 Select the file type whose association you want to change. Look at the File Type Details section to verify that you've selected the correct type of document.

4 Click the Edit button.

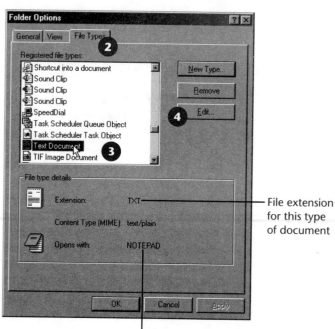

File extension for this type of document

Program associated with this type of document

Edit the Association

1 Select Open in the Actions list.

2 Click the Edit button.

3 Click the Browse button.

4 Navigate through your folders and select the program in which you want your document to open. (Most programs reside in subfolders of the Program Files folder.)

5 Click Open to specify the program.

6 Click OK to set the association.

7 Click Close in the Edit File Type dialog box to end the editing.

8 Click Close to close the Folder Options dialog box.

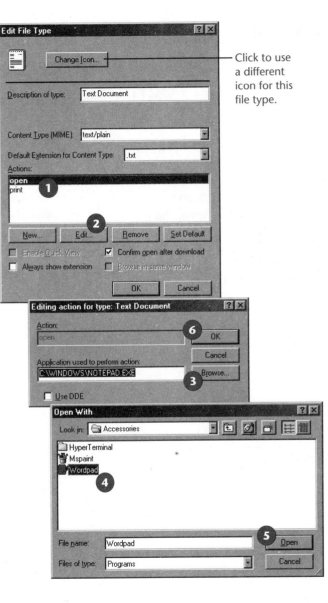

Click to use a different icon for this file type.

14

File Associations, File Extensions, and Registered Programs

Windows tries hard to let your work be *docucentric*—that is, you concentrate on keeping your *documents* organized and Windows will do the work of figuring out which *programs* your documents need to run in. To do this, Windows needs three main pieces of information:

♦ The programs you have installed

♦ The types of documents that are to be opened in each program

♦ The file type of the document you want to use

Windows keeps track of all this information in a special database called the *registry*. Whenever you run Setup to install a software program, Setup adds information to the registry, including the name and location of the program and the types of documents and files the program will open.

To link a document with a program, Windows uses the file's *extension*—the three-character code that follows the document's name—to identify the document as a specific file type. The file's extension, which is usually added automatically when you save a document in a program, might or might not be visible, depending on your settings, but Windows is always aware of it. (See "Displaying Paths, Extensions, and Hidden Files" on page 217 for information about displaying a file's extension.) By recognizing the file extension, Windows knows the file type of the document and its associated program.

You can identify the file type of a document by its icon and, when you're in Details view, by the description in the Type column. Because a document is identified by its extension, you shouldn't change the extension when you create a document or when you are conducting any file management. Sometimes, alas, things don't work out as they're supposed to. Some programs are installed without the use of Setup or a similar program and thus might not be registered. Other programs can grab a file extension that "belongs to" another program. And sometimes, even when Setup is used, a program somehow still doesn't register itself correctly.

When a program isn't properly registered, whatever the reason, you can often solve the problem by rerunning Setup for the program or by changing the file extension's program association, as described in "Specifying Which Program Opens a Document" on page 244. If neither of these methods works, contact the people who sold you the software. They might be able to supply you with updated software that properly registers the program, or they might tell you how to fix the problem with a workaround. But remember—it is *very* dangerous to edit the settings in the registry. If anyone suggests that you do this, the first thing you should do when you run RegEdit is to make a copy of the registry, using the Export Registry File command on the File menu. That way, if something goes wrong, you can restore the original registry.

EXAMPLES OF FILES AND THEIR EXTENSIONS

Document type	Icon	Filename with extension	Typical associated program
Text document	Events	Events.txt	Notepad
Bitmap image	Humpback	Humpback.bmp	Paint
TIFF image	Little one	Little one.tif	Imaging
Rich Text Format document	My mystery story	My mystery story.rtf	WordPad
Internet document (HTML)	My Own Page	My Own Page.htm	Internet Explorer
Mail message	Out-of-office	Out-of-office.eml	Outlook Express

Adjusting Mouse Actions

Few things are more frustrating than an uncooperative mouse that doesn't do what you want it to do. A dirty—and thus unhappy—mouse is often the cause of many problems, but, if you've attended to your mouse's *toilette* and you're still having problems, you can make some simple adjustments for better mouse performance.

SEE ALSO

"Changing Your Click" on page 230 for information about specifying the way Windows responds to your mouse clicks.

"Changing Your Input" on page 238 for information about using the keyboard to control mouse movements.

"Wheeling Around with Your Mouse" on page 250 for information about using a wheel mouse.

Switch Buttons

1. Click the Start button, point to Settings, and choose Control Panel from the submenu.

2. Double-click the Mouse icon.

3. On the Buttons tab, select the Right-Handed or Left-Handed configuration.

Text shows the button assignment for the selected configuration.

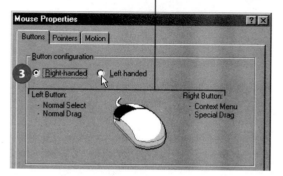

Set the Double-Click Speed

1. Drag the Double-Click Speed slider to set your double-click speed.

2. Double-click the jack-in-a-box. If it doesn't pop up, change the double-click speed and repeat the test.

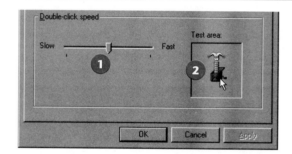

You have many more settings options with the Microsoft IntelliPoint software installed. Although the IntelliPoint software isn't part of Windows, it's often installed when the Microsoft IntelliPoint Mouse with Wheel or the Microsoft IntelliPoint Trackball with Wheel is installed. With IntelliPoint software installed, the Mouse Properties dialog box contains additional tabs that let you fine-tune mouse speed, improve pointer visibility, customize the way you select items, and even set the pointer to wrap around your screen from top to bottom or side to side.

SEE ALSO

"Switch Themes" on page 224 for information about changing all your mouse pointers in one fell swoop.

"Changing the Mouse Pointers" on page 226 for information about using different mouse pointers and customizing them for standard Windows events.

Set the Pointer Speed

1 Click the Motion tab and drag the Pointer Speed slider to set the speed at which the pointer moves.

2 Click the Apply button, and move the mouse around to observe its speed. Reset the speed if necessary.

Make the Mouse More Visible

1 Turn on the Show Pointer Trails check box.

2 Drag the slider to set the length of the trails.

3 Move the mouse around to observe the length of the trails, and adjust them if necessary.

4 Click OK.

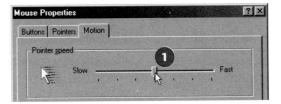

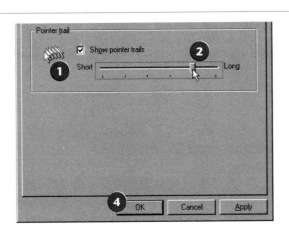

14

Wheeling Around with Your Mouse

With a *wheel mouse,* such as the Microsoft IntelliMouse, the functionality of both the wheel and the wheel button is determined by the individual program. The wheel button functions in the same manner as a third mouse button, so if the program has features that work with a third mouse button, those features will work with the wheel button. Rotating the wheel, however, is a feature unique to the wheel mouse, so the program must be designed to work with a wheel mouse.

> **TIP**
>
> *If you have Microsoft Intelli-Point software installed, you can change what happens when you click the wheel button. To do so, double-click the Mouse icon in the Control Panel, and adjust the setting on the Wheel tab.*

Find Out What the Wheel Does

1. Read the program's documentation and online help.

2. If the information is inadequate, experiment! Try the methods shown in the table at the right and see how your program responds to the wheel action.

EXAMPLES OF USING THE WHEEL	
Action	What it does
Rotate the wheel.	In a folder window and most applications: scrolls up and down or left and right.
Shift+rotate the wheel.	In a Web-style folder window, or in Internet Explorer or Windows Explorer: acts like the Back and Forward buttons to browse through windows. Function varies depending on the program.
Ctrl+rotate the wheel.	In Internet Explorer, Windows Help, and other HTML viewers: changes the font size.
Click the wheel button and move the mouse.	In Internet Explorer and some other applications: scrolls in the direction the mouse is moved. Click again to turn off scrolling.

Running Programs While You Sleep

Task Scheduler will run a program when you schedule it—a convenient way to use your computer or the network during off hours. Be sure, though, that the program can run unattended, with no ill effects if it's suddenly terminated.

TIP

If a program you run interferes with other scheduled programs, right-click the program in the Scheduled Tasks window and choose Properties. Reschedule the program on the Schedule tab or, on the Settings tab, set Stop The Scheduled Task After to a duration that will stop the program before another scheduled program starts.

SEE ALSO

"Optimizing Your System" on page 264 for more information about setting up maintenance programs and scheduling programs.

Schedule a Program to Run

1. Double-click Scheduled Tasks in the My Computer window.

2. Double-click Add Scheduled Task. Click the Next button to run the Scheduled Task Wizard.

3. Select a program or click the Browse button to locate a program. Click Next.

4. Specify when you want the program to run, and click Next.

5. If necessary, provide additional scheduling information. Click Next.

6. Verify the schedule, and click Finish.

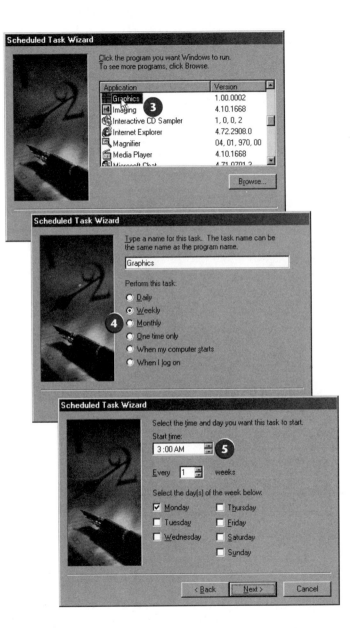

14

Using Two Monitors

Desktop not big enough for you? Well, you can literally spread it out on two—or more—monitors. You need to have a PCI or an AGP video adapter card installed for each monitor, but, once the card is installed, you can set each monitor to its own color and screen resolution settings and spread your work out over a *big* desktop.

TIP

If you're not sure which monitor is which, point to the picture of the monitor in the Display Properties dialog box, and press and hold down the left mouse button. A large number will appear on your monitor's screen to identify which monitor it is.

Set Up the Monitors

1 Right-click a blank spot on the Desktop and choose Properties from the shortcut menu.

2 On the Settings tab, click monitor 1 and adjust the color, screen area, and any advanced settings for that monitor.

3 Click monitor 2. If you're asked whether you want to enable the monitor, click Yes.

4 Adjust the colors, screen area, and any advanced settings for that monitor.

5 Drag the monitors into the arrangement you want.

6 Click OK.

When one monitor is above the other, the Desktop is taller than it is wide. When the monitors are side by side, the Desktop is wider than it is tall.

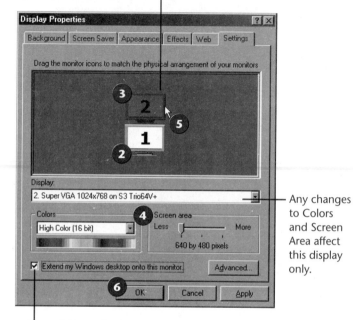

Any changes to Colors and Screen Area affect this display only.

Turn off if you don't want the secondary monitor to be active.

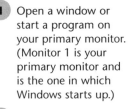

TIP

When you maximize a window, it expands to the dimensions of the monitor, not the dimensions of the multi-monitor Desktop. You can, however, position or size a window so that it extends across the two monitors.

TIP

A full-screen MS-DOS program, or the MS-DOS Prompt running in full screen, can appear in the primary window only.

TIP

If you've removed the secondary monitor and started a program that had been in the second window, but you don't see the program, there's a good chance that it's positioned beyond the existing Desktop. To bring the program back, try changing the screen resolution to increase the size of the Desktop. If the program still isn't visible, right-click the program name on the taskbar and choose Move from the shortcut menu. Use the arrow keys to move the title bar onto your monitor, and then press Enter.

Work on the Desktop

1 Open a window or start a program on your primary monitor. (Monitor 1 is your primary monitor and is the one in which Windows starts up.)

2 Drag the program to whichever edge of the primary monitor is adjacent to the other monitor, as shown in the Display Properties dialog box. Continue dragging the program until you see it on the second monitor, and then drop the program.

3 Arrange your windows, programs, and toolbars on the two monitors.

4 Use standard techniques to switch between programs—pressing Alt+Tab, using shortcut key combinations, or clicking items on the taskbar, for example—regardless of which monitor the programs are located on.

With the monitors arranged one above the other, you see this on your secondary monitor...

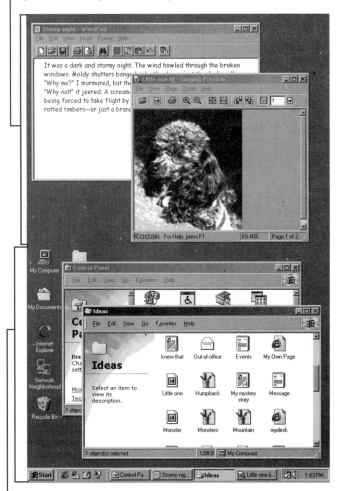

...and this on your primary monitor.

15

Tuning Up and Adding On

Everything needs a tune-up once in a while—a car runs better, a piano sounds sweeter. So it is with a computer. When you tune up your computer, you might or might not make it work faster but you'll make it work better. Because computers, programs, and peripheral devices are continually changing, Windows 98 provides an Update Wizard that compares what you have with what's available and then installs the most recent files for you over the Internet. Windows also provides disk-maintenance tools that you can schedule to run period-ically (even while you sleep!)—they'll find and re-order bits of files that have become scattered or lost, and they'll delete unused files and test for disk errors. You might also be able to change your hard disk's file system from the standard FAT16 to FAT32, which can speed up your system *and* use fewer of your computer's resources.

We'll show you how to add or remove Windows components, create more disk space, and what you can do if—heaven forbid—disaster strikes. And what if you have a problem and can't find the information you need in this book? Although we've tried really hard to cover a broad range of problems, it's possible that you'll come up with a question about Windows 98 that we haven't answered. If so, we'll direct you to the place where you're most likely to find the answer. Read on.

Adding or Removing Windows Components

As you work, you might find that some Windows 98 components you'd like to use aren't installed on your computer. Or perhaps there are Windows components installed that you never use, and they're just occupying valuable disk space. You don't have to rerun the rather lengthy Windows Setup program again—you can use one of the tools Windows provides to install and remove any Windows components.

Add or Remove a Component Group

1 Save any documents you're working on, and close all your running programs.

2 Click the Start button, point to Settings, and choose Control Panel from the submenu.

3 Double-click the Add/Remove Programs icon.

4 On the Windows Setup tab, turn check boxes on or off to add or remove all the items in the component group.

Click a checked box to turn off the option and remove all items from a group.

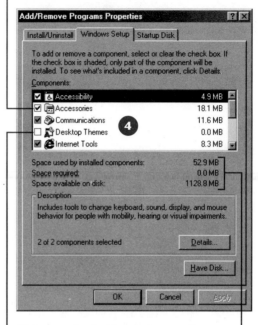

Click an unchecked box to turn on the option and add all items to the group.

Displays how much disk space was saved or how much is required, based on your selections.

Add or Remove an Item in a Component Group

1 Select the component group in which you want to add or remove an item.

2 Click the Details button.

3 Click a checked box to remove the item, or click an unchecked box to add the item.

4 Click OK when you've finished adding or removing the item or items.

5 Repeat steps 1 through 4 for each component group you want to change.

6 Click OK to close the Add/Remove Programs Properties dialog box. Depending on which items you selected to install, you might need to restart Windows.

Installing a Software Program

Most software programs come with an installation program that copies the required files to your hard disk and tells Windows which files are installed, where they are, and what they do. Windows simplifies the installation of most Windows-based programs and of many MS-DOS–based programs with the helpful Installation Wizard. Before you start, look at the program documentation for installation instructions. It's better to avoid problems in the beginning so that you don't have to fix them later.

TIP

Caught in the Net. *If you're installing a program over a network, check with your network administrator before you begin. Some programs can't be installed over a network, and others require that special software be run by the network administrator.*

Install a Program

1. Save any documents you're working on, and close all your running programs.

2. If you're installing from a CD, place the CD in the drive, wait for it to start, and then follow the instructions that appear on the screen.

3. If the CD didn't start, or if you're installing from a different location—over a network or from a floppy disk, for example—click the Start button, point to Settings, and choose Control Panel from the submenu.

4. Double-click the Add/Remove Programs icon.

5. Click Install.

6. Place the installation disk or the CD in the drive, and click Next.

7. If the correct Setup program filename is displayed, click Finish. If not, click Browse, locate the Setup program, and then click Finish.

8. Follow the Setup program's instructions.

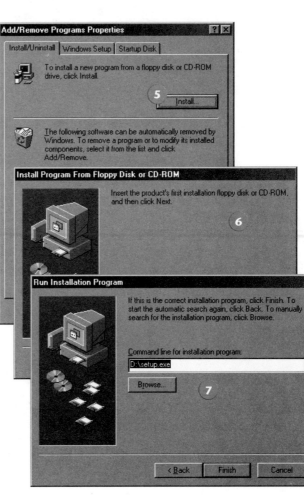

Removing a Software Program

Most programs are *registered* with Windows when you install them. You can—and should—use Windows tools when you want to remove a program. If you simply delete the files, you might leave accessory files you don't need, or delete files you need for other programs. When you use Windows tools to uninstall a program, Windows keeps track of the files you need. When a file is no longer needed by any of your programs, Windows deletes the file.

SEE ALSO

"File Associations, File Extensions, and Registered Programs" on page 246 *for information about registered programs.*

"Adding or Removing Windows Components" on page 256 *for information about removing programs that are part of Windows.*

Uninstall a Program

1. Save any documents you're working on, and close all your running programs.

2. Click the Start button, point to Settings, and choose Control Panel from the submenu.

3. Double-click the Add/Remove Programs icon.

4. On the Install/Uninstall tab, select the program to be uninstalled. (Programs that are components of Windows—Paint and WordPad, for example—aren't listed here. You can remove them using the Windows Setup tab.)

5. Click Add/Remove. If the program you want to remove isn't listed, see the program's documentation for removal instructions.

6. Follow the instructions that appear on the screen.

7. Click OK when you've finished.

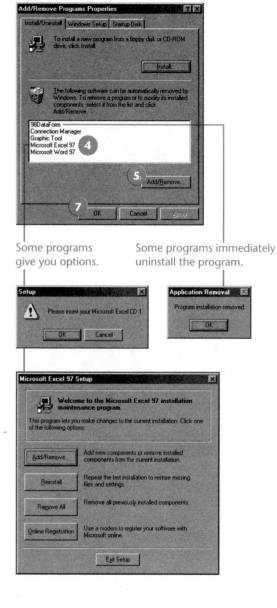

Some programs give you options.

Some programs immediately uninstall the program.

Adding Fonts to Your System

Fonts are styles of lettering whose different designs add personality and feeling to our words. Some programs offer many fonts on CD that you can install as you need them. Windows makes it easy to install fonts and to view them on screen. If you want to, you can print very nice sample sheets and store them in a binder—a handy reference tool when you're trying to decide which fonts to use.

Add a Font

1 Click the Start button, point to Settings, and choose Control Panel from the submenu.

2 Double-click the shortcut to the Fonts folder.

3 Choose Install New Font from the File menu.

4 Navigate to the drive and folder containing the font to be installed. (If there are many fonts in the folder, you might need to wait a few seconds until all the font names have been retrieved.)

5 Select the font or fonts. (To select several fonts, hold down the Ctrl key and click each font.)

6 Click OK.

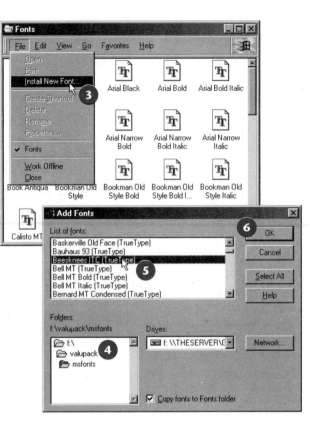

View and Print a Font

1. Double-click the font name to view a font sample.

2. Click the Print button to print a font sample sheet.

3. Click the Done button.

4. Repeat steps 1 through 3 to view and print additional font samples.

15

Hooked on Fonts

When you open the Font drop-down list on a program's toolbar, you might be surprised to see how many fonts you already have. Where did they all come from? Well, Windows 98 comes with quite a few fonts, and if you've installed other programs, you've probably installed their font collections too. Depending on where your fonts came from, you'll see various icons—or in some cases no icon at all—next to their names in the Font list. The two icons you'll see most frequently represent *TrueType fonts* and *printer fonts*. (Windows also includes a few other fonts that are provided for compatibility with some older programs.)

◆ TrueType fonts are WYSIWYG (what-you-see-is-what-you-get) fonts, which means that the printed output looks exactly the same as what you see on your screen. TrueType fonts are outline fonts: the shapes of the letters are drawn with lines and curves rather than with patterns of dots. TrueType fonts were designed to print well at any size on almost any printer, even at low resolutions.

◆ Printer fonts are usually stored in your printer, not in your computer's Fonts folder. When you install a printer, these fonts are made available to your programs, and their names appear in your Font list. Be aware, if you're using a printer font, that what you see on your screen might not exactly match your printed output—sometimes you'll see a look-alike font instead.

What these rather dry facts don't tell you is what a delight it is to be able to transform the look and the personality of your text with a few mouse-clicks. Try it! Select some text, open your Font drop-down list, click a font name, and see what you get. Open the Font Size list and click to change the size. For a real surprise, try one of the picture fonts. Your words will change into little pictures (called *dingbats*), and you can enlarge them, italicize them, and so on, just as you can with words. It can be a lot of fun.

If you feel like a kid with a new toy, just keep in mind that you *can* have too much of a good thing. A document with too many different fonts can be very difficult to read and instantly marks you as an amateur in the world of graphic design. Keep things simple. Professional designers seldom use more than two or three different fonts in a document—a *display font* for head-lines or anything that's meant to attract attention, a *text font* for the body of the document, and perhaps a third font for elements such as captions, pull quotes, sidebars, and so on. A discussion about the best fonts to use for display or text is beyond the scope of this book, but you won't go wrong if you use a big, bold font for display and a plain, readable font for text.

There are literally *thousands* of fonts, and new ones are being created all the time. To learn more about fonts and their history, check the shelves of your local library or bookstore—they're overflowing with books about this fascinating art form.

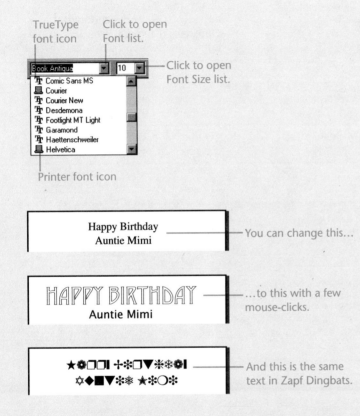

TrueType
font icon

Click to open
Font list.

Click to open
Font Size list.

Printer font icon

You can change this...

...to this with a few
mouse-clicks.

And this is the same
text in Zapf Dingbats.

Stormy Night

It was a dark and stormy night. The wind howled through the broken windows. Moldy shutters banged relentlessly against the dank walls. "Why me?" I murmured, but the shrieking wind carried my voice away. "Why not!" it jeered. A scream—or was it just a gull complaining about being forced to take flight by the storm? A hand ripping at the door's rotted timbers—or just a branch brushing against the house?

Stormy Night

It was a dark and stormy night. The wind howled through the broken windows. Moldy shutters banged relentlessly against the dank walls. "Why me?" I murmured, but the shrieking wind carried my voice away. "Why not!" it jeered. A scream—or was it just a gull complaining about being forced to take flight by the storm? A hand ripping at the door's rotted timbers—or just a branch brushing against the house?

Stormy Night

It was a dark and stormy night. The wind howled through the broken windows. Moldy shutters banged relentlessly against the dank walls. "Why me?" I murmured, but the shrieking wind carried my voice away. "Why not!" it jeered. A scream—or was it just a gull complaining about being forced to take flight by the storm? A hand ripping at the door's rotted timbers—or just a branch brushing against the house?

Three different looks created with display and text fonts

15

Optimizing Your System

The Maintenance Wizard sets up a group of disk-maintenance tools to run periodically. Once these tools are set up and Task Scheduler is active, you can schedule tasks to run at certain times, customize how they'll run, or stop running specific tasks.

Run the Wizard

1 Click the Start button, point your way through Programs, Accessories, and System Tools, and choose Maintenance Wizard from the submenu.

2 Complete the wizard to activate Task Scheduler and schedule the maintenance programs you want it to run. The Task Scheduler icon appears on the taskbar.

Control Task Scheduler

1 Double-click the Task Scheduler icon on the taskbar to open the Scheduled Tasks folder.

2 From the Advanced menu, choose

◆ Stop Using Task Scheduler to deactivate Task Scheduler. To reactivate it, choose Start Using Task Scheduler.

◆ Pause Task Scheduler to stop running all scheduled tasks. Choose Continue Task Scheduler to resume running the tasks.

MAINTENANCE TOOLS RUN BY TASK SCHEDULER	
Program	**What it does**
Maintenance Defragment	Re-orders the items on your hard disk so that files are not separated into several noncontiguous parts. Optionally rearranges programs on the disk for maximum access efficiency. Can take a long time to run but speeds up disk performance.
Maintenance Disk Cleanup	Checks your hard disk for unused files that can be deleted.
Maintenance ScanDisk	Conducts a quick test to check for disk errors in any files or folders.

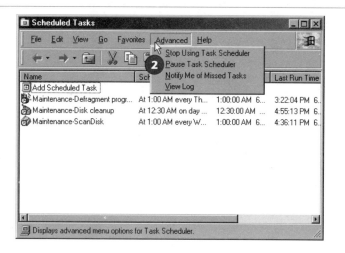

SEE ALSO

"Running Programs While You Sleep" on page 251 for more information about scheduling programs to run unattended.

TIP

Microsoft Plus! 98—an add-on to Windows 98 that's available separately—contains additional programs to protect your computer and optimize its performance.

TIP

If you don't see the Task Scheduler icon on the taskbar, you can open the Scheduled Tasks folder from My Computer or Windows Explorer.

TIP

You can run any of the maintenance programs without using Task Scheduler. Each program is listed on the System Tools submenu of the Start menu. To run all the maintenance programs, choose Maintenance Wizard from the System Tools submenu, select the Perform Maintenance Now option, and click OK.

Control a Program

1. Open the Scheduled Tasks folder if it's not already open.

2. Double-click the program.

3. Do either of the following:

   ◆ On the Schedule tab, specify when you want the program to run.

   ◆ On the Task tab, turn off the Enabled check box to prevent the program from running until you turn the option back on.

4. Click OK.

Click to see a greater range of scheduling options.

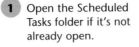

Click to customize the way the program runs.

15

Changing Your Disk File System

You can change your hard disk's file system from the standard FAT16 to the advanced FAT32. This conversion can save you disk space, speed up program loading, and use fewer of your computer's resources. However, you'll pay a price in terms of compatibility and flexibility: you won't be able to use disk-compression programs or some disk utility programs, and you won't be able to uninstall Windows 98 or use a dual-boot setup to run previous versions of Windows.

TIP

What Is FAT? *It's the acronym for File Allocation Table.*

Check Your FAT

1 Double-click the My Computer icon on the Desktop.

2 Right-click the hard-disk icon and choose Properties from the shortcut menu.

3 On the General tab, take a look at the type of FAT listed next to File System.

◆ If *FAT* is listed, the disk uses FAT16.

◆ If *FAT32* is listed, the disk already uses FAT32, and you don't need to make any changes.

4 Click OK.

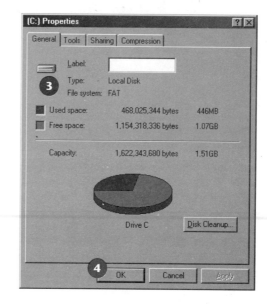

Convert Your FAT. *Windows doesn't offer a tool to convert FAT32 to FAT16, mainly because errors can occur and data can be lost during conversion. However, if you really need to convert back, there are programs made by other companies that will allow you to do so. Check with your computer store for details.*

If there are bad sectors on your hard disk, you probably won't be able to convert to FAT32. You might be able to fix the bad sectors by using ScanDisk or some other disk-repair tool, or by reformatting the hard disk, but you'll probably end up using FAT16.

Expect the conversion to take anywhere from a few minutes to several hours to be completed.

Convert to FAT32

1. Close any running programs.

2. Click the Start button, point your way through Programs, Accessories, and System Tools, and choose Drive Converter (FAT32) from the submenu.

3. Click Next to start the Drive Converter Wizard.

4. If more than one drive is listed, select the drive you want to convert, and click Next.

5. If you see any programs listed as incompatible, but they're programs you can't do without, click Cancel, and continue using the FAT16 system. Otherwise, click Next.

6. Back up your files if you haven't already done so, and click Next.

7. Click Next to start the conversion.

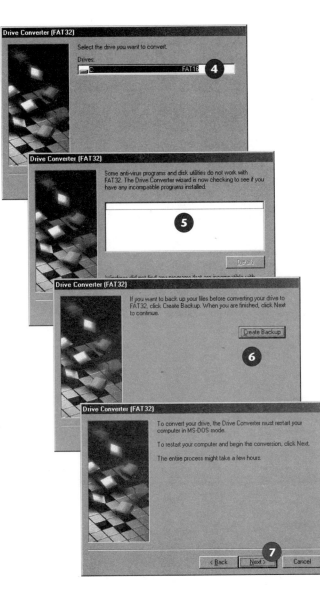

15

Updating Your System

Everything gets outdated eventually, even Windows! To obtain free updates to programs or to find fixes for buggy software, just connect to Microsoft's Windows Update Web page and let the Windows Update Wizard compare what you have with what's available. It's as simple and convenient as that!

TIP

If you install an update and your system starts misbehaving, return to the Update Wizard and click the Restore button to remove the new files and restore the old ones.

TIP

Because Web pages are changed so frequently, what you see on your screen might look different from what's shown here.

Start the Wizard

1. Close any running programs.

2. Click the Start button, and choose Windows Update to go to the Windows Update Web page.

3. Click Update Wizard to start the wizard. (If you haven't registered your copy of Windows 98, you'll need to register it before you can use the Update Wizard.)

4. Click Update. Wait while the wizard examines your system files.

5. Select the update you want.

6. Read the description.

7. Click Install.

8. Follow any instructions to complete the installation.

Conserving Power

Most of today's computers have power-saving features, which give you the ability to switch to a low-power standby mode, shut down the monitor, and even shut down the hard disk. These handy features are great for conserving power, but sometimes they're a little too zealous! If you find that the system shuts down just as you're reaching for the mouse or the keyboard, you can customize the power-saving settings.

Define a Scheme

1. Click the Start button, point to Settings, and choose Control Panel from the submenu.

2. Double-click the Power Management icon.

3. On the Power Schemes tab, specify when you want the system to go into standby mode.

4. Specify when you want the monitor to be turned off.

5. Specify when you want the hard disk (or disks, if you have more than one) to be turned off.

6. Click Save As, name the scheme, and click OK.

7. Click OK to close the Power Management Properties dialog box.

15

Creating More Disk Space

When disk space is at a premium, you can create additional free space by compressing your files. You can do this automatically by compressing the hard disk with DriveSpace 3. What you end up with are two drives: your compressed drive and an uncompressed host drive (usually drive H, and often hidden).

TIP

It can take several hours to compress a drive.

TIP

You can't compress a drive that uses the FAT32 file system.

SEE ALSO

"Changing Your Disk File System" on page 266 for information about disk compression and the FAT32 file system.

Compress Your Drive

1. Click the Start button, point your way through Programs, Accessories, and System Tools, and choose DriveSpace from the submenu.

2. Select the drive to be compressed.

3. Choose Compress from the Drive menu.

4. Click Start. When prompted, create an updated startup disk if necessary.

5. Back up your files if you haven't already done so.

6. Start the compression.

7. Click OK when Windows tells you to restart the computer.

8. Click OK when Windows tells you that DriveSpace has finished. DriveSpace creates an additional drive, usually drive H.

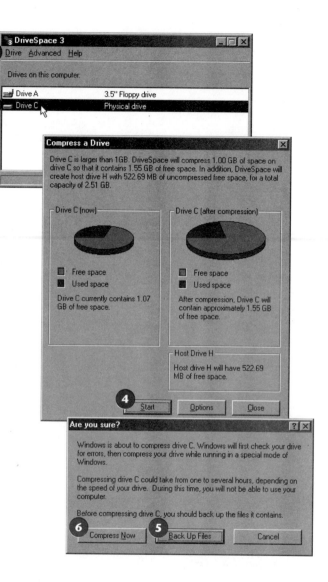

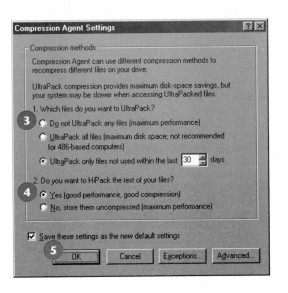

TIP

UltraPack compresses files up to approximately 33 percent of their original size but slows down the performance of those files. HiPack compresses files to just under 50 percent of their original size but slows down file-writing performance. If you don't use UltraPack or HiPack, files will be compressed using standard compression. Standard compression compresses files to less than 50 percent of their original size but doesn't usually reduce file-reading and -writing performance.

TIP

You can create a new compressed drive instead of compressing drive C by choosing the Create Empty command from the Advanced menu in the DriveSpace 3 window. From the same menu, you can also change the drive letter of the new drive or of the host drive.

SEE ALSO

"Running Programs While You Sleep" on page 251 and "Optimizing Your System" on page 264 for information about setting up and using Task Scheduler.

Modify the Compression

1 Click the Start button, point your way through Programs, Accessories, and System Tools, and choose Compression Agent from the submenu.

2 Click Settings.

3 Specify whether you want to use UltraPack compression and, if so, for which files.

4 Specify whether you want to use HiPack compression for the remaining files.

5 Click OK.

6 Click Start.

Finding System Information

When your system isn't working properly and you need to contact someone for help, you're going to have to supply that helpful person with some information about your system. You can quickly and easily obtain and print a comprehensive listing of your system settings. Although most of the information is nearly indecipherable to the average computer user, there is some valuable information you can use, together with useful details for the support person.

SEE ALSO

"Send a Print File to a Printer" on page 91 for information about printing documents at a later date when you've turned on the Print To File check box in the Print dialog box.

Print System Settings

1 Click the Start button, point to Settings, and choose Control Panel from the submenu.

2 Double-click the System icon.

3 Click the Device Manager tab.

4 With Computer selected, click the Print button.

5 With the System Summary option turned on, click OK.

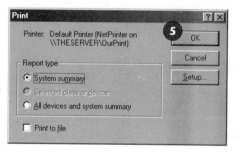

You can also use the device's Properties dialog box to update any drivers. Click the Driver tab, and then click Update Driver. The wizard will let you specify where to look for the new driver.

"Updating Your System" on page 268 for information about installing updated drivers for your system.

If you decide to modify any of the system properties, such as the interrupt, first use the Hardware Profiles tab of the System Properties dialog box to create a copy of your hardware profile. Then, if your changes make the system unstable, restart Windows, select the copy of your original hardware profile, and change the profile back to the original settings. After you verify that the system is stable, delete the copy you made of the profile so that you won't be prompted for it each time you start the computer.

Check the Device

1 Display the information for the type of device that you think might be causing a problem, and look for any symbols that seem to indicate a device isn't working or is in conflict with a resource.

2 Double-click the device.

3 Review the Device Status information.

4 Click the Hardware Troubleshooter button, if it's available, and step through the wizard to try to resolve your problems.

5 Click OK to save any changes or Cancel to discard changes.

6 Click OK to close the System Properties dialog box.

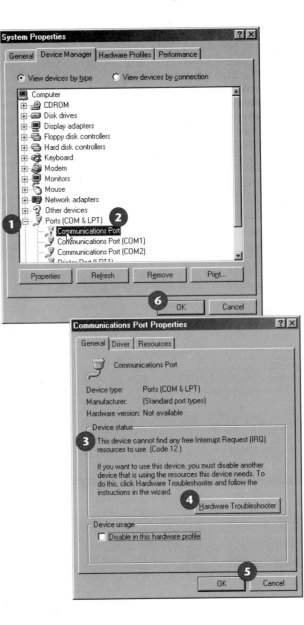

15

If Disaster Strikes...

Is there a computer user anywhere who hasn't suffered the frustration of losing or damaging documents that represent hours of work? A power surge, a virus, a worn-out hard disk, or some other component can wreak havoc. With a little advance preparation and some routine procedures, you can minimize the damage and drive out your computer's demons.

Protect yourself from invaders. If you use files from outside sources, install and *use* a virus-protection program. Windows provides security features in Internet Explorer and Outlook Express, and many programs contain features that protect you from viruses.

Back up your data. Create separate copies of all your data and update the files regularly. Windows has an excellent utility called Backup that you can use to back up your data on tape or on network drives—if the utility is installed, it's on the Start menu's System Tools submenu. Check with your network administrator for preferred network backup tools.

Document the configuration. If your computer has problems, you'll need to know how it was configured when it was working properly. See "Finding System Information" on page 272.

Use the right tools. If a program is misbehaving, you might need to access its setup files to reinstall the program. If the problem is in Windows, you'll probably need the Windows 98 Startup Disk to start the computer and run diagnostic and repair programs.

Diagnose the problem. When Windows is running, several tools are available. "Check the Device" on page 273 describes how to find which device is malfunctioning; "Updating Your System" on page 268 describes how to find and replace outdated system files and drivers. Windows has more advanced programs for documenting and diagnosing problems: System Information, on the Start menu's System Tools submenu, creates a detailed record of your system that you can save or export as a text file for review by a technician. The System Information program also gives you access from its Tools menu to several useful tools. However, these tools are powerful enough to cause serious problems, so, unless you really know what you're doing, you should use them only in consultation with a trained computer technician. For information about these tools, see Windows Help.

Get help. "Using Help to Solve Problems" on the facing page describes how to use Help's Troubleshooters to fix problems. The Help window also has a Web Help button that takes you to the Windows 98 Web site, where you'll find information and services offered by Microsoft.

Fix the problem. After you've talked to the experts, read the Help topics and articles in the Microsoft Knowledge Base, and prowled the Internet, you should find the solution. Very often, it will entail reinstalling or updating a program or a Windows component. Thankfully, because you've backed up all your data, you have nothing to lose but a little time and effort.

Using Help to Solve Problems

The Windows 98 Help system contains many Troubleshooter topics that provide interactive support for common problems. These topics help you narrow down the possible causes for the problem you're experiencing, and in many cases they provide jumps directly to the dialog box in which you can fix the problem.

TIP

If you have access to the Internet, click Web Help to go to Microsoft's support pages for additional help.

SEE ALSO

"Searching the Knowledge Base" on page 280 for information about seeking answers to problems the Troubleshooters were unable to solve.

Start the Troubleshooter

1. Click the Start button, and choose Help from the Start menu.

2. On the Contents tab, click the Troubleshooting topic.

3. Click the Windows 98 Troubleshooters topic.

4. Click the topic that's the most relevant to your problem.

5. Read the text, and click the option that best describes the problem. Click Next.

6. Continue reading the text, taking the recommended actions, clicking the most appropriate options, and clicking Next. Use the Back or Start Over button to modify or redo your responses.

7. Close Help after you've solved the problem.

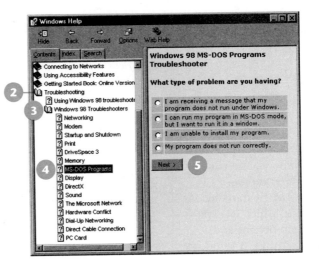

Starting Up When There's a Problem

If there's a serious problem with Windows, and you restart the computer, Windows often starts in Safe mode, which lets you diagnose problems and change settings. If Windows won't start in the normal way, you can modify how it starts, or you can start the computer without Windows. If the system won't start at all, you can try starting it from a floppy disk.

SEE ALSO

"Creating an Emergency Disk" on page 278 for information about creating that valuable emergency disk.

Control the Startup

1 Turn on your computer.

2 Hold down the Ctrl key while the computer starts.

3 When the Windows 98 Startup menu appears, type a number or use the arrow keys to select an option, and press Enter. Use the following selections to start Windows:

◆ Logged to record which elements are loaded

◆ Safe mode to change system settings from within Windows

◆ Step-by-step config-uration to select which configuration files and drivers are installed

STARTUP OPTIONS	
Option	**What it does**
Normal	Starts Windows in standard manner.
Logged (\BOOTLOG.TXT)	Starts normally; records system information in file Bootlog.txt.
Safe mode	Starts Windows with no network connections and without most of its drivers.
Step-by-step configuration	Questions which startup config-uration elements are processed.
Command prompt only	Loads MS-DOS and uses all settings in the Autoexec.bat and Config.sys files.
Safe mode command prompt only	Loads MS-DOS only without configuration files or drivers.
Previous version of MS-DOS	Loads previous version of MS-DOS if installed.

Boot from a Disk

1. Turn off the computer.

2. Place the emergency startup disk in your floppy drive.

3. Start the computer.

4. Select the type of CD drive support you need.

5. Note the information on the screen about the drive letter for the CD drive and the location of the tools that have been extracted from the startup disk.

6. Do either of the following:

   ◆ Use the tools to fix your disk or computer, and restart Windows.

   ◆ Place the Windows 98 CD in the drive, switch to your CD, and run Setup.exe to reinstall Windows.

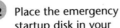

Program	What it does
Attrib.exe	Changes the attributes of programs so that you can copy, move, or delete them.
Debug.exe	Serves as a primitive text editor for modifying system files.
Edit.com	Serves as a simple text editor for modifying system files—easier to use than Debug.exe.
Format.com	Deletes all content and reformats hard disk. System files, Windows 98, and all programs must be reinstalled. Files not backed up to removable media or to another computer will be lost. (Do not use unless all other options have failed and you have consulted a technician.)
Scandisk.exe	Examines hard disk and repairs errors.
Uninstal.exe	Uninstalls Windows 98 and replaces it with the previous version of Windows. (Uninstall option must have been selected during initial installation of Windows 98.) Do not use unless instructed to do so by a technician.

15

Creating an Emergency Disk

If your computer won't start with Windows, you might need to start your computer from a floppy disk. If you didn't create an emergency disk when Windows was installed, or if you need to update the emergency disk due to system changes, or if you simply can't find it, Windows can make you a new one. We can't stress this enough: create an emergency disk *before* you experience any problems!

TIP

Many new computers come with a startup disk. If you make substantial changes to the system, however, you'll want to create a new disk.

Create the Disk

1 Click the Start button, point to Settings, and choose Control Panel from the submenu.

2 Double-click the Add/Remove Programs icon.

3 On the Startup Disk tab, click Create Disk.

4 If prompted, insert the Windows CD or specify the location of the files, and click OK.

5 When prompted, insert a blank disk into your floppy drive, and click OK.

6 After the disk has been copied, click OK.

7 Remove the disk, label it *Windows 98 Emergency Disk,* and store it in a safe place.

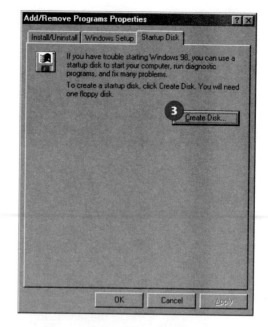

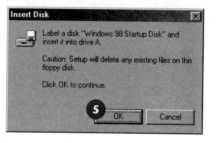

Finding More Software

The Windows CD contains a lot more than the Windows system and accessory programs. It's chock-full of useful tools and other items. When you wander around the CD, you'll find folders that contain tools, and there'll usually be a text file that will explain what to do or how to use the items.

Browse the CD

1. Insert the CD and wait for it to start. When the Windows 98 window appears, click Browse This CD.

2. Examine the contents of the different folders and read the informational text files.

3. Do either of the following to install a program:

   ◆ Double-click the Add/Remove Programs icon in the Control Panel, and, on the Windows Setup tab, click Have Disk. Locate the program's INF file, turn on the item in the Components list in the Have Disk dialog box, and click Install to start the Setup program.

   ◆ For programs without an INF file, double-click the program to run it or to execute the self-extraction and installation.

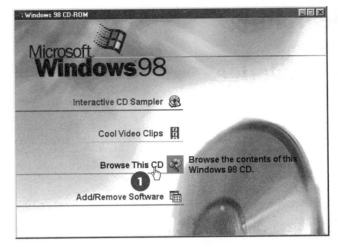

15

SOME USEFUL RESOURCES ON THE WINDOWS 98 CD	
Program or folder	**What it does**
PWS	Turns your computer into a Web site.
Reskit	Installs the Microsoft Windows 98 Resource Kit Sampler, which contains advanced tools for maintaining, optimizing, and customizing your system.
Clipbook	Allows you to store, view, and use multiple items from the Windows Clipboard.

Searching the Knowledge Base

Microsoft has gathered all documented Windows-related problems—and, in many cases, the techniques for solving them—and placed them in the Microsoft Knowledge Base. This is the same tool that's used by Microsoft's support engineers, and it's also the "secret weapon" of many consultants. By using good keywords and a couple of search techniques, you should find the solution to most of your problems in the Knowledge Base—and it's free!

TIP

The first time you connect to the Microsoft Knowledge Base, you'll need to register by completing the online forms.

Access the Knowledge Base

1 Do any of the following:

◆ From Windows Help, click the Web Help button.

◆ From the Microsoft Home Web page (*www.microsoft.com*), click Support, and follow the links to Support Online.

◆ Use an Internet browser to connect to *http://support.microsoft.com/support,* and follow the links to Support Online.

2 Select the product you want information about.

3 Type a keyword or key phrase.

4 Click Find.

5 Review any articles relevant to your problem that are returned by the search.

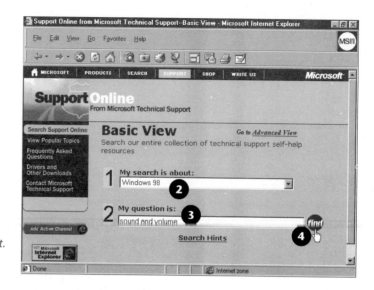

Refine the Search

1 Click the New Search button or use the Back button to return to the main search page.

2 Select the product if necessary.

3 Use more precise keywords, and use any of the operators shown in the table at the right to create a more specific search. (Replace the examples with your own keywords.)

4 Click Find.

SEARCH STATEMENTS

Statement	What it does
keyword1 AND keyword2 (sound AND volume)	Finds article that includes both keywords.
keyword1 OR keyword2 (sound OR volume)	Finds article that includes either keyword1 or keyword2 or both keywords.
keyword1 keyword2 (sound volume)	Finds article that includes keyword1 followed immediately by keyword2.
keyword1 NEAR keyword2 (sound NEAR volume)	Finds article in which keyword2 occurs within 50 words of keyword1.
keyword1 AND NOT keyword2 (sound AND NOT volume)	Finds article that contains keyword1 but not keyword2.
"keyphrase" ("sound and volume controls")	Finds article that contains the entire keyphrase, even if it contains operators AND, OR, NEAR, or NOT or special characters.
startofkeyword* (count*)	Finds article that contains words that start with the startofkeyword characters (country, countenance, counting).
keywordstem (sit**)	Finds article that contains any word form of the keywordstem (sit, sat, sitting).

15

Index

Italicized page numbers refer you to information you'll find in a Tip or a Try This entry.

G

game players, using with WebTV *121*
GIF graphics as Desktop backgrounds *109*
graphics images. *See* pictures
grayed options in dialog boxes 17
groups of e-mail addresses, adding to Address Book 165

H

hard disks. *See also* drives (disk)
 creating more space on 270–71, *277*
 Defragment (maintenance tool) 264
 Disk Cleanup (maintenance tool) 264
 saving space on 266–67
 ScanDisk 264, *267*
headers, creating 53
help
 with dialog boxes 17, 19
 with MS-DOS commands 126
 reading while working with windows *19*
 using 18–19, 274, 275, 280–81
hibernation settings *269*
hidden files and folders *37,* 217
hiding
 Call Status dialog box *207*
 Channel Bar 183
 dates (calendar) *239*
 filenames 217
 icons 213

hiding, *continued*
 taskbar 100–101
 time (clock) *239*
 toolbars 35, 100–101
 wallpaper on Windows Desktop *109*
High Contrast accessibility feature 238
HiPack compression 271
History button, returning to Web pages with *176*
home pages, creating 186–87.
  See also Web
Home Page Wizard 186–87
host computers
 using cable connection 204–5
 on networks 66
hosting Web sites 186–87
HTML format in e-mail *157,* 160
hyperlinks, obtaining addresses of *69*
HyperTerminal 200–203
hypertext document icons 247

I

icons
 arranging 23, 24, *25,* 106
 background color *109*
 changing size of 23
 customizing 225
 deleting from Start menu 233
 dragging and dropping 13, 232
 for file types 247
 hiding and displaying 213
 location on screen 6, 7
 organizing 23, 24, 25, 106
 for programs *132*
 resizing on toolbars *103*

icons, *continued*
 selecting 230
 on Start menu 233
 starting programs using 10
 styles of 6, 7, 230
 views of 23, 24, 25, 106, 225, 246
images. *See* pictures
Inbox Assistant (Outlook Express) 151. *See also* e-mail
information
 adding to headers and footers 53
 displayed in Address Book *164*
 linking to changing 48–49
 losing after closing a program 63
 storing on floppy disks 40–41, 194–95
infrared communication ports *204*
input devices 116, 238
inserted material, editing 50
inserting special characters 51
Installation Wizard 258
installing and uninstalling programs *39,* 258, 259, 268
IntelliMouse. *See* Microsoft IntelliMouse
international settings 242–43
Internet. *See also* e-mail; Web
 bulletin boards 200–201
 conversations on 188–91
 getting information using WaveTop 192
 intranets compared with 171
 newsgroups 152, 153–55, 156
 Windows support on 280–81

Internet Connection Wizard 142, 143
Internet Explorer. *See* Microsoft Internet Explorer
intranets
 described 171
 directory servers for 188
 going to Web pages on *172*
 shortcuts to locations on *33*
Intro Play (music CDs) 118

J

JPEG graphics as Desktop backgrounds *109*

K

keyboard
 Accessibility features 238
 adjusting for typing speed *243*
 controlling mouse using 238
 customizing layout 243
 ignoring repeated characters 238
 mouse compared with 12
 pressing key combinations one at a time 238
 setting language 242, 243
Knowledge Base. *See* Microsoft Knowledge Base

L

labeling
 floppy disks 40, *41*
 toolbars *103*
language settings 242, 243
Large Icons view 23

Jerry Joyce has had a long-standing relationship with Microsoft: he was the technical editor on numerous books published by Microsoft Press, and he has written manuals, help files, and specifications for various Microsoft products. As a programmer, he has tried for many years to make using a computer as simple as using a toaster, but he has yet to succeed. Jerry's alter ego is that of a marine biologist; he has conducted research from the Arctic to the Antarctic and has published numerous scientific papers on marine-mammal and fisheries issues. In his spare time he enjoys traveling, birding, boating, and wandering about beaches, wetlands, and mountains.

Marianne Moon has worked in the publishing world for many years as proofreader, editor, and writer—sometimes all three simultaneously. She has been editing and proofreading Microsoft Press books since 1984 and has written and edited documentation for Microsoft products such as Microsoft Works, Flight Simulator, Space Simulator, Golf, Publisher, the Microsoft Mouse, and Greetings Workshop. In another life, she was chief cook and bottlewasher for her own catering service and wrote cooking columns for several newspapers. When she's not chained to her computer, she likes gardening, cooking, traveling, writing poetry, and knitting sweaters for tiny dogs.

Marianne and **Jerry** own and operate **Moon Joyce Resources**, a small consulting company. They are co-authors of *Microsoft Word 97 At a Glance, Microsoft Windows 95 At a Glance,* and *Microsoft Windows NT Workstation 4.0 At a Glance.* They've had a 17-year working relationship and have been married for 7 years.

The manuscript for this book was prepared and submitted to Microsoft Press in electronic form. Text files were prepared using Microsoft Word 97 for Windows. Pages were composed using QuarkXPress 3.32 for the Power Macintosh, with text in ITC Stone Serif and ITC Stone Sans, and display type in ITC Stone Sans Semibold. Composed pages were delivered to the printer as electronic prepress files.

Cover Design and Illustration
Tim Girvin Design
Gregory Erickson

Interior Graphic Designers
designlab
Kim Eggleston

Interior Graphic Artist
WebFoot Productions

Interior Illustrator
s.bishop.design

Typographer
Blue Fescue Typography & Design

Proofreader
Alice Copp Smith

Indexer
Bero-West Indexing Services

Take the
whole family
siteseeing!

For Microsoft® Windows® 95 and Windows NT®

The Reference for Everyday Use in Home, School, and Office

1998 Edition
Regular
Online
Updates

CD-ROM included

Official
Microsoft® Bookshelf®
Internet
Directory

Searchable on
CD-ROM—with direct
links to thousands of
the best and most
useful Internet sites

Microsoft *Press*

U.S.A.	**$39.99**
U.K.	£37.49 [V.A.T. included]
Canada	$55.99
ISBN 1-57231-617-9	

Want to update your stock portfolio? Explore space? Recognize consumer fraud? Find a better job? Trace your family tree? Research your term paper? Make bagels? Well, go for it! The OFFICIAL MICROSOFT® BOOKSHELF® INTERNET DIRECTORY, 1998 EDITION, gives you reliable, carefully selected, up-to-date reviews of thousands of the Internet's most useful, entertaining, and functional Web sites. The searchable companion CD-ROM gives you direct, instant links to the sites in the book—a simple click of the mouse takes you wherever you want to go!

Developed jointly by Microsoft Press and the Microsoft Bookshelf product team, the OFFICIAL MICROSOFT BOOKSHELF INTERNET DIRECTORY, 1998 EDITION, is updated regularly on the World Wide Web to keep you informed of our most current list of recommended sites. Microsoft Internet Explorer 4.0 is also included on the CD-ROM.

Microsoft Press® products are available worldwide wherever quality computer books are sold. For more information, contact your book or computer retailer, software reseller, or local Microsoft Sales Office, or visit our Web site at mspress.microsoft.com. To locate your nearest source for Microsoft Press products, or to order directly, call 1-800-MSPRESS in the U.S. (in Canada, call 1-800-268-2222).

Prices and availability dates are subject to change.

Microsoft *Press*

Microsoft Press has titles to help everyone— from new users to seasoned developers—

Step by Step Series
Self-paced tutorials for classroom instruction or individualized study

Starts Here™ Series
Interactive instruction on CD-ROM that helps students learn by doing

Field Guide Series
Concise, task-oriented A–Z references for quick, easy answers— anywhere

Official Series
Timely books on a wide variety of Internet topics geared for advanced users

All User Training All User Reference

Quick Course® Series
Fast, to-the-point instruction for new users

At a Glance Series
Quick visual guides for task-oriented instruction

Running Series
A comprehensive curriculum alternative to standard documentation books

Microsoft Press® products are available worldwide wherever quality computer books are sold. For more information, contact your book or computer retailer, software reseller, or local Microsoft Sales Office, or visit our Web site at mspress.microsoft.com. To locate your nearest source for Microsoft Press products, or to order directly, call 1-800-MSPRESS in the U.S. (in Canada, call 1-800-268-2222).

Prices and availability dates are subject to change.

start faster and go farther!

The wide selection of books and CD-ROMs published by Microsoft Press contain something for every level of user and every area of interest, from just-in-time online training tools to development tools for professional programmers. Look for them at your bookstore or computer store today!

Professional Select Editions Series
Advanced titles geared for the system administrator or technical support career path

Microsoft Certified Professional Training
The Microsoft Official Curriculum for certification exams

Best Practices Series
Candid accounts of the new movement in software development

Microsoft Programming Series
The foundations of software development

Professional   Developers

Microsoft Press® Interactive
Integrated multimedia courseware for all levels

Strategic Technology Series
Easy-to-read overviews for decision makers

Microsoft Professional Editions
Technical information straight from the source

Solution Developer Series
Comprehensive titles for intermediate to advanced developers

Microsoft Press

mspress.microsoft.com

Here's how to **better define** *your*

computing experience.

A Use-Every-Day Computer Reference

The Concise Standard for Business, School, Library and Home

Over 4,700 Entries!

Microsoft Press
Computer User's Dictionary

- Clear, up-to-date definitions of the terms you need to know
- Entries cover the Internet, hardware, software, operating systems, and more
- Online updates keep information current

Microsoft Press

U.S.A.	$14.99
U.K.	£13.99
Canada	$21.99

ISBN 1-57231-862-7

The MICROSOFT PRESS® COMPUTER USER'S DICTIONARY gives you fast, easy explanations of terms covering the most recent trends in computing, including the Internet, the Web, multimedia, virtual reality, hardware, networks, and workgroup computing. In 400 pages, you get over 4,700 terms, along with concise versions of the in-depth definitions featured in the third edition of the *Microsoft Press Computer Dictionary,* described by *Booklist* (12/1/97) as "The Webster's of computer dictionaries." In addition, you can view regular quarterly updates to the dictionary on the Microsoft Press Web site.

Microsoft®*Press*

Register Today!

Return this
Microsoft® Windows® 98 At a Glance
registration card for
a Microsoft Press® catalog

U.S. and Canada addresses only. Fill in information below and mail postage-free. Please mail only the bottom half of this page.

1-57231-631-4   *MICROSOFT® WINDOWS® 98 AT A GLANCE*   *Owner Registration Card*

NAME

INSTITUTION OR COMPANY NAME

ADDRESS

CITY   STATE   ZIP

Microsoft®*Press*
Quality Computer Books

**For a free catalog of
Microsoft Press® products, call**
1-800-MSPRESS

MICROSOFT PRESS REGISTRATION
MICROSOFT® WINDOWS® 98 AT A GLANCE
PO BOX 3019
BOTHELL   WA   98041-9946